IN THE MATTER OF BLACK LIVES:
WOMANIST PROSE

To Ed,

My Precious brother!!!

Best Wishes

[signature]

1/11/2021

ARICA L. COLEMAN

IN THE MATTER OF BLACK LIVES: WOMANIST PROSE

Library of Congress Control Number: 2021901797

Trade paperback ISBN: 978-1-883435-02-8

E-book ISBN: 978-1-883435-03-5

Jacket and interior design by Stephanie Vance-Patience

Published in the United States by
I Womanist Publishing, an imprint of *SistahGurl Books*

I Womanist
Publishing
An Imprint of SistahGurl Books

Unless otherwise indicated, all in-text citations of book references are taken from the Kindle format.

To my husband Tracy, my children Julienne (Steve), and Manny,
and my grandson Stephen,
You are my first, my last, my everything

And

To My People throughout the African Diaspora

"Black Lives Matter is an ideological and political intervention in a world where Black lives are systematically and intentionally targeted for demise. It is an affirmation of Black folks' humanity, our contributions to this society, and our resilience in the face of deadly oppression.
— *Patrisse Cullors, Alicia Garza, and Opal Tometi,*
BLM Founding Sistahs

FOREWORD

BY MARITA GOLDEN

In the Matter of Black Lives: Womanist Prose by Arica L. Coleman is a brilliant, energetic, and energizing meditation on Black history, American History, and the past decade of tumultuous, inspiring, radical and marginal change in this country we call America. Coleman is a scholar and public intellectual dedicated to relentless inquiry and the shattering of mythology and the challenging of conventional wisdom. As I read these essays which range from a journey to the plantation where her enslaved ancestors were held in bondage, to moving memorials to sheroes (journalist Gwen Ifill and Ida B. Wells among them) and heroes (W.E.B. Du Bois, James Baldwin among many) to incisive political analysis that makes the past feel absolutely present, I wondered where else could a reader encounter discourse on Beyoncé, the mass murderer Dylan Roof, a discussion of the legacy of Black-Native relations, Black Lives Matter, discover the abolitionist Cassius Clay, whose namesake became Muhammad Ali, and a bracing examination of media coverage of Michelle Obama?

This is a book that is necessary for anyone who cares about this country, its past and especially its future. As I read these essays and as they stayed with me for days after, I thought how appropriate this collection would be for young people to read. Why should readers of *Time Magazine*, *The Crisis* and *The Washington Post* have all the fun and be the only ones to experience the exhilaration of witnessing a questioning and questing mind at work? These essays are jam-packed with historical facts, critical thinking, and the kind of contextual analysis that too few young minds are exposed to.

Coleman examines the major cultural and political schisms and changes of the last decade in essays that perfectly capture the frenzied roller coaster of change and retrenchment, the promise and failure of our political system and the courage of those who keep on pushing against it and forward every day, while keeping their eyes on the prize of justice and equality in a society addicted to instant gratification. This book is a map of where we have been and a GPS system for where we need to go, to survive, and to finally "discover" the America that has yet to be America to me.

Arica L. Coleman is an old-fashioned Race Woman whose vision is grounded in the search for integrity and respect, honesty and truth in public discourse, historical accounts and in the ways we as citizens live with one another. As readers we can answer the question "Can I get a witness?" with a resounding yes and thank Arica L. Coleman for witnessing and challenging and speaking what has been silenced, hidden, erased. This is a woman on fire. Arica, thank you for this collection.

May 2019

INTRODUCTION:
LONG STORY SHORT

*We are all worthy; we are all significant and we all matter
because we exist.*

—India Arie

I had no idea that when I began publishing political commentary at *History News Network* (HNN) during the historic 2008 Clinton-Obama presidential primary, that these essays were the building material for my second book. At that time I was a tenure-track assistant professor at a major research university struggling to complete my first book *That the Blood Stay Pure: African Americans, Native Americans, and the Predicament of Race and Identity in Virginia* with the mantra "publish or perish" weighing on my shoulders.[1]

The 2008 presidential primary officially began on January 20, 2007, when Hillary Clinton announced her candidacy for the Democratic nomination. My brain said "Yes" to this historic moment, but my heart said "No" to HRC. Bill Clinton had used Black people as political pawns and played us like a banjo by duping us into believing that he was pro-Black and had our backs. Yet, much of the legislation enacted under his administration such as the 1994 Crime Bill and the Welfare Reform Act of 1996 reified stereotypes of Black pathology and caused untold devastation to Black families and communities. Frankly, I was not feeling HRC who as First Lady vocally supported many of her husband's policies even characterizing

Black youth as "super predators" based on a theory by political scientist John Dilulio of unbridled youth criminals terrorizing the streets, a theory which had been rejected by numerous academics. Dilulio would later recant his assertions but the damage had already been done. Consequently, numerous Black youths received life sentences based on Dilulio's devastatingly erroneous theory. Notwithstanding, like everyone else, I knew that HRC had the nomination in the bag. My plan was to skip the political circus, pull the lever for HRC, if only to fulfil my voting obligation in the November general election, and keep it moving.[2]

But what a difference a year made. Obama won the Iowa Caucus, HRC did not seal the deal in February's Super Tuesday primary sweep as was predicted, and by late March *Slate Magazine* created "The Hillary Death Watch Widget" which featured her cartoon image on a sinking ship. HRC's inevitable win had turned into an inevitable defeat as Obama's reach for the nomination was unstoppable.[3]

By this time, I was on primary election overdrive reading and listening to every political commentary and following every election poll as the Clinton-Obama contest thrusted gender, race, and class politics center stage like no other time in American history. While there was no shortage of excellent analysis (and some bad ones too), I believed a historical context of this historic moment from a womanist perspective was necessary as a corrective to the numerous blind spots evident in mainstream commentary. I dived head long into the political fray and soon my commentaries became classroom material on college campuses across the nation. Connecting the historical and contemporary dots to demonstrate to my readers that the past is prologue, or to borrow from HNN's slogan "Because the past is the present and the future too," was beyond thrilling.

By the summer of 2009, however, on the advice of a mentor who stated that senior university colleagues viewed the work as unscholarly, I abandoned writing historio-political commentary. Incidentally, I published and perished in spring 2013. "Your work sucks: Tenure Denied," was the institution's response to my body of award-winning work. It took a while, in fact several years to regain my confidence; to quiet the nagging voice in my head screaming "You're damaged goods," which I awoke to every morning because I no longer had a job to go to. But I kept writing and kept hoping that I would find my way back to myself. An invitation to contribute to *Time Magazine's* "The 25 Moments That Changed America" in 2016 (I missed 2015 because I deleted the email thinking it was a subscription offer. What?) was the boost I needed to finally let go of the academy. Being an independent scholar suits me fine. And as they say the rest is history. Well herstory in my case.

It is now the year 2020 and what a rollercoaster ride it has been so far. There is a saying, "When White America catches a cold, Black America catches pneumonia." At this moment Black America finds itself in survival mode as it struggles against a double pandemic: 1) the novel virus COVID-19, a worldwide pandemic which has had a disproportionate effect on Black communities due to disparities in the U.S. healthcare system; and 2) the legacy of structural racism (not so novel) resulting in the state sanctioned violence and murder of Blacks at the hands of police and white vigilantes for the "crime" of breathing while Black. As historian Peter Wallenstein opines, "Look up, in a dictionary, the definition of 'pandemic.' And ponder whether racism is not well characterized as such. It affects everyone. It kills many." Kareen Abdul-Jabbar expressed the same sentiment in a *Los Angles Times* op-ed regarding the fall out in the Black community after the murder of George Floyd.

COVID-19 has been slamming the consequences of all that [systemic racism] home as we die at a significantly higher rate than whites, are the first to lose our jobs, and watch helplessly as Republicans try to keep us from voting. Just as the slimy underbelly of institutional racism is being exposed, it feels like hunting season is open on blacks. If there was any doubt, President Trump's recent tweets confirm the national zeitgeist as he calls protesters "thugs" and looters fair game to be shot. [4]

The poison of anti-Black racism, like the novel virus, suffocates Black Americans both literally and figuratively so much so that our collective cry "We Can't Breathe" has ignited protest across the nation and the world. Even ultra-rightwing *Fox News* commentator Sean Hannity experienced a moment of sanity during his radio and televised opinion broadcasts when he criticized white police officer Derek Chauvin who settled his knee on the neck of George Floyd, a Black man who allegedly purchased cigarettes from a convenience store in Minneapolis, Minnesota with a counterfeit $20 bill. Seventeen-year-old Darnella Frazier captured the 8 minutes and 46 seconds of the Memorial Day cold-blooded murder which immediately went viral on social media. "The tape, to me, is devastating," Hannity stated. "I watch it, I get angrier every time." In July of 2016 a video titled "23 Ways You Could Be Killed If You Are Black In America" featured celebrities from numerous genres highlighting how normal everyday activities such as a routine traffic stop, jaywalking, selling CDs or loose cigarettes on the street, seeking help after a car accident, walking towards police, walking away from police, or wearing a hoodie can result in a death sentence. Added to this list are the current high profile cases of Rashad Brooks (Atlanta, Georgia) who fell asleep at a Wendy's Drive Thru, Breonna Taylor (Louisville, Kentucky), for being at home during the execution of a suspicious "no knock" warrant (pun intended), Elijah McClain (Aurora, Colorado) for wearing a face mask outdoors in mid-August to stay warm as a result of his anemia, Ahmaud Arbery (Glynn County, Georgia) for jogging, and Jacob Blake Jr. (Kenosha, Wisconsin) for attempting to deescalate a fight between two women. Blake was shot in the back multiple times (and paralyzed) by an officer as he was getting into his car where three of his children were waiting to go to a birthday party.

In addition, the rise of indiscriminate calls by whites to the police for mundane things such as selling water in front of your own house while

Black, BBQing while Black, sitting in Starbucks while Black, building a patio on the back of your own house while Black, and bird watching while Black has raised awareness of not only police overreach, but how the privilege of whiteness is weaponized against Black bodies. As Amy Cooper threatened birdwatcher Christian Cooper (no relation) in Central Park, "I am going to call the police," she stated, "and tell them that an African American man is threatening my life." It is within the context of this current movement for Black lives that I have compiled this collection of 40 short essays published from 2008-2020 (except for the first essay which was published in 2002) on a wide range of current issues faced by Black America from a historical and womanist perspective.

In the Matter of Black Lives: Womanist Prose unabashedly and unapologetically takes the humanity of Black people for granted. In these essays, presented in the order in which they were originally published (with added postscripts where updated information is available), I examine the ways in which structural racism underscores issues of gender, education, colonialism/neocolonialism, the environment, gun control, human rights, mental health, patriotism, protest, and religion to demonstrate that the struggle for Black liberation continues in this very hour. Abdul-Jabbar continued making the case for Black lives stating:

> I don't want to see stores looted or even buildings burn. But African Americans have been living in a burning building for many years, choking on the smoke as the flames burn closer and closer. Racism in America is like dust in the air. It seems invisible — even if you're choking on it — until you let the sun in. Then you see it's everywhere. As long as we keep shining that light, we have a chance of cleaning it wherever it lands. But we have to stay vigilant, because it's always still in the air.[5]

Indeed. Although Dr. King believed that riots were counterproductive, he nevertheless believed, "A riot is the language of the unheard."

The long and short of womanism is this: it is not nor is it related to feminism despite the often quoted or rather misquoted definition of the term coined by

Alice Walker in the early 1980s who asserted, "Womanist is to feminist as purple is to lavender." Yet, while there are some commonalities between the two, womanism should not be conflated with feminism which continues to privilege the historical and cultural experiences of middle and upper class white women or with Black feminism, a Black expression of feminism which focuses on eradicating misogynoir within the Black community and beyond.[6]

First, as Walker states and I concur, "An advantage of using 'womanist' is that, because it is from my own culture, I needn't preface it with the word 'Black' (an awkward necessity and a problem I have with the word 'feminist') since Blackness is implicit in the term." Second, unlike feminism, on which theories and activism focus to eradicate sexism and patriarchy, womanism is a worldview which takes a holistic approach to societal ills. As Layli Maparyan asserts in *The Womanist Reader*, "*Womanism does not emphasize or privilege gender or sexism*" but "*rather, it elevates* **all sites and forms of oppression,** whether they are based on social-address categories like gender, race, or class, to a level of equal concern and action (emphasis mine)." Having grown-up within the throes of matriarchy on my paternal and maternal sides, and my life experiences as an adult, particularly within the academy, have left me wary of assumptions that women exercise power in more equitable ways than their male counterparts.[7]

Maparyan identifies five overarching themes of the womanist idea: anti-oppression, vernacular (anti-elitist), nonideological, communitarian (collective wellbeing), and spirituality. The latter cannot be overstated. Historically, spirituality has been part and parcel to the liberation struggles of Black peoples, what scholar Ana Louise Keating calls "spiritualized politics." Or as South Asian Feminist Lata Mani aptly states, "the personal is social, and spiritual." Indeed. womanism does not seek a seat at the table but rather like the historic Jesus, who entered into the halls of power and overturned the tables and seats of those who exploited the masses, our mission is to overturn and drive out all structures of oppression leaving no stone unturned. The womanist idea assumes that everything and nothing is sacred. All ideologies are equally interrogated and deconstructed.[8]

I am so grateful to my mentor and sister-friend Marita Golden who came up with the idea for the book and wrote this gracious foreword.

A big thank you to my long-time sister-friend Stephanie Vance Patience (*Stefani Vance*) for the cover art and interior book design. Yours are indeed "gifted hands."

I am also grateful to editors Rick Shenkman of *History News Network* (who started this whole mess, LOL); Dick and Sharon Price of *LA Progressive and Hollywood Progressive;* Brian Ross and the Made By History editorial team at the *Washington Post*; Jabari Asim, former editor of *The Crisis Magazine*, Keisha Blain, former editor-in-chief for *The North Star Newsletter*, and last but certainly not least Lily Rothman at *Time Magazine.* Thank you all for providing spaces to express progressive views.

TABLE OF CONTENTS

1

SLAVERY UP CLOSE & PERSONAL

ANCESTRY MAGAZINE, JULY/AUGUST 2002

Prior to the Civil Rights Movement, many of my family members joined the thousands of African Americans who migrated from the rural south to northern cities in search of a better life. By the close of the twentieth century, however, a substantial number of African Americans had resettled in the South. Among them was my mother Dorothy Kendall who in the mid-1980s moved back to her childhood home of King George County, Virginia. My grandmother Frances James joined her in 2005. This county, which is known as the gateway to the Northern Neck, is a peninsula surrounded by the Potomac and Rappahannock Rivers. It is the earliest known residence of my ancestors William and Mildred (McGruder) Thompson. who possibly endured the arduous middle passage across the Atlantic Ocean in slave ships sometime before 1798.

In the winter of 1998, as I interviewed relatives about our family history, my grandmother told me about the narrative her maternal uncle Jacob Thompson (Uncle Jake) had written which recorded the family history as it was told to him by his mother Eliza Stuart Thompson, a former slave. Before that time, I was unaware of my family's personal connection to slavery. Even as we sat around the television in 1976 watching Alex Haley's *Roots*, the memory of our slave past remained unspoken.

In 1997 I asked one of my grandmother's older sisters about our slave ancestors; she laughed nervously and told me we were descended from free people. Thankfully when I asked my grandmother, the youngest of fifteen children, she told me the truth. "Lethy knows good and well our grandparents were slaves," she snapped. I knew my grandmother was not simply irritated that her sister had lied about our ancestry. These two women never got along and that was even before Auntie bought Mommy's West Baltimore restaurant from under her. Oh, but I digress.

I quickly changed the subject back to our ancestors. "What were their names," I asked?

"Who," Mommy responded.

"Your grandparents," I responded and stated the question more deliberately. I knew I was about to hit pay dirt and needed for my grandmother to focus on the issue at hand. "What-were-their-names?"

"Oh yeah," she responded now remembering the initial conversation. "Well, Papa's father was Cornelius Gray but I don't know his mother's name. She burned up on a boat when Papa was just a baby, you see, so we never knew who she was." I later found out that her name was Alethea Garnett Gray. She and Cornelius, both descendants of Black and Indian peoples in Caroline County, Virginia married in King George County in 1868. They had three children Lucy, Laura, and George Allen. Tragically when their son was only 10 months old, Alethea known as Lethy, was a victim of the Wawaset ship explosion which occurred on the Potomac River on August 8, 1872.

"Now Mama," my grandmother continued, "was a Thompson. Her father was Joshua Thompson and her mother was Eliza. They were slaves you know?"

No, I did not know. While growing up I only heard my grandmother and her siblings talk about their parents George Allen and Mary Frances Gray (Papa and Momma). Now I was learning about the generations before and that we were indeed descended from slaves. A few days later, I read Uncle Jake's narrative *The History of the Thompson Family*, which filled in gaps from my conversation with my grandmother. I was eager to take a trip to the King George County Circuit Courthouse for additional information.

Immediately when I saw the sign, "Welcome to King George County–The Gateway to the Historic Northern Neck," I was overcome with nostalgia. Memories of childhood summers I spent with my siblings away from Baltimore and "down the country" caused my insides to dance with childlike excitement. We used to love roaming the thirty-eight acre farm my grandmother and her nine older siblings inherited from our great-grandparents. During those playful days of tire swinging, baseball playing, tree climbing, and tractor riding, I was unaware that the county that had been home to six generations of my family was indeed historic. Yet, as I now stood gazing up at the words, "King George County Circuit Courthouse," I would soon come face to face with that history in a more intimate way. I entered a room and immediately noticed the clerk's counter to my right. I was eager to find any information I could regarding my family during the antebellum years. I was told that some courthouses still had slave and plantation records. Since my ancestors had been slaves in King George County, I wanted to see if I could locate any of them.

"May I help you?" asked the friendly white woman behind the counter.

It never occurred to me that the subject of slavery was ultra-sensitive, hostile even, to white people so I simply asked the clerk if there were slave schedules and/or plantation records available in the courthouse. The woman responded that she believed there were some records available, but she did not know where they were located; and of course, the clerk who usually handled "those types of records" was not in. I was told that I might be able to catch her at the King George County Museum the next morning.

Not only was I a bit disappointed, I was also unsure what step to take next. My heart had been set on spending the morning, and part of the afternoon, combing through those musty records. Now I would have to wait.

Early the next morning, I arrived at the King George County Museum. The museum located next door to the courthouse had, in former days, been the county jail. I entered the museum and walked around the room gazing at various items that had been donated to the museum: a saddle from World War I, a late-eighteenth-century water barrel, various oil paintings of prominent people of the county. There was nothing about slavery except a three-panel cardboard display of a family who had been freed and relocated to Philadelphia, not Liberia as the American Colonization Society advocated. Soon a white woman emerged from a back room, "May I help you?" she asked.

"Yes," I responded. I again inquired about the slave schedules and plantation records. But this woman was not the woman the courthouse clerk had told me about the previous day and she too did not know where the records were kept. Nonetheless, she invited me to a tiny research room. We searched all the file cabinets and drawers, but we found nothing. Afterwards, I asked the woman if she had any information on Spy Hill, the plantation that Uncle Jake indicated was the place where my ancestors had been slaves.

She assured me that there was nothing at the museum about it, but that I should check the Virginiana Room at the regional library in Fredericksburg.

But my visit to the museum was not a total bust as something prompted me to ask this woman about the boat accident my grandmother alluded to. "By the way," I asked as I walked back around to the customer side of the counter, "Do you have any information about a boat accident which occurred in the county around the early 1870s. "Oh yes, she stated. She disappeared into a back room and returned shortly with a brief article about the tragedy.

I left the museum and headed to my car. Fredericksburg was thirty miles north of King George County. But as I walked towards my car I noticed the King George County Library across the street. The librarian eagerly responded to my inquiry concerning Spy Hill. "Do you know where it is?" she asked.

"No," I responded.

"Wait one moment, my husband can tell you better than I can how to get there."

I could feel the anticipation building within me as the librarian dialed the phone. Her husband gladly gave me directions. "By the way," he said as we concluded our conversation, "There's an old cemetery there."

Just then, the librarian handed me a small document containing information about Spy Hill. "It isn't much," she said, "but there's a bit of history here I'm sure you will find interesting."

Interesting indeed. Spy Hill, formerly known as Round Hill, was purchased in 1655 by John Washington, the grandfather of President

George Washington. Lawrence Washington, John's son, inherited Round Hill and acquired the land adjoining the estate. The property remained in the Washington family until it was sold in 1828 to Thomas Baber. Not far from the main house on what had been formerly known as the Round Hill Estate was a hill that provided a panoramic view of the Potomac River from Colonial Beach to Mathias Point. The hill was used as an observation post to spy out British troops sailing up and down the river during the American Revolution and the War of 1812. So, Thomas Baber changed the name of the estate to the Spy Hill Plantation.

"I definitely need to see this place," I said to the librarian, my heart leaping with excitement.

"I know Ruth Talliaferro [Tolliver] who lives at Spy Hill. Let me call to see if she's home."

The librarian thumbed through a card index on the counter and then dialed a number. After a brief introduction, she handed me the phone. I explained to the kind voice on the other end that I was working on a family history project. I told her about my uncle's narrative which named Spy Hill as the place where my ancestors had been slaves. Ruth invited me to her home. Fifteen minutes later, I was on a long driveway that stretched up a hill. At the top of the hill was an old, large, dilapidated house. "That must have been the big house where the slave master and mistress used to live," I thought as I continued past an old tobacco barn standing to the left. I drove a half-mile down the road and turned into a smaller driveway that led to a beautiful contemporary house—the home of the descendants of the family who had once owned mine.

Ruth was a middle-aged woman. Her hair was cut in a neck-length bob with strands of gray running sparingly through it. She had a kind face and welcoming smile. I liked her immediately. Ruth greeted me warmly and invited me into her home. We stepped into a hallway that revealed a beautifully decorated living room to the right and an equally elegant dining room to the left. She led me through the dining room and into a modest kitchen. After we enjoyed a hot cup of tea and a bit of small talk, she went to another room and came back with a large manila folder and a black loose-leaf notebook. As she laid the items in front of me, Ruth explained that she was related to the Baber family by marriage (her husband Edward is a direct descendant), and that due to her love of history, the family had appointed her the family historian. The information she was about to share with me was information she had spent the past twenty-five years gathering. Ruth began going through the various documents, telling me the history of Spy Hill and the families–the Babers and subsequently the Garnetts–who had owned the property. Much of the information was familiar thanks to Uncle Jake's narrative.

My great-great-grandfather, Joshua Thompson, had been owned by the Baber family and my great-great-grandmother, Eliza Stuart Thompson, had been owned by the Garnetts, a prominent family in Westmoreland County, which lies southeast of King George. Thomas Baber's daughter, Emma Baber, married Thomas Stuart Garnett, a physician and later a Brigade General in the Confederate Army, who was killed during the Battle of Chancellorsville in May 1863. After losing a husband and two brothers to the war, another brother to alcoholism, and her father, Thomas Baber, to illness, Emma Baber Garnett became the sole heir of Spy Hill. She returned to her childhood home in 1871, bringing her domestic servant Eliza Stuart with her. On August 3, 1873, Eliza and Joshua Thompson were married. It was Eliza who had passed on to her son the oral history of our family. As I sat listening to Ruth confirm that history, I quietly thanked my great-great-uncle and great-great-grandmother for the enormous gift they left me.

Once we had gone through the documents, Ruth escorted me to her living room and showed me family pictures. I could hardly believe that I was staring into the faces of the people who had once owned my family. They were a good-looking family, genteel, and without a hint of malice in their eyes. It was hard to imagine these people had ever owned slaves. Later, Ruth gave me a tour of what is now a 500-acre estate. Our first stop was a wooded area that stood to the right and left of the driveway leading up to what was once the big house.

"This is where the slave quarters used to be," Ruth said.

We stopped for a few moments and I gazed at the area that had been home to my slave ancestors. Several hundred feet away from the old slave quarters and across the road was the slave cemetery, which contained the remains of slaves who had died before the year 1843. I was glad Ruth was there to show it to me. Had I driven there on my own, I would have never guessed it was a cemetery. The area was just a blanket of leaves surrounded by trees. There were no markers or signs to indicate that it was a cemetery. Ruth parked the car on the side of the road, and we walked a short distance to another cemetery. This burial plot, which began in 1843, was an appendage to the original slave cemetery and had been used as a segregated burying place for African Americans until 1943. Although there were only three headstones, it was easy to see the burial impressions in the ground. The graves without headstones were marked with wooden stakes.

Ruth and I drove back up the hill, passed the big tobacco barn, and turned down a little road to the Spy Hill family cemetery. There, beneath lovingly inscribed tombstones, lay the remains of the masters and mistresses of my ancestors. I believe this is the cemetery the librarian's husband spoke of. It was a small cemetery surrounded by a cast-iron fence. The bars reminded me of the oppression that had once held my ancestors captive. Our tour concluded at the old antebellum house that was much too dilapidated for an inside tour. But Ruth and I walked along the grounds, and she allowed me to take pictures.

As we concluded the tour, it was hard to determine my feelings. Initially, I was excited. It was as though I had walked through a time capsule and had taken an excursion through history that few African Americans will ever experience. It was not until I returned to my home in Delaware the following afternoon that I felt the pain of that experience surface without warning. Slavery was no longer something that had happened to unknown Black people. It had happened to my family, my ancestors, people whose names and faces are no longer those of strangers. No, slavery was no longer an intangible historical event; it had become a tangible reality. ▪

POSTSCRIPT: In 2005, descendants of Amelia Thompson (sister of Joshua Thompson) and James Washington held a family reunion on the Spy Hill property. Then in 2016, The Spy Hill House was disassembled and moved to Stevenson Ridge, an 87-acre historical property in Spotsylvania County, Virginia where it was restored by Spear Builders-Custom Homes & Historic Preservation. It is one of nine 1 to 2-bedroom historic cottages on the property which date from the 18th and 19th centuries. In September 2020, Ruth and I climbed together once again into the African American cemetery which is currently under consideration for a Virginia Highway Marker.

2

HILLARY CLINTON AND THE POSSESSIVE INVESTMENT IN WHITENESS

HISTORY NEWS NETWORK, MAY 19, 2008

Now that the North Carolina/Indiana primaries are over, many are hearing the death knell of the Clinton campaign as Barack Obama's path to the Democratic nomination appears imminent. Notwithstanding her overwhelming defeat in North Carolina and narrow victory in Indiana, which did nothing to bring her closer to narrowing the delegate gap, Clinton is not ready to cede the race. In her victory speech, even while the news outlets were still reporting that Indiana was "too close to call," Clinton assured her supporters, "It's full speed on to the White House."[9]

But with the math, the money, and the momentum against her, California Congresswoman Dianne Feinstein (D-Cal), a staunch Clinton supporter, inquired of the New York senator "What's your game plan?" According to Mike Barnicle, Clinton's only recourse is to deploy a racialize strategy as his article title suggests: "Race Is The Only Thing The Clintons Have Left." Barnicle asserts, "Now, faced with a mathematical mountain climb that even Stephen Hawking could not ascend, the Clintons — and it is indeed both of them — are just about to paste a bumper sticker on the rear of the collapsing vehicle that carries her campaign. It reads: VOTE

WHITE." Such a plan became apparent within hours after the May 6 primary results were in, making it the most talked about news story of the day. Nevertheless, while Hillary's strategy holds significance for the present, the precedents for her campaign tactic can be found in the late 19th century women's suffrage movement as white women, in competition with Black men for the vote, argued if they could not be given the vote because they were women, they should be given the vote because they were white.[10]

Race baiting has been a recurring feature of the Clinton campaign as efforts were begun early to brand Barack Obama the "Black" candidate, thus raising questions about his electability. In addition, racially tinged comments made by the Clintons regarding Obama's candidacy were viewed as personal attacks against the Illinois senator and criticized by many as playing the race card. Consequently, the strategy proved costly for the Clinton campaign and the couple as African American voters, feeling a sense of betrayal, withdrew their support. Blacks had helped the Clintons win the White House, twice. They stood with them uncompromisingly during the Lewinsky scandal and impeachment proceedings. They had even dubbed Bill "the first black president." To employ "the big black scare," to use the words of Ofari Hutchinson, was viewed by many African Americans as a slap in the face. Certainly, a percentage of Blacks would have defected to the Obama camp as his chances for the nomination increased. Nevertheless, at best the two Democratic candidates would have split the Black vote. Well, at least until the Clintons botched things up.[11]

Now that her chances of winning the nomination are down to 2.3% as of this writing as calculated by *Slate*, it appears that Hillary has assumed a more overt racialized strategy by appealing directly to whites to woo superdelegates and voters in remaining primaries to favor her as the Democratic nominee to face John McCain in November. Assessing the North Carolina defeat and slim win in Indiana, the Clinton campaign stated, "We are pleased with the outcome." Why? Because the exit polls, according to their interpretation of the data, demonstrated Hillary's increasing appeal among white voters. Ben Smith of Politico and other analyst have contested this interpretation. Nevertheless, as reported by M. S. Bellows, who participated in a press telephone conference the morning following the primary:

The Clinton campaign's analysis of yesterday's results was largely based on exit polling and a careful parsing along demographic — mainly racial — lines that seemed to track the campaign's recent strategy of dispatching Bill Clinton to speak to small groups of rural, almost exclusively white, Southern voters.[12]

To continue the racialized strategy to reinvigorate the campaign, the day after the telephone press conference in an interview with *U.S.A. Today*, Hillary spoke of her appeal to white voters stating, "I have a much broader base to build a winning coalition on." As evidence, Clinton cited an Associated Press article "that found how Sen. Obama's support among working, hard-working Americans, white Americans, is weakening again, and how whites in both states who had not completed college were supporting me."[13]

Hillary in a last ditch effort to clinch the nomination is spinning the election narrative to demonstrate her appeal to white Americans and to appeal to white Americans in staunch language which suggests that a vote for Hillary Clinton is a vote for whiteness. Because whiteness is constructed in this society as the norm, race is often viewed as something people of color have, but that white people do not. Hence, Clinton, throughout this protracted campaign has been given a pass on her race. As writer Alice Walker stated:

One would think she is just any woman, colorless, race-less, past-less, but she is not. She carries all the history of white womanhood in America in her person; it would be a miracle if we, and the world, did not react to this fact. How dishonest it is, to attempt to make her innocent of her racial inheritance.[14]

Hillary's attempt to claim her racial inheritance, by appealing to white solidarity, has its historical precedents in the 19th century suffrage movement led by Susan B. Anthony and Elizabeth Cady Stanton. During Reconstruction, as the issue changed from abolition to equal rights, the question of racial equality and women's rights became competing ideals in American politics. At this time, the 15th amendment was being considered which would grant voting rights to Black men, excluding women regardless of race. Although white women had a gender disadvantage, they benefited from the patriarchal system of white supremacy, granting them a status in American society only second to white men. However, the ratification of the 15th Amendment, as white women saw it, would threaten that status. Therefore, it was upon the premise of race and not gender that the woman question emerged. If Black men were enfranchised leaving white women disenfranchised what would be the status of white women?

Anthony and Stanton approached long time abolitionist and women's rights advocate Frederick Douglass about forging an alliance that would bring before Congress the issue of the enfranchisement of Blacks and women jointly. The women approached Douglass not only because he was a Black male leader, but also because Black men supported women's suffrage far more than did their white male counterparts. In 1867, Douglass, along with various Black male activists, attempted an alliance with Anthony and Stanton by forming the American Equal Rights Association (AERA). Anthony and Stanton, to gain the support of Black women, encouraged them to seek the vote lest they become slaves to Black men. According to Paula Giddings's *When and Where I Enter: The Impact of Black Women on Race and Sex in America*, "Stanton warned that if black women weren't given the ballot, they would be fated to a triple bondage that man never knows.

… It would be better to be the slave of an educated white man, than of an ignorant black one." Ironically, Stanton's statement subordinated gender to race by placing a premium on whiteness, betraying a less than genuine concern for the interest of Black women as women.

While Black women activists varied in their views concerning their support of the 15th Amendment, a majority were not ready to align themselves with white women in the name of gender solidarity. Suffragist, such as Frances E. W. Harper, believed the plight of Black people in general, and Black women, would fare no better by locking arms with white women. Harper believed Black women's activism was based on the uplift of the race, while white women's activism sought to uplift themselves. Harper saw this as counterproductive. "The white women all go for sex [gender], letting race occupy a minor position … but … being black means that every white, including white workingclass women, can discriminate against you."

Anthony and Stanton proved Harper's assessment of Black women's double jeopardy to be correct. When it became apparent that Congress would not grant both Black men and white women the vote but rather would choose between the two, Stanton and Anthony laid claim to their racial inheritance by urging Congress to grant them the vote not because they were women, but because they were white. After the 15th amendment was ratified on February 3, 1870, Anthony published an article in the feminist newsletter *The Revolution* which she and Stanton launched with the financial backing of a wealthy Democrat stating:

While the dominant party [Republican party] have with one hand lifted up TWO MILLION BLACK MEN and crowned them with the honor and dignity of citizenship … with the other they have **dethroned** FIFTEEN MILLION WHITE WOMEN … and cast them under the heel of the lowest orders of manhood.

Anthony's articulation of the defeat of women's suffrage in such staunch racial terms was not uncommon in the 19th century and for much of the 20th century. Her disappointment reflected not only her frustration of a dream deferred, but more important the failure of Congress to uphold the possessive investment in whiteness, to use George Lipsitz's term, a racial inheritance that would be denied to white women for another fifty years.

Yet, in this first decade of the 21st century, as America continues to struggle with its racist past and present, Hillary's use of the same overt language to garner support for the Democratic nomination has been widely criticized as reckless. Her statements violated a code of silence by articulating what many believe should remain unspoken. As Lipsitz states in his book *The Possessive Investment in Whiteness: How White People Profit From Identity Politics*, "As the unmarked category against which difference is constructed, whiteness never has to speak its name, never has to acknowledge its role as an organizing principle in social and cultural [and political] relations." As Lipsitz further explains, "Since the passing of civil rights legislation in the 1960s, whiteness dares not speak its name, cannot speak on its own behalf, but rather advances through a color-blind language radically at odds with the distinctly racialized distribution of resources and life chances in U.S. society." Hence, the wide condemnation Hillary Clinton received for deploying 19th century Anthony/Stanton politics was not because she laid claim to her racial inheritance, but rather because she violated the code of modern-day polite society by voicing it in public.

Whether the results of the current Democratic primary will parallel the results of the 19th century political schism between Black men and white women remains to be seen. While Black men indeed gained the suffrage before white women, for most the emergence of Jim Crow delayed their ability to exercise the franchise for almost a century. The struggle for women's suffrage continued for another fifty years before white women nationwide received the franchise with the ratification of the 19th amendment in 1920. The pressure for Hillary to cede the race for the Democratic nomination is mounting. Many believe the longer she remains in the race, the more she hurts Obama's chances of defeating McCain in the general election. If that happens, we will once again squander a historic moment which may take generations to recapture. Let's hope not.

POSTSCRIPT: Hillary Clinton made history in 2016 when she became the first woman to receive the Democratic Nomination for President; she won the popular vote by approximately 3 million votes but lost to Republican nominee Donald Trump who won the presidency with 304 Electoral College votes to Clinton's 227. Ironically, Trump invoked the same racialized politics to stoke white fears of a post-Obama Democratic Party win with a slogan "Make America Great Again." The slogan was widely interpreted as code meaning "Make America White Again." Hence, despite his ultra-racist and sexist rhetoric, Trump's win was largely based on the 54% of white female voters, regardless of social status, who chose him over Clinton. In 2020 Trump lost to former Vice President Joe Biden who chose Senator Kamala Harris as his running mate making her the first woman (and Black/South Asian descent) to be elected as Vice President of the United States. Notwithstanding, Trump received 70 million votes comprising 57% of the white vote overall and 55% of the white female vote. ■

3

DOES BARACK OBAMA HAVE TESTICULAR FORTITUDE?

HISTORY NEW NETWORK, JUNE 1, 2008

During this protracted Democratic primary season, issues of race and gender have taken center stage. Race and gender politics are no stranger to the political trail; however, they have become the competing elephants in the room now that the final choice for the nomination has come down to an African American male, Barack Obama, and a white woman, Hillary Rodham Clinton. While this is undeniably a historic moment in American politics, the analysis of race and gender within the body politic, for the most part, has followed precedence. As whiteness is constructed as the norm so that race is seen as something only possessed by people of color, so too maleness is constructed as the norm so that gender is seen as something only possessed by women. Hence, in mainstream discussions, race and gender are often oversimplified. Constructed within an either/or paradigm, the two systems are viewed as polar opposites rather than as an interlocking system, a double stitch, if you will, threaded throughout the American fabric.

In recent days, charges of sexism have been leveled against the news media and even the Obama campaign as a number of Hillary Clinton surrogates have cited gender discrimination as the cause of the New York senator's second place showing in the primary race. The purpose here is not to refute or reinforce this allegation, but rather to insist that issues regarding gender have not been exclusive to the Clinton campaign. Unfortunately, there has been a persistent silence within recent feminist discourse regarding gender issues as it pertains to Barack Obama.

Nowhere is this more evident than in the commentary surrounding the comments made by Paul Gipson, president of a local steel workers union in Indiana, in his endorsement speech for Hillary Clinton during an April 30, 2008, campaign event. Gipson spoke of the type of leader the unions would need to perfect the provisions in NAFTA stating, "I truly believe that that's going to take an individual that has testicular fortitude … That's exactly right. That's what we gotta have." Gipson's overt masculine language lent credence to the image of Hillary Clinton as the "fighter" in the Democratic race, a portrayal her campaign began to nurture during the weeks leading up to the Pennsylvania primary. Yet, Gipson's statement asserting "That's exactly right," goes one step further. He emphasizes to his audience in unambiguous terms precisely what he wants to convey, and that is, Hillary Clinton got balls.[15]

The reaction to Gipson's statement was swift. Catherine Price, a writer for *Salon.com*, responding to questions regarding whether Gipson's comment was a compliment or an insult to Hillary Clinton, or if it was sexist, thought the discussion was much ado about nothing. Price believed that Gipson's comment merely reflected our male centered society in which his wording only demonstrated an inability to articulate characteristics that are widely associated with masculinity yet are not gender specific. Price asserts:

> Instead of simply saying that we want a strong leader who can stay calm in a crisis, be assertive, bring people together, negotiate and evaluate issues rationally and intelligently (a description that, incidentally, includes both "masculine" and "feminine" traits), we say that we need

someone with "testicular fortitude," because we associate leadership with masculinity. Historically, this makes sense; most of our leaders have been male.[16]

I would almost agree with Price except that she, and incidentally others who have joined this conversation, have viewed Gipson's comment without any consideration for how his words should be interpreted in relation to Clinton's male opponent Barack Obama. Are we to assume that these comments bear no insult to the senator? Could such comments be viewed as sexist? Consequently, by assuming that issues of gender only relate to women, Obama has become, at least in this conversation, the invisible man, to use the words of Ralph Ellison. This is a gross error. For it stands to reason that to state unequivocally that Hillary Clinton has the testicular fortitude to run the country, is to also state unequivocally that Barack Obama does not.

This sentiment was expressed several days later by reporter Eleanor Clift, who in a recent *Newsweek* article questioned Obama's manliness due to his refusal to respond to Hillary Clinton's "kitchen sink" strategy by indulging in a proverbial appliance free-for-all, the type of gutter politics Obama has sought to avoid. Clinton surrogate James Carville's contribution to the article at once challenged Obama's machismo while subordinating his masculinity to the supposed masculinity of his female rival stating, "If she [Clinton] gave him [Obama] one of her cajones they'd both have two."[17]

Gipson's, and subsequently Carville's, comments coupled together demonstrate far more than an inability to articulate leadership in gender neutral terms. Theirs was a direct and deliberate assault on Obama's masculinity, shaping a narrative to raise doubts in the minds of voters regarding whether or not the Illinois senator possesses the temperament needed to make the tough decisions required by the president. Price is correct when she stated that historically our leaders have been men, thus, leadership and masculinity become synonymous. In the same token, historically, our leaders have also been white. Thus, whiteness and masculinity have also become synonymous. Hence, Obama was feminized while Clinton was branded "the man" in the match up for the Democratic nomination. Clinton's portrayal as being more masculine than Barack Obama has historical significance in that it articulated a racialized gendered narrative rooted in 19th century ethnology which theorized whiteness as masculine and blackness as feminine.

During the mid-nineteenth century, American intellectual thought turned away from the universalism of the Enlightenment to embrace a racialist romanticism that generalized about the diversity of national character of peoples with whom they came in contact. American historiographers of romantic thought such as William H. Prescott, Francis Parkman, and John Lothrop Motley made general comparisons of national characteristics between the Spanish and the conquered natives of Mexico, the Anglo Saxon and the "Celtic" French, and Germanic- Celtic stocks which comprised the Dutch nation, respectively. What emerged, according to George Fredrickson's *The Black Image in the White Mind: The Debate on Afro-American Character and Destiny, 1817–1914,* was a celebration of the Anglo-Saxon whose innate character was born of "a love of liberty, a spirit of individual enterprise and resourcefulness, and a capacity for practical and reasonable behavior, none of which his rivals possessed." Yet others such as Theodore Parker, an anti-slavery advocate, also recognized a dark side to Anglo-Saxon character which he described as "his restless disposition to invade and conquer other lands; his haughty contempt of humbler tribes which leads him to subvert, enslave, kill, and exterminate." Although numerous terms were used to describe American ethnologic identity such as Anglican, Anglo-Saxon, and Celtic-Anglo Saxon, mid-nineteenth century Anglo-Saxonism came to differ from its late nineteenth century counterpart in that the former was inclusive of diverse European stocks making no distinction between various groups. At this time, they were all placed under one umbrella: Caucasian.[18]

Simultaneously, as the national character of the Anglo–Saxon was becoming popular, the slavery debate turned the focus of discussion towards the African American population. During this time, there were two schools of thought regarding Black character. As Fredrickson notes, "The biology school saw the Negro as a pathetically inept creature who was a slave to his emotions, incapable of progressive development and self-government because he lacked the white man's enterprise and intellect." Nevertheless, others whose thoughts were based in romanticism and evangelical religion provided a different assessment. "Where scientists and other 'practical' men saw weakness," stated Fredrickson, "others discovered redeeming virtues and even evidence of black superiority."

The evidence of Black superiority, as espoused by romantic racialist thinkers, was embraced by abolitionists, both Black and white, who viewed the African race as the redeemer race whose innate character as a natural Christian differed sharply from that of the "Angry" Saxon. For example, Harriet Beecher Stowe in the preface of her book *Uncle Tom's Cabin*, described her characters as possessing "a character so essentially unlike the hard and dominant Anglo-Saxon race." The depiction of Blacks as the polar opposite of whites comprised a racialized gendered persona which viewed Black traits as interchangeable with those attributed to women. Stowe's most famous character Uncle Tom, the embodiment of Christian virtue, differed little from the author's white female character Mary in *The Minister's Wooing*. The stark similarity between the two caused Helen Papashvily to conclude in *All the Happy Endings: A Study of Domestic Novels in America* that "Uncle Tom might have been a woman." Romantic racialist thought advanced the notion that Blacks, and white women shared the same traits. As philosopher

Alexander Kinmont declared, "the black race was more 'feminine and tender minded' than the whites."

Mid-nineteenth century Black ethnologists, while not fully accepting the concept of racial difference, embraced the romantic notions of the redeemer race, according to Mia Bay's *The White Image in the Black Mind: African American Ideas About White People, 1830–1925*, "present[ing] the races in counterpoint." Most Black ethnologists during this period believed that each race possessed traits uniquely their own. Blacks were:

> moral, pious, and benevolent … less aggressive than Anglo-Saxons. A Redeemer race, people of African descent were destined by both Providence and their God-given gifts to endure and survive slavery and oppression, and to lead mankind toward a millennium. By contrast, whites were all but irredeemable. Greedy and warlike, whites had been savages in Europe, and they still terrorized blacks and other people of color.

The preeminence of the femininity of blackness proved counterproductive to Black men seeking to define themselves on an equal footing with white men; while morality may have bolstered their status within the racial hierarchy, such a position proved tenuous. Consequently, within the male dominated discussion of racial difference, white men shaped the narrative which perpetuated the stereotype of Black men as cowardly, weak, emotional, and irrational, traits attributed to women. While Black racialist thought embraced the romanticism of a racialized gendered notion of difference contrasting "between the feminine black race and masculine white race," whites were far more emphatic in emphasizing the so-called womanly traits of the African than their Black male counterparts.

Such an image proved problematic for Black men during the Civil War as romanticized notions of racial difference cast Black men as unfit for military duty. Despite the fact that Black men had fought in the Revolutionary War and the War of 1812, romantic racialist thought of the 1850s cast doubts in the minds of even the staunchest abolitionists regarding whether Black men were tough enough to assume the duties of a soldier. Black men were eventually allowed to enlist, though few could serve as officers. Nevertheless, they used the war to not only demonstrate their patriotism, but also to demonstrate their manhood. Despite serving in the Civil War with distinction, Black men continued to war against the ideals of romantic racialist thought which cast doubts upon their masculinity for much of the twentieth century.

As we near the end of the Democratic primary season, the historic race between Barack Obama and Hillary Clinton serves as metaphor for the progress as well as for the failure of America to come to terms with issues of race and gender. While Carville's comment was an overt attack on Obama's masculinity, Gipson's comment, though overt in its use of masculine terminology, proved subtle in its effort to subordinate the Illinois senator's masculinity to the supposed masculinity of his white female contender, something nineteenth century romantic racialist thinkers never attempted to do. Taken together, such statements articulate in staunch terms that the historical privilege of whiteness and maleness remains a stronghold in American society. Hence, while this historic moment demonstrates a decisive move towards transcending race and gender stereotypes in American politics, it also demonstrates the long journey which remains in putting such infantile ideas away. ▪

POSTSCRIPT: Republicans continued their gendered assault on Obama throughout his tenure as president. They often compared Obama to Russian President Vladimir Putin showing pictures of Putin bare chested riding horseback and performing Judo maneuvers to contextualize him within a masculinist narrative as the strong/stronger leader. In counterpoint, Obama was characterized as weak. A picture of him riding a bike wearing a helmet and "Mom" jeans, which he also wore to throw out the first pitch at a baseball game, was widely circulated in mainstream and on social media. There were no shortages of memes. Sarah Palin's diss during a Fox News broadcast was indicative of the type of criticism heaped upon the president for his "poor" casual fashion choice. "People are looking at Putin as one who wrestles bears and drills for oil," Palin stated to Sean Hannity. "They look at our president as one who wears mom jeans and equivocates and bloviates." Yet, as Obama stated in an interview with Ryan Seacrest and I concur, "I have been unfairly maligned."

4

THOUGHTS ON A BLACK FIRST LADY IN WAITING

HISTORY NEWS NETWORK, AUGUST 25, 2008

"Barack has a handicap the other candidates don't have: Barack Obama has a black wife. And I don't think a black woman can be first lady of the United States. Yeah, I said it! A black woman can be president, no problem. First lady? Can't do it. You know why? Because a black woman cannot play the background of a relationship. Just imagine telling your black wife that you're president. 'Honey, I did it! I won! I'm the president.' 'No, we the president! And I want my girlfriends in the Cabinet! I want Kiki to be secretary of state! She can fight!"

—Chris Rock, comedian

There is an old saying, "Many truths are told in jokes." Unfortunately, Rock's "joke" fails to warrant any comedic merit. Notwithstanding, it lends credence to a glaring truth in this historical moment of America's anxiety regarding the potential of a Black woman becoming first lady. Rock's statement is underscored by the late twentieth century stereotype of the Black Matriarch, the domineering Black woman who refuses to allow her male partner to assume his rightful position as patriarch. Hence Rock's characterization of Michelle Obama as a "handicap" echoes Daniel Patrick

Moynihan's thesis in his late 20th century treatise *The Negro Family: The Case of National Action*, which reified the representation of Black women as castrators and emasculators of Black manhood.[19]

Rock is not alone in articulating the anxiety some Americans feel in relation to the idea of a Black woman assuming the role of first lady. *New York Times* opinion writer Maureen Dowd in her recent article "Mincing Up Michelle" explores America's perceptions of Mrs. Obama's supposed unsuitableness for the role. "There are some who think it will be harder for America to accept a black first lady ... than a black [male] president." Leonce Gaither, in a *Huffington Post* article, "Michelle Is Ungrateful? For What?," also challenges assertions that the potential first lady displays ingratitude towards America. "Sometimes it seems that many Americans fear a black First Lady," he stated, "more than a merely half-white President."[20]

It is precisely Barack's ability to straddle racial boundaries, invoking an illusion of a post-racial America, that has caused many, who may have otherwise discounted his candidacy, to embrace the idea of his presidency. Michelle, however, is another matter as she is undeniably, and to some, unforgivably Black, a racialized gendered marker which renders the term Black first lady a contradiction in terms. Barack implicitly demonstrates this in his seminal speech on race, "A More Perfect Union." While he locates his own heritage from the trajectory of his immediate parentage, "I am the son of a black man from Kenya and a white woman from Kansas," he locates his wife's heritage from the trajectory of American slavery. "I am married to a black American who carries within her the blood of slaves and slave owners - an inheritance we pass on to our two precious daughters."

Barack's latter statement is no mere acknowledgment of his and Michelle's shared mixed-race heritage which at first glance appears to be the legacy being passed on to daughters Malia and Sasha. A closer reading, however, indicates that bundled within this legacy is a racialized gendered inheritance which ties all Black women to the inescapable stereotypes which have defined Black womanhood from slavery to the present (e.g. The Obama girls labeled "Nappy Headed Hos in Art"). As Black feminist critic Barbara Christian once asserted, "In America the enslaved African woman became the basis for our society's Other." More specifically, the image of the sexually wanton Black female, the Jezebel, the foundation upon which white American conceptualizations of Black womanhood are built, has informed white perceptions of women of African descent since time immemorial contrasting it with the myth of the ultra-virtuous conception of white womanhood. Such myths were codified in the "cult of the southern lady" and the "cult of true womanhood." These parallel nineteenth century ideologies reinforced a hierarchy among women based on race and class to maintain a white supremacist patriarchal agenda. America's present anxiety with Michelle Obama is located within this historical framework.[21]

Gloria Steinem, in a *New York Times* op-ed, "Women are Never Front-Runners," states, "Gender is probably the most restricting force in American life, whether the question is who must be in the kitchen or who could be in the White House." While one cannot argue with Steinem regarding the prevalence of gender discrimination in the United States," such an illusion of a shared experience based on gender alone is self-serving and obscures the ways in which gender, race and class (not excluding sexuality) interlock to construct a nuanced reality of what it means to be a woman in American society. As Vanessa Tyson contends, "the combined discrimination of being 1) black, 2) female and 3) poor may be greater than the sum of each of the three parts." Steinem's gross generalization fails to acknowledge that race has equally played a role in who must be in the kitchen (read: black female domestics) or who could be in the White house (read: white women).[22]

As the office of the president has been exclusively reserved for white men, the role of the first lady has been exclusively reserved for white women. While her role has never been clearly defined, as she is neither paid nor elected, nevertheless the president's wife has had and can have tremendous influence over the social and political life of the nation. Far more than a hostess or keeper of the presidential residence, American history abounds with examples of first ladies who indeed proved their political weight in gold. While not serving in an official capacity, women such as Abigail Adams, Eleanor Roosevelt, Roslyn Carter, Nancy Reagan, and Hillary Clinton proved instrumental in broadening the boundaries of the first ladies' circle of influence within the political arena. Nevertheless, the first lady figures prominently on the national landscape as the female embodiment of the reigning virtues of American society. As such, from the beginning of our nation, white women have been held forth as the quintessential "lady," the icon of true womanhood and American female royalty to which all women should aspire.

Black women, on the other hand, were presented in counterpoint. Subjected to a barrage of disfigured images, stereotypes of African American women perpetuated notions that they were, as historian Adele Logan Alexander contends, "[un]deserving of the courtesy and esteem automatically bestowed on white women." As one southern boy responded to his younger friend who suggested that they step aside for a Black woman and let the lady pass, "She's no lady," the older boy quipped, "she's a nigger." However, such sentiments transcended region, as the North and South invoked the language of the lady to articulate the incompatibility of Black women with this ideal.[23]

In 1804 as the North began implementing its policies for the gradual emancipation of slaves, the South's effort to forge a regional identity as a pro-slavery defense against growing sentiments of abolition intensified. During this period, "the cult of the southern lady" served as the cornerstone of nineteenth century white Southern identity. While the origins and function of the ideal of white southern womanhood to southern ideology continues to be debated among historians, they generally agree that the function of the myth served to lend credence to the hegemonic ideals which normalized race, class, and gender dominance. Southern slaveholding women were placed upon a proverbial pedestal, the base of which was racial slavery.

The value in southern women was the embodiment of unadulterated Southern identity. Through her role as submissive wife, caring mother, guardian of the patriarchal social order and of the Southern ideal itself, "Such basic myths," according to Anne Goodwyn Jones, "polarized woman into ... the clustering of images — goodness and light with virginity and evil and darkness with sexuality" which were "reified and confirmed when white planters owned black slave women." While the Black female body was exploited as a ready resource for white male sexual gratification, the cult of the southern lady demanded that white women be the icon of female virtue and purity. This moral double standard prized white female fertility as the reproducer of the legitimate heirs to southern white privilege; therefore, white female sexuality had to be protected at all cost. As W. J. Cash asserted, "For as perpetuator of white superiority in legitimate line, and as a creature absolutely inaccessible to the males of the inferior group, she inevitably became the focal center of the fundamental pattern of proto-Dorian pride."[24]

She also inevitably became the central justification in pro-slavery literature as demonstrated in the works of Thomas R. Drew, William Harper, and George Fitzhugh. Consequently, slavery and women's subordination become two sides of the same Southern identity coin. As Anne Firor Scott contends it was "no accident that the most articulate spokesmen for slavery were also eloquent exponents of the subordinate role of women." Nevertheless, white southern women internalized the mythology of the southern feminine mystique and reveled in the power it granted them over their Black subordinates, both male and female.[25]

Womanhood was also central to the abolitionist argument as slavery's degradation of Black women fueled Northerners' arguments against the peculiar institution. Despite this, Northern Black females fared no better than their Southern counterparts when it came to Northern perceptions of Black womanhood. Perceptions of Black female immorality were also pervasive in Northern society. Neither Northern emancipation nor abolitionist sentiments proved useful in abating it. As Gerda Lerner asserts, "Just as the cult of white womanhood in the South served to preserve a labor and social system based on race distinctions, so did the cult of the lady in an egalitarian society serve as a means of preserving class distinctions." Hence free Northern Black women, faced with what has been popularly dubbed "the cult of true womanhood," found themselves struggling against the conventional wisdom of moral aptitude and its relationship to race and socio-economic status.[26]

By the 1830s with the rise of Northern industrialization, stark class distinctions, due to the differing lifestyles of women, began to emerge. The burgeoning middle-class, with its sights ever pressed toward obtaining upper class status, believed the avenue to women's privilege and prestige rested in her ability to strictly adhere to what Barbara Welter identifies as the four cardinal virtues of true womanhood: "piety, purity, submissiveness and domesticity. Put them all together and they spelled mother, daughter, sister, wife—woman. Without them no matter if there was fame, achievement, or wealth, all was ashes. With them she was promised happiness and power."[27]

Domesticity was central to the cult's cardinal tenets as expressed in the slogan "a woman's place is in the home." The home, according to conventional wisdom, provided a protective shield from corrosive forces which all but guaranteed a woman's adherence to the remaining tenets. Such women were viewed as ladies of leisure; a concept once proscribed was now viewed as a status symbol. Lerner suggests, "The women of the newly middle and upper classes could use their newly gained time for leisure pursuits: they became ladies." Leisure pursuits were not confined to merely serving as hostess or attending afternoon teas. Ladies, both North and South, being relieved of domestic chores and motherly duties, by relegating them to the lower classes of women, namely Black women, had more time to focus on the higher responsibilities of life such as religious refinement and perfecting moral character.[28]

Ironically, the virtues of domesticity were trumpeted during a time when poorer women, more specifically immigrant women, were entering the work force as factory workers by the droves. It also occurred at a time when the abolition of slavery in the North sent large numbers of Black women into the wage labor force. Consequently, Black women were shut out of factory employment. As Harriet Martineau asserted, white women viewed the factories as "a more welcome resource to some thousands of young women unwilling to give themselves to domestic service." The majority of the white female wage labor force was comprised of single women, but Black women, both single and married, worked as washer women or domestics, cared for children, and performed domestic chores in white households while often neglecting the same responsibilities in their own homes. Most Black women could hardly afford to adhere to the cardinal tenets of the cult of the lady as often they were the breadwinner of the family. This was a consequence of the systematic discrimination of Black men in the employment arena, a pattern that would persist well into the twentieth century.[29]

Nevertheless, a Black middle class emerged in the antebellum North and Black women attempted to adhere to the tenets of the lady even as they challenged its racist and classist premise. As historian Paula Giddings observed, "they organized Black ladies' literary, intelligence, temperance, and moral improvement societies in this period as a reaction to that pressure." Their aim was to prove that they were able to acculturate white middle class values. Nonetheless, the stereotype of the lascivious Black female proved a formidable stronghold. While the Victorian ethic applied to the so-called

better classes of women during this time (white working class women were
also viewed as sexually indiscreet), Black women regardless of their socio-
economic status were viewed as innately amoral, even by their white female
counterparts who excluded them from their ladies' societies. Unfortunately,
white female abolitionists were not immune to such racialized sentiments.[30]

The fight against the assault on Black womanhood intensified during
the post-Civil War era as noted by Harvard professor Evelyn Higginbotham
who contends that the intersections of race and class conflated with gender
to construct the contours of ladyhood which continued to exclude Black
women regardless of socio-economic standing. In the post war South
Black women "playing the lady" were criminalized as violating laws against
"loaferism" for attempting to adhere to the ideal of domesticity by remaining
in the home while their husbands and fathers worked to support the family.
Such efforts were viewed as "unnatural" and "evil." Although working class
white women also fell outside of the mainstream definition of the lady, class
was racialized to subordinate working-class Black women as demonstrated
in a North Carolina tobacco factory. While white working-class women
labored under conditions deemed "suitable for ladies," Black women,
however, were relegated to unsanitary and hazardous working conditions.
Moreover, segregation came to "exemplify the trope of the lady," which
further racialized class as Black women, despite their ability to purchase
first-class tickets, were not allowed to ride in the first car on public trains
also known as "the ladies car." If a Black woman insisted on sitting in the
ladies' car, her resistance to Jim Crow was met with unrequited violence. For
example, when anti-lynching activist Ida B. Wells refused to give up her seat
in the ladies car after having paid her fare, she was dragged by three men to
the smoking car as "the white ladies and gentlemen in the car even stood
on the seats so they could get a good view and continued applauding the
conductor for his brave stand."[31]

The racialization of class invoked ideas of Black women as possessing a morality lower than white prostitutes as expressed by an anonymous Africa American woman in an article that appeared in the *Independent* on September 18, 1902:

> I am a colored woman, wife, and mother … A colored woman, however respectable, is lower than the white prostitute. The Southern white woman will declare that no negro women are virtuous, yet she places her innocent children in their care… Southern railway stations have three waiting rooms and the very conspicuous signs tell the ignorant that this room is for "ladies," and this is for "gents," and that for the "colored" people. We are neither "ladies" nor "gents" but "colored."[32]

While the above statement identifies the degradation shared by both Black men and women alike, Adele Logan Alexander, nevertheless, observes that the lack of separate bathroom facilities for African American men and women served as a fundamental insult to Black women "thereby deliberately denying African American women the basic courtesies they unquestioningly accorded white women." This practice was only discontinued in the late 1960s. Alexander further observes that other courtesies such as being referred to by one's proper title in places of business was also denied Black women. During business transactions, Black women were not granted the simple courtesy of being addressed as "Miss" or "Mrs." though Blacks faced retaliation if they did not extend such courtesies to whites. Black female domestics even had to address the white children they cared for as "Miss" or "Mr." while the children merely addressed them by their first names. One elderly housekeeper complained that "the child I work for calls me 'girl.'"[33]

In fact, of the myriad of names Black women have been called throughout American history, lady is not one of them. As literary historian

Trudier Harris quipped in her book *From Mammies to Militants: Domestics in Black American Literature*:

> Called Matriarch, Emasculator and Hot Momma, Sometimes Sister, Pretty Baby, Auntie, Mammy and Girl, Called Unwed Mother, Welfare Recipient and Inner City Consumer, The Black American Woman has had to admit that while nobody knew the troubles she saw, everybody, his brother and his dog, felt qualified to explain her, even to herself.[34]

Reflecting on the historical misconceptions of Black womanhood indelibly etched in the psyche of American society, African American feminist Michelle Wallace stated in her book *Black Macho and the Myth of the Super Woman*, "Black women have a hell of a history to live down." It is this hell of a history outlined above that Michelle Obama must contend with and overcome. As Ed Kilgore aptly points out, Michelle Obama has now become a part of "the long pedigree of presidential spouse-bashing." Nevertheless, her unique position as the first African American spouse with the potential to become first lady has invoked racially tinged representations by both the conservative and liberal media which are clearly informed by the historical stereotypes of Black womanhood. This is no joke as such representations aim to demonize Michelle as the bad Black woman undeserving of the respect afforded the litany of white women who have come before her, despite isolated comparisons to Jacqueline Kennedy Onassis.[35]

From the misinterpretation of her "proud statement" by numerous media outlets, to Fox News Channel's label of her as "Obama's baby momma," to a teasing segment of MSNBC's *Hardball* which featured silhouetted female dancers to represent Michelle's supposed image makeover, to the most recent caricature on the front cover of the *New Yorker*, which depicts the Princeton-Harvard Law graduate as an Afro hairdo wearing, rifle toting militant, are all deliberate attempts to ghettoize her image and reinforce the historical stereotypes of Black womanhood which continue to define the status of African American woman as outsiders. Hence, the notion that Black women, despite their level of education or socio-economic status, lack the refinement to be ladies is a hurdle which remains to be overcome.

The full-frontal assault against Michelle notwithstanding, she also belongs to a long pedigree of African American women who have resisted the cultural misrepresentation of Black womanhood and triumphed despite its continued prevalence in American society. From Sojourner Truth who challenged the racism of the 1854 Women's Rights Convention in Akron, Ohio, by asking the question, "A'int I a Woman?," to the activism of Frances E. W. Harper and others who struggled to speak for themselves at the 1893 World's Congress of Representative Women, to the open defiance of Ida B. Wells and Mary McLeod Bethune who dared to trespass the segregated boundaries in public train stations, to the bravery of Anita Hill who despite the Jezebel stereotype refused to remain silent about sexual harassment, to the indomitable spirit of Gwen Ifill who challenged the complicity of the corporate media in degrading Black professional women as "cleaning women" and "nappy headed hos," Black women continue to forge ahead triumphantly in spite of racialized gendered bigotry. It is indeed a testament to the resilience of the African American female spirit.

It is this resilience which Maya Angelou celebrates in her famous poem *Still I Rise* that provides the metaphor for the resilience of Michelle Obama. Her historic role as "candidate" for first lady of the United States exemplifies the audacity of hope demonstrated by her forbears as she:

Rise[s] out of the huts of history's shame ... from a past that's rooted in pain ... leaving behind nights [and days] of terror and fear.

Michelle can indeed claim ownership to the final words of Angelou's poem:

Bringing the gifts my ancestors gave,
I am the dream and the hope of the slave.
I rise

As I conclude my thoughts on this Black first lady in waiting under
the gaze of my great-great-grandmother Eliza Stuart Thompson, a former
Virginia slave, whose portrait stares at me from the place where I write, I say,

Rise Michelle
Rise ▦

POSTSCRIPT: Mrs. Obama remains immensely popular. In November
2018, her memoir *Becoming* was released to critical acclaim. She was also
widely praised for her 2020 Democratic National Convention speech
in support of Joe Biden for the Democratic Nomination for President
impressing Fox News panelists Juan Williams, Chris Wallace, and Dana
Perino. Perino did not mince words in her praise of the former first lady.
"She has that voice, she has clarity," stated Perino, "and she knows what
she is out there wanting to do. I think that the DNC, if they look over
the course of the night, the first virtual convention of our history, I think
they would say that Michelle Obama stuck the landing." Indeed, a few
weeks later the former first lady broke the internet with a 24-minute video
"Michelle Obama Closing Argument: Joe Biden For President 2020," which
confirmed her rock star status.[36]

5

WE WERE EIGHT YEARS
IN A BEER SUMMIT:
AN AMERICAN TRAGEDY

HISTORY NEWS NETWORK, JULY 29, 2009

When the presidential election campaign began two and a half years ago, I was a reluctant Hillary Clinton supporter. I supported Clinton not so much because she was a woman or that I believed she was the best candidate. I supported her because I believed the hype that she had the Democratic nomination in the bag. I always believed The United States of America would have a white female president before it had a Black male president (a Black female president may have to wait until the next century) and so I did not want to waste my vote. But there was another reason I initially supported Clinton over Obama which goes to the heart of my essay and can be summed up in two words: race matters.

My reluctance to support Obama stemmed from what I believed was the former Senator's reluctance to honestly confront issues of race. I was as excited as many about Obama after witnessing his stirring keynote address at the 2004 DNC convention. I believed a run for the presidency might not be a far-fetched idea. But I later became disillusioned during the Katrina crisis as Obama, in an effort to defuse racial tensions, stated that the shortcomings in response to that horrific event were a matter of class. "Race had nothing to do with it," he stated.[37]

I believed Obama's response was cowardly and dishonest. Anyone who knows the history of New Orleans knows that race cannot be separated from the events before and after Katrina. It was astonishing to watch a Black politician engage in such blatant denial for his own political gain. Black candidates and elected officials seeking state and national office know they must scale the racial mountain to assure their white constituents that they are not in it to advance the "Black cause." In doing so, Black politicians all too often campaign or govern at the expense of their Black constituents, downplaying racially charged issues so as not to offend whites. But Obama well knows that race and class are not mutually exclusive and are often intersecting factors. Racial inequality is real and often has life and death consequences as we witnessed during and after Katrina. For those of us at the bottom of the racial food chain, achieving racial equality is just as important as health care, the economy, and education as race determines access and quality of access. Obama's willingness to obscure these complexities amid such human suffering gave me pause. I honestly did not think I could support a candidate who, to use the words of Kanye West, "doesn't care about Black people." Despite my misgivings, however, I eventually came around when some of my colleagues, namely a white middle-aged female friend, urged me to listen to Obama's stump speeches. After listening to both Clinton and Obama, I was convinced that Obama was the better candidate. By December 2007 I was well on my way to becoming an Obama supporter and took the full leap, as many others did, after the Iowa Caucus.

While Obama tried his best throughout the primary election to appear race neutral, quelling the flames of unrest whenever racial animosities attempted to hijack his campaign, the Jeremiah Wright controversy brought race front and center. Hence, Obama was faced with having to do something he had long tried to avoid: address the issue of race head on. Like many

Obama supporters, I was nervous about what he would say in the "race" speech he reluctantly delivered in Philadelphia on March 18, 2008. Not only was I nervous because of what this could mean to him politically, I was also nervous because of what this could mean for Blacks all over the country. In addition to his Katrina comments, I had read Obama's book *The Audacity of Hope* and frankly was unimpressed with his chapter on race. While he addressed issues of institutional and structural racism, unfortunately, the chapter quickly descends into a discourse on so-called Black pathology. His memoir *Dreams From My Father,* written a decade prior, dealt far more honestly with the issue of race. But that was written before he became a politician.

And so, I sat nervously in front of the TV waiting for the speech. Would Obama yield to the status quo and simply say what was necessary to appease white anxieties? Or would he truly give voice to the reality of continued racial inequality in America? The speech was indeed as MSNBC anchor Chris Matthews stated, "Brilliant . . .one worthy of Lincoln." Obama nevertheless managed to let whiteness off the hook by, in the words of novelist Adam Mansback, "fudg[ing] the difference between institutional racism and white bitterness." Despite this shortcoming, I felt Obama had done what was necessary to keep his campaign afloat while at the same time not throwing Black folk under the bus.[38]

My disillusionment with Obama would return again as his visits to various Black churches during the general election yielded didactic speeches of personal responsibility, a message many felt condescending and only designed to garner white votes (i.e. the controversial Father's Day speech). As appalled as I was at Rev. Jesse Jackson's remarks that such condescension made him want "to cut his [Obama's] nuts off," I could identify with Rev. Jackson's frustration. Why is it that Obama and others resort to scolding Black parents for not doing their part to insure their children's success, but never acknowledge that there are Black parents who are actively engaged in their children's lives? Yes, there are fathers who need to "step up," but what about acknowledging those who have indeed stepped up and are taking care of their parental responsibilities? Such people are not an exception, but rather the rule in Black communities all over the country.

Consequently, I was apprehensive about listening to the President's recent speech at the NAACP centennial anniversary for fear that he would once again get on his personal responsibility soap box. Such rhetoric plays well with the media. As expected, his "no excuses" sound bite was the only part of the speech that made the news cycle and was played ad nauseam. While I agree that we need to teach our children that racism is no excuse for poor school performance, I also believe that academic and professional achievement does not immunize anyone from racism, which has indeed stifled the potential of countless young people in this country. How one successfully navigates a system which automatically assumes he or she is intellectually inferior or is an affirmative action baby undeserving of his or her achievements (i.e. Geraldine Ferraro's comments about Obama during the primary election) is a lesson parents must provide young people as well. But once again Obama's gross generalizations about Black parenting and Black underachievement lent credence to the time worn assertion that Black anti-intellectualism and the dysfunctional Black family lay at the root of what ails Black communities.

Therefore, I was not a little shocked by the President's pointed response on July 21, 2009, to a question posed by Chicago journalist Lynn Sweet regarding the arrest of renowned Harvard scholar Dr. Henry Louis "Skip" Gates, Jr. While on the one hand I thought some of his remarks crossed the line, on the other hand I thought, "Finally, he provides an unambiguous response to a question on the dilemma of race in this country." While Obama rightfully stated that he did not know if race played a part in the Gates controversy, his exposé on the reality of racial profiling and the disproportionate targeting of Blacks and Latinos by law enforcement made him the advocate, however unintentional, for those at the bottom of the racial food chain. By doing so, Obama transgressed polite politics before a majority white audience as he gave voice to the current dilemma of the abuse of police authority in minority communities. As one writer quipped, "Finally, Obama sounded like a Black Man." Witnessing such a rare occurrence caused me to proclaim with glee, "Indeed change has truly come to America."

But that was on Tuesday.

Obama stated in his book *The Audacity of Hope* that he learned early how not to make white people feel their whiteness to avoid white backlash. In his subsequent remarks at an impromptu White House press conference on July 24, 2009, the President once again demonstrated his mastery of appeasing white anxieties for political gain. Unfortunately, his effort to tamp down racial tensions generated from his earlier remarks came at the expense of those at the bottom who are most vulnerable to aggressive policing. To state that Black people are sensitive to racial issues because of a history of past wrongs without acknowledging that we have legitimate concerns about the present state of racial inequality in this country relegated such concerns to the category of Black paranoia. While he maintained that Gates was wrongfully arrested, Obama also stated that both Gates and Crowley, the arresting officer, no doubt overreacted. Then Obama provided a possible explanation for Gates's alleged over-the-top behavior. He attributed it to a misunderstanding between Blacks and officers which often happens during law enforcement encounters with communities of color (though Ware Street where Gates resides can hardly be defined as a minority community). He never provided an explanation for why Crowley may have overacted. But what was most astonishing was that Obama invited the arresting officer along with Gates to the White House for a beer and conversation as though such a gesture were a panacea for police misconduct.[39]

My first reaction was "WTF?!" So, the teachable moment that Obama talked about in his revised comments is that the dilemma of over-aggressive policing can be solved by a bottle of beer, a slap on the back and a good laugh about it all. That strategy might indeed work for Gates, a renowned Harvard Scholar, but what about the rest of us? What about those who do not have the name recognition to have their story make the news cycle? Who do not have the connections to get the charges dropped? Who do not have a personal friendship with the president who will speak out on their behalf? If Obama went too far in his initial remarks by saying that Cambridge police "acted stupidly," he certainly went way too far in his later remarks to defuse the controversy. His acknowledgment that he should have calibrated his earlier remarks more carefully so as not to appear to disparage the police department was a sufficient attempt to silence his critics. But engaging in reductionist reasoning regarding the intersection of race and law enforcement and then offering to have a beer with the arresting officer, whom he never identified in his remarks, all in the name of taking the high road, goes a bit too far. This merely trivializes police misconduct which far too often results in the false incarceration, physical injury and death of people of color in this country.

I understand that Obama, as the first African American to assume the presidency, must walk a racial tight rope, a burden no other American president has had to bear. But as an African American woman who cried the night he was elected and cried the day he was inaugurated, I feel a deep sense of betrayal. It is the same sense of betrayal I felt when I heard and read his comments regarding Katrina. Yes, he must be the president for all the people; but this should not come at the expense of people of color. African Americans are deeply shaken by Gates's arrest. As a wife, mother, sister, aunt, cousin, daughter and friend of Black men, my anxiety for them has now increased tenfold. And should they fall into the hands of an officer who refuses to disengage from a situation even after it has been established that no crime is in progress or has been committed, they undoubtedly will not be as lucky as Gates. Obama asserted that we should all step back and realize that Professor Gates and Officer Crowley are two decent people. Fine. But perhaps we should also step back and realize that our collective reaction to this event clearly demonstrates that the idea that the election of a Black president is evidence that America has moved beyond race is very premature. As Gates pointedly stated in his most recent interview, and I concur, "I thought the whole idea that America was post-racial and post-black was laughable from the beginning. . . But the only black people who truly live in a post-racial world in America all live in a very nice house on 1600 Pennsylvania Avenue." Indeed. I guess the rest of us at the bottom will have to fend for ourselves.

POSTSCRIPT: This article was originally published under the title "What's Been Missing From Obama's Response to the Arrest of Henry Louis Gates." During the second term of his presidency, as the body count of unarmed or legally armed Black men, women, and children piled up across the nation, Obama proved to be woefully ambivalent; he chided the leaders of the Black Lives Matter Movement who refused his invitation for a 15 minute meeting in the Oval Office. In 2016, when police officers were ambushed in Dallas, Texas and Baton Rouge, Louisiana by two Black male veterans in the wake of the killing of Ashton Sterling and Philando Castile (see the essay "When American Soldiers Become American Vigilantes"), Obama made the problem of police brutality an issue of gun control and expressed his sympathy to America's Law Enforcement Community in an open letter. "At the end of the day, you have a right to go home to your family, just like anybody else," he stated. So, do we Mr. President. So, do we. His post-presidential 700 page autobiography *A Promised Land*, mentions police brutality twice but only in relation to the Arab Spring Uprising. The book is woefully deficient in addressing racial tensions in the U. S.

6

SUICIDE FOR WHITES ONLY?

LA PROGRESSIVE, MAY 28, 2016

It goes without saying that the February 8, 2016, suicide of MarShawn McCarrel II, is beyond heartbreaking. Although the police reported that they are not clear why this Black Lives Matter activist took his own life, the fact that he shot himself on the front steps of the Ohio Statehouse indicates that there was a political motive behind this tragic act. Those on the front lines of Black activism must not ignore the psychological consequences of activism and seek ways to buffer friends and colleagues from the trauma resulting from society's continuous denigration and dehumanization as we engage in the never ending struggle of social activism.

It is our responsibility to look out for the mental wellbeing of ourselves and our fellow comrades. The media's *ad nauseum* looping of the brutalization of Black bodies by the police state coupled with our constant push back against the criminalization of what I call Breathing While Black, leaves us as a community forced to deal with the perpetual trauma of resistance to a society that refuses to recognize the humanity of Blacks, and other people of color.

If we do not keep ourselves mentally and yes physically fit, we will not survive; and if we don't survive, oppression and the oppressor will win. McCarrel's untimely demise by his own hands must be a wakeup call to mental health professionals and other community healers that they must aid those activists on the front lines of the movement for Black Lives. The myth that suicide is a "white thing" must be dispelled. While death by suicide is higher for whites, nonetheless Blacks are not immune. According to a 2010 CDC report:

> Although Black suicide rates are lower than the overall U.S. rates, suicide affects Black youth at a much higher rate than Black adults. Suicide is the third leading cause of death among Blacks ages 15-24. Since the Black community in the United States is disproportionately young, the number of deaths among youth may have a particularly strong impact on the Black community. Black Americans die by suicide a full decade earlier than White Americans. The average age of Black suicide decedents is 32, and that of White decedents is 44.

The numbers for American Indian youth are even more dismal.

McCarrel is not the first or only Black activist to lose to his demons brought on by the trauma of oppression. In her intriguing book *Homelands and Waterways: The American Journey of the Bond Family, 1846-1926*, historian Adele Logan Alexander writes about the December 12, 1915, suicide of Black female Adella Hunt Logan, an ardent suffragist and devoted Tuskegee educator. Hunt Logan became disillusioned when Alabama legislators "defeated a bill that summer that would have required a statewide referendum on women's suffrage." Hunt Logan continued undeterred in her activism, but later became "noticeably disagreeable, increasingly irritable, and her emotional deterioration no longer could be ignored when she ignited a fire one night in her husband's office." She was placed in a mental facility which was of little help. Sadly, like McCarrel, Adella Hunt Logan's demons won and she flung "herself from a top-floor window of an administrative building" and "jumped to her death as administrators, teachers, visitors, and many young people (including, most lamentably, two of her own children) watched in horror. A decade earlier, Hunt Logan had prophetically written that a woman's compound frustrations could lead her "to cry, to swear, or to suicide."[40]

And lest we forget the young, awesomely beautiful, and talented Karyn Washington, creator of the Brown Girls Blog "which sought to empower chocolate-complexioned black women." Washington committed suicide on April 8, 2014.

Of course, these are just a few examples. Suicide and mental illness remain a taboo and a stigma among African Americans; many of us are simply walking around with our eyes wide shut refusing to engage with the problem of mental health issues within our own communities. The macho man and the myth of the super woman, to use the words of Michelle Wallace, is literally killing us. We must take care of ourselves and each other by pushing back against the taboo and the stigma of mental illness. As comrades in struggle, checking in with one another to ask, "How you doing? Are you okay?" This must become part and parcel to Black activism.

Work cycles which provide activists space for some R&R so that they do not get mentally and physically burned out must be a central part of activism. We must also be able to recognize and ACT when a comrade is in distress and work toward getting him/her the help she/he needs. Activists who are having coping issues must be honest about how they are feeling and what is going on with them. They should be able to express when they are burned out and need a time out without fear or shame. This is not the time to go it alone. Everyone needs help every now and then. Seeking help is not a sign of weakness; it is a sign of strength and maturity!

As activists, we must work smarter, not harder. The liberation struggle is not a sprint, but a cross country marathon. It is a test of endurance. *Aesop's Fables* taught us the lesson of the hare and the tortoise. Slow and steady wins the race. It is a matter of life and death my friends. Choose life! ▪

7

MELISSA HARRIS PERRY
BURNING

LA PROGRESSIVE, MARCH 3, 2016

"We younger Negro artists who create now intend to express our individual dark-skinned selves without fear or shame. If white people are pleased, we are glad. If they are not, it doesn't matter. We know we are beautiful. And ugly too. . . If colored people are pleased we are glad. If they are not, their displeasure doesn't matter either. We build our temples for tomorrow, strong as we know how, and we stand on top of the mountain, free within ourselves."

—*Langston Hughes*

On Wednesday, March 2, 2016, Melissa Harris Perry's relationship with MSNBC came to a climatic end with one anonymous executive characterizing the former weekend anchor as "a complicated, unpredictable personality." Harris-Perry wasn't having none of it as she took to Twitter in an "I'll show you a complicated unpredictable personality" sistah girl style take down which earned her the headline "Melissa Harris-Perry Leaves MSNBC in a Blaze of Glory!"

On Friday, February 26, 2016, Harris-Perry walked out of the MSNBC studio after sending an email to her staff which lambasted the network for preempting her show to provide additional coverage of the presidential primary; but Harris-Perry saw something more sinister at work:

> Here is the reality: our show was taken—without comment or discussion or notice—in the midst of an election season. After four years of building an audience, developing a brand, and developing trust with our viewers, we were effectively and utterly silenced. Now, MSNBC would like me to appear for four inconsequential hours to read news that they deem relevant without returning to our team any of the editorial control and authority that makes MHP Show distinctive.[41]

Harris-Perry did not mince words in expressing her frustration at the network's preemption of the show that bears her name. "I will not be used as a tool for their purposes. I am not a token, mammy or little brown bobble head. I am not owned by Lack, Griffin or MSNBC. I love our show. I want it back." Of course, that is not going to happen now; and even though the show bore her name, one wonders if it was ever really her show.[42]

I had the pleasure of meeting Dr. Harris-Perry a little over a year ago when she was the keynote speaker at a 2015 Black History Month event in Delaware. As we chatted for a few moments prior to her talk, she seemed a bit frustrated that she was not able to steer the show in the direction she wanted. I had asked her if she would consider doing a segment about women of color in the academy. Her response was candid. "I get this request all the time." She stated that she had approached the producers on several occasions about a segment on the topic with a focus on tenure and how it tied in with the growing tendency to hire adjuncts instead of tenure-track faculty. "But they," she stated, "don't think it's important." It seems to me that the struggle between Harris-Perry and the network began long before last Friday's showdown. Certainly in the last few weeks as the focus of her show shifted from social justice issues to the presidential primary, she felt she was being pushed out; so in a fierce effort to reclaim her voice she pushed back.

A similar scenario played out this past December when Tony Award winning actress Tonya Pinkins abruptly departed the off-Broadway production *Mother Courage and Her Children* because of creative differences with director Brian Kulick. Pinkins also articulated her frustration in unambiguous racialized language stating that her role had been "'neutered,' 'subordinate' and created through 'the filter of the white gaze'. . .My Mother Courage was left speechless, powerless, history-less and even cart-less . . . Why, in 2015, in the arts, is there a need to control the creative expression of a black woman?. . .Am I a dog or a slave to be misled so as to be controlled in my artistic expression?"[43]

Harris-Perry and Pinkins are not the only ones staging their own personal riots to bring attention to the continued systematic oppression of Black people. With the hopes of a post-racial America dashed, much of Black activism has taken on the persona of fighting fire with fire and it seems that Black women are leading this effort. Baltimore prosecutor Marilyn Mosby, the Founding Sistahs of Black Lives Matter, Confederate flag destroyer Bree Newsome, anti-"super predator" Ashley Williams, and yes, Michelle "don't even think about heckling me" Obama, are only a few examples of Black women who have refused to be defined or controlled by "the politics of respectability." Consequently, Harris-Perry has been criticized in some circles for her "undignified" and "riotous" departure from MSNBC. Meanwhile, the network has played the innocent as if the former anchor's disgruntlement was merely a figment of her imagination. Yet, as Dr. King stated regarding riots:

> But it is not enough for me to stand before you tonight and condemn riots. It would be morally irresponsible for me to do that without, at the same time, condemning the contingent, intolerable conditions

that exist in our society. These conditions are the things that cause individuals to feel that they have no other alternative than to engage in violent rebellions to get attention. And I must say tonight that a riot is the language of the unheard. And what is it America has failed to hear? … It has failed to hear that the promises of freedom and justice have not been met. And it has failed to hear that large segments of white society are more concerned about tranquility and the status quo than about justice and humanity.[44]

For the past four years, Harris-Perry gave voice to those victimized by the contingent, intolerable conditions that exist in our society, only to have her show snatched from under her without notice. She felt "worthless" and "betrayed." So, what's a Black woman to do when faced with such devaluation? I know what she was expected to do. She was to remain silent and assume the role of the long-suffering Black woman willing to submit to the white male executive agenda so as to maintain the myth of Black progress and the hope for better opportunities for herself and those of her community which her presence afforded. But Harris-Perry refused to allow the network to continue to indulge this illusion at her own expense. Rather than do the expected, she took the complicated, unpredictable route. With a series of tweets, concluding with a photo of the iconic scene from *Waiting to Exhale* of Bernadine Harris (Angela Bassett) nonchalantly strolling away from the risen flames after setting her cheating husband's luxury car on fire, Harris-Perry told MSNBC what to kiss and where to go, freeing herself in that moment from the perils of preemption. ■

8
WHAT'S IN A NAME: MEET THE ORIGINAL CASSIUS CLAY

TIME MAGAZINE, JUNE 10, 2016

When Sonny Liston failed to return to the ring after the seventh round, ceding the heavyweight boxing championship in 1964, the media—which had largely bet against his rival—was forced to deal with, as *TIME* put it, the "mouth and magic" of Cassius Marcellus Clay. Clay wasted no time rubbing his win into the faces of a naysaying media, shouting, as the magazine reported:

> "Hypocrites!" yelled Cassius Clay at the press conference. "Whatcha gonna say now, huh? Huh? Who's the greatest?" "Cassius," came the faint reply—too faint to satisfy the new champ. "Let's really hear it!" he hollered. "Who's the greatest? I'll give you one more chance: Who's the greatest?" The chant was loud and clear. "You, Cassius, you. You're the greatest.[45]

But Cassius Clay would not be the greatest for long. Weeks after that Feb. 25, 1964, win, the champ had a new religion, Islam, and a new name, Muhammad Ali. When the media rejected his new identity, Ali hit back hard as Alexandra Sims noted in a recent article for the *Independent*. "Cassius

Clay is a slave name," he said. "I didn't choose it and I don't want it. I am Muhammad Ali, a free name — it means beloved of God, and I insist people use it when people speak to me."[46]

The idea of rejecting a "slave name" has been a resonant one for many, but it comes with a twist in Ali's case. Truth is, Ali's father — Cassius Marcellus Clay, Sr. — was named after a Kentucky slave owner turned emancipationist.

The original Cassius Marcellus Clay (1810-1903), nicknamed Cash, was the son of Kentucky Revolutionary War veteran, politician, and slave-owner General Green Clay. While at Yale College, Cash heard a speech by abolitionist William Lloyd Garrison, who influenced the aspiring politician's anti-slavery sentiments. Unlike Garrison, who called for the immediate end to slavery, Cash became an emancipationist supporting gradual emancipation.

During the 1840s, Cash was elected to the House of Representatives and twice won reelection; but his anti-slavery views cost him his House seat and almost his life, as he survived two assassination attempts. The death threats continued when he freed his slaves and began publishing the anti-slavery newspaper *The True American* in Lexington, Kentucky. When vandals stole his publishing equipment, Cash relocated the office to Cincinnati.

In the 1850s, Cash gave abolitionist John G. Fee a ten-acre homestead on the edge of his property where Fee built Berea College, the first integrated institution of higher learning in the South; Cash was also a founding member of the Republican Party and was pivotal in the campaign to elect Abraham Lincoln in 1860. Cash served as Lincoln's minister to Russia, where he witnessed the Tsar's edict of emancipation, which liberated 23 million people from serfdom.

It is often the case in American history that Black and white families from the same regions who share the same surname have familial ties, and in fact Clay family lore does say that the boxer was descended from a cousin of his namesake. In any case, they shared their flamboyant personalities and gifts of gab. According to biographer David Smiley in his book *The Lion of White Hall*, Cash was braggadocious and continuously talked about his military exploits in the Mexican-American War to anyone who would listen. No stranger to controversy, Cash ignited a firestorm on his return from Russia in 1862 during the Civil War when he publicly rejected the president's offer of a military command. Cash accused Lincoln of "trying to conquer the rebellion with the sword in one hand and the shackles in the other" because he refused to liberate slaves in Confederate territories. "You allow four million of good Union men in the South," he chided, "who are your natural allies, to cut your own throats, because you cannot lay aside a sickly prejudice." The media had a field day as newspapers all over the country reprinted the speech.

Cash believed he had scored a major political victory on Sept. 22, 1862, when Lincoln issued a preliminary proclamation warning the Confederates of his intention to free all slaves within territories still in rebellion against the Union. The ambassador no doubt bragged that he had finally brought the president to his senses — but Cash would receive no sign of appreciation from Lincoln. According to the diary of Illinois Senator Orville Browning, Lincoln thought Cash was "conceited" and wanted "to control everything— conduct the war on his own plan and run the entire seat of government." After the Emancipation Proclamation went into effect on January 1, 1863, Cash resigned his commission and returned to Russia where he remained until 1869.

The parallels between Cassius Marcellus Clay the emancipationist and the boxing heavyweight champion of the world who once bore his name, while remarkable, also make Ali's rejection of that name more appropriate. After all, self-naming is one of the pillars of self-liberation. Cassius Clay was the name of an emancipator, and Muhammad Ali was the name of a free man. ■

9

REMEMBERING
THE CHARLESTON NINE

LA PROGRESSIVE, JUNE 17, 2016

I vividly remember where I was a year ago today when I first heard the news of the massacre at Emanuel African Methodist Episcopal Church in Charleston, South Carolina. It was about 2 a.m. and I had just finished an op-ed urging those who were angry about the Melissa Harris Perry-Rachel Dolezal interview to cut the former weekend anchor some slack. No sooner had I submitted the post; news of the church shooting appeared in my Face Book newsfeed. CNN was the only news outlet at that time reporting the horrific incident:

"Breaking News: shooter on the run after fatally wounding nine church members during a prayer service."

Listening to the news reports was surreal. I wanted Dolezal's fifteen minutes of fame to be over, but not like this. As the saying goes, "Be careful what you pray for!"

THE FALLEN

The following day, we learned the names of the fallen:

- **Cynthia Marie Graham Hurd** (54) – Bible study member and manager for the Charleston Public Library system.
- **Susie Jackson** (87) – a Bible study and church choir member.
- **Ethel Lee Lance** (70) – the church's sexton.
- **Depayne Middleton-Doctor** (49) – a pastor who was also employed as a school administrator and admissions coordinator at Southern Wesleyan University.
- **Clementa C. Pinckney** (41) – the church's pastor and a South Carolina state senator.
- **Tywanza Sanders** (26) – a Bible study member and grandnephew of Susie Jackson.
- **Daniel Simmons** (74) – a pastor who also served at Greater Zion AME Church in Awendaw.
- **Sharonda Coleman-Singleton** (45) – a pastor, speech therapist and track coach at Goose Creek High School.
- **Myra Thompson** (59) – a Bible study teacher.

On that same day we learned the name of the murderer, Dylann Roof, a white supremacist who targeted the church on the anniversary of the failed slave insurrection organized by Denmark Vesey, a freed slave and founding member of the historic congregation. Roof confessed that he committed the act in the hope of igniting a race war. Roof made his motive clear to his victims when he stated, "I have to do this. You rape our women and you're taking over our country. And you have to go." Ironically, six of the nine victims were women. His words echoed the sentiments of post-Civil War white southern extremists. White womanhood must be protected by any means necessary, which often included the lynching of Black men, while the protection of Black womanhood was of no relevance to the southern cause.

To show our solidarity, on the Sunday following the tragedy, my husband Tracy and I attended services at Mother Bethel African Methodist Episcopal Church, the original A.M.E. pioneered by Rev. Richard Allen in 1794 in

Philadelphia. Allen started the denomination when Black parishioners of St. George's United Methodist Church were no longer welcomed there to worship. It was an honor to attend this historic house of worship. The church's atmosphere, the singing, the reading of scripture, and the preaching were refreshing and cleared away the toxic energy which had engulfed us.

Roof's callous act of murder stirred much debate in the mainstream and social media about gun control, mental illness, racism, and domestic terrorism. But the salient debate sparked during the aftermath concerned the relatives of the victims who expressed sentiments of forgiveness during Roof's arraignment two days after the massacre. "I forgive you," stated Nadine Collier, the daughter of 70-year-old Ethel Lance. "You took something very precious from me. I will never talk to her again. I will never, ever hold her again. But I forgive you. And have mercy on your soul." While their actions drew praise from some corners of Black America, it enraged others as if, according to Meeke Addison, "their grief isn't black enough." There were also some who shook their heads at those of the Christian faith who continued to pray and seek spiritual guidance and solace. "Weren't the nine victims praying when they were shot down?" some asked.

I indeed understood the anger, pain, and frustration many felt at the country, the world, and even "white Jesus" but no one has the right to dictate to others their process for coping with tragedy. No one has a right to criticize people for peacefully practicing their religious faith, and certainly no one has the right to demand that they stop practicing that faith. This criticism was a violence perpetrated upon the loved ones already reeling from the unspeakable violence visited upon their family members. Dr. Maya Angelou stated it best. "Hate. It has caused a lot of problems in this world but has not solved one yet." The victims' families understood this as they stood in the courtroom that day looking in the eyes of the man who had stolen from their loved ones the greatest gift of all: life. On this first anniversary of the Emanuel A.M.E. tragedy, let us honor the victims and their loved ones by remembering their acts of kindness shown to one who proved himself to be so undeserving. ▪

10

THE PULSE NIGHT CLUB MASSACRE WAS NOT AN ACT OF GOD

LA PROGRESSIVE, JUNE 16, 2016

I remember the day I began to question the hellfire and brimstone sermons I had heard on Sunday mornings (and later preached) about LGBTQ people. I was watching members of Westboro Baptist Church on television as they were picketing at the funeral of Matthew Shepard, a gay student at the University of Wyoming who had been brutally tortured and left for dead on October 6, 1998. Two men took turns pistol whipping Shepard on the head with a .357 Magnum revolver. Eighteen hours later, two bicyclists found a near frozen comatose Shepard, who they first thought was a scarecrow, tied spread-eagled to a roughhewn deer fence. According to *Losing Matthew Shepard* by Beth Loffreda, "Matt was suffering from hypothermia, and there was severe trauma to the brain stem ... one side of Matt's head had been beaten in several inches ... the neurosurgeon was quite frankly surprised that he was still alive." Shepard died six days later from his injuries.

On October 18, 1998, as mourners gathered in St. Mark's Episcopal Church for Shepard's funeral, Westboro Baptist Church held a nearby protest with picket signs that read, "God Hates Fags!" I was shocked as I stood in the middle of my living room floor watching one hate-filled sign after another pass before my eyes. My mind briefly drifted back to the scene I witnessed days earlier when medical personnel carefully removed Shepard from the fence. His mother Judy Shepard was on site and witnessed the horrific scene. The compassion I felt for this stranger was overwhelming. I wanted to climb though the television and comfort her in her unimaginable mother's grief. Now refocused on the hate-filled signs, I shouted at the television, "That was no fag, that was somebody's son!" For certain, Westboro won the day. The media focus and subsequent sensationalism helped catapult the religious hate group to international fame. I do not think, however, that Westboro ever imagined that their message would transform the life of a Black Christian woman who saw through their hate, and her own.

Blacks have been falsely characterized as more homophobic than those of other communities. I do agree that we are arguably the most hypocritical on the subject because for most African Americans, our first encounter with gay people is at church. Whether Baptist, Christian Methodist Episcopal, Church of God in Christ, Holiness/Apostolic, African Methodist Episcopal. or non-denominational, the music ministry in numerous Black churches is comprised of LGBTQ people. The best singers, musicians, and choir directors are most often also queer. Their presence as LGBTQ, however, is never openly acknowledged; but church members constantly whisper about those presumed to be queer, whether real or imagined.

Every Sunday, Black preachers across America sermonize about the sin of homosexuality and its consequence, hell; they preach to the straight members while proverbially (and in some cases literally) winking at the gay members.

Notwithstanding, the church's anti-gay message and shameless exploitation of the talents of its queer members has been extremely hurtful. As gospel great Kirk Franklin recently stated in his apology to the LGBTQ community on behalf of the Black church:

I want to apologize for all of the hurtful and painful things that have been said about people in the church that have been talented and gifted and musical, that we've used and we've embarrassed…and all this other horrible crap that we've done…We have not treated them like people. We're talking about human beings, men and women that God has created … It is horrible that we have made it where the Bible is a homophobic manual… That's not what the Bible is. I mean you want to talk about things that God gets at … pride and jealousy and envy and arrogance. But what we also see is God sending his son to save us all, because we were all … straight, gay or whatever, lost and in need of a savior, and there's room at the cross for all of us.[47]

Indeed, LGBTQ people are human beings who deserve the love, compassion, and respect that all of God's children deserve. The dead and wounded in Orlando's Pulse nightclub were/are mothers, fathers, sisters, brothers, sons, daughters, nieces, nephews, and friends. Just as the song "You Were Loved" sung by the late Whitney Houston attests these victims "were loved by someone, touched by someone, held by someone, meant something to someone, loved somebody, touched somebody's heart along the way." Early Sunday morning, loved ones gathered near Pulse nightclub crying, holding their heads and hearts, beating their chests and later the wall trying to make sense of a senseless tragedy. As news of the mass shooting made national headlines, Westboro and others of the religious wrong called it an act of God.

This tragic episode, however, was no more an act of God than the massacres which occurred at Columbine, Virginia Tech, Sandy Hook, and Emanuel African Methodist Episcopal Church. This was the act of Omar Mateen, an American citizen who chose to commit mass murder at a LGBTQ nightclub he had frequented the past three years. Anyone who considers her/himself a member of the faith community yet believes that God approves of this heinous act because the victims were LGBTQ, has no understanding of the true meaning of Christianity. As Florida Attorney

Chuck Hobbs stated in a Face Book post, "You are not a real Christian. You are a damned fool!" In other words, you need a come to Jesus moment! ■

11

THE W. E. B. DU BOIS ARGUMENT FOR NOT VOTING IN A "PHONY" ELECTION

TIME MAGAZINE, AUGUST 18, 2016

As President Obama made an impassioned case for a Hillary Clinton presidency on the third night of the Democratic National Convention in Philadelphia, Pennsylvania, some delegates booed at the mention of Republican opponent Donald Trump. Obama quipped in response, "Don't boo, vote!" Yet, now that the two major parties are facing off in the general election, for many voters a question still remains: vote for whom? As Michael Barbaro, writing for the *New York Times,* stated, a Clinton vs. Trump contest "represents the first time in at least a quarter-century that majorities of Americans held negative views of both the Democratic and Republican candidates at the same time."[48]

As a result of the hard-fought and continuing battle for universal suffrage, voting has become a sacred duty for many Americans. For certain, some dissenters will remain loyal and vote within their own party, while others will vote across party lines or for a third-party candidate. Yet, there are an increasing number of dissenters from both parties who are choosing to exercise their right not to vote.

Eddie Glaude, chair of the Department of African American Studies at Princeton University, has written for *TIME* that his values are informed by the quest for economic and racial justice. He wants a president who "fundamentally transforms the circumstances of the most vulnerable in this country" and believes that the Democrats have failed miserably in addressing these issues. Come November, while not completely abandoning the franchise, Glaude—like so many others—has said that he will leave the ballot for president blank. But, as unusual as the 2016 election may seem, those dissenters are not the first to come to such a conclusion.[49]

A similar sentiment regarding the presidential election was expressed 60 years ago by renowned intellectual and civil rights activist W. E. B. Du Bois: In 1956 he declared "I shall not go to the polls." When Du Bois' article "I Won't Vote" appeared in *The Nation* on October 20, 1956, the seasoned scholar-activist was 88 years old and had exercised the franchise since reaching the age of eligibility in 1889. The Fifteenth and Nineteenth Amendments enfranchised Black men and all women in 1870 and 1920 respectively, at which points Northern Blacks — like Du Bois — could vote, though their counterparts in the South were often prevented by discriminatory regulations. And voting was no small thing to him. Du Bois' deep commitment to political and civil rights for African Americans was poignantly expressed in a scathing rebuke of his intellectual rival, Booker T. Washington, in his 1903 classic *The Souls of Black Folk*, which expressed his belief that economic advancement was unattainable without political and civil rights.

Du Bois saw presidential politics as a means to achieving racial and economic justice. He was a strategic voter. He supported (and rejected) candidates based on his perception of their "attitude toward Negroes," he wrote, rather than on their party affiliation. As long as he had been old enough to vote, he had expressed those preferences by voting "for a third party even when its chances were hopeless, if the main parties were unsatisfactory; or, in absence of a third choice, voting for the lesser of two evils."[50]

From Reconstruction to the turn of the 20th century, Republicans had courted Black voters, which had guaranteed the party's political dominance; but when Theodore Roosevelt "dodge[d] the Negro Question," at his Bull Moose convention in 1912, Du Bois and other Black leaders encouraged the Black electorate of 500,000 to cast their ballots for Woodrow Wilson. According to Du Bois biographer David Levering Lewis, Wilson "hinted that under his inspiring leadership, the Democratic Party and the African American could find a modus vivendi." But within six months of Wilson taking office, the new president had segregated federal civil service workers. Under his administration many Blacks lost their jobs. Du Bois wrote to Wilson asking the president to rescind his policies, but Wilson refused.[51]

During the decades that followed, Du Bois continued his strategic voting like a square dancer switching from one partner to the next. In 1920 he voted for Republican Warren Harding, in 1924 for Republican turned Progressive Robert La Follette, in 1928 for Socialist Norman Thomas and in 1932 for Democrat Franklin Roosevelt. When he returned to the North after teaching in the South from 1934 to 1944, Du Bois joined the Progressive Party, voting for nominees Henry Wallace and Vincent Hallinan in 1948 and 1952 respectively. By 1956, Du Bois said, "Enough!"

Du Bois believed the rematch between Republican Dwight Eisenhower and Democrat Adlai Stevenson was a contest of "one evil party with two names and it will be elected despite all I can do or say ... Democracy is dead in the United States." The eminent scholar anticipated his critics' responses to his decision to not vote, asserting, "Is the refusal to vote in this phony election a counsel of despair? No, it is dogged hope. It is hope that if twenty-five million voters refrain from voting in 1956 because of their own accord ... this might make the American people ask how much longer this dumb farce can proceed without even a whimper of protest."[52]

Eisenhower won by a landslide, carrying 41 states and over 57% of the vote; the two-party political system has remained unchanged. And yet, today many Americans, irrespective of party affiliation, have again said "Enough!" Despite criticism, they view the right not to vote as a democratic exercise of conscience that reimagines a politics unchained from the mere act of casting a ballot. ▪

12

SLAVERY ON AMERICA'S COLLEGE CAMPUSES WENT BEYOND BUYING AND SELLING

TIME MAGAZINE, SEPTEMBER 15, 2016

Not long after Georgetown University President John J. DeGioia announced a plan to atone for the school's active participation in slavery — which included the 1838 sale of 272 slaves, which kept the school financially afloat — the descendants of those slaves are now calling on the school to do more. Beyond the proposed monument and admission preferences, they are asking the university to partner with them to raise $1 billion to finance a reconciliation project. The group first raised $115,000 in seed money, which was the amount Georgetown received for the slave sale.[53]

Their effort to extend the conversation beyond DeGioia's statement is fitting, as it is worth remembering that the relationship between the slave economy and America's academies did not stop at the sale of human beings. That continuing transaction is one of the points underlined by the research of Craig Steven Wilder, the foremost expert on the topic and the author of *Ebony and Ivy: Race, Slavery and the Troubled History of America's Universities.*

Georgetown was founded in 1789 by John Carroll, the first Catholic Bishop in the U.S. As noted by Wilder in his chapter "War and Priest:

Catholic Colleges and Slavery in the Age of Revolution" in *Slavery's Capitalism: A New History of American Economic Development*, members of the Catholic clergy relied on the profits from several plantations for funding of church and campus alike. For the first 40 years of Georgetown's existence, the college was tuition free, with the help of the funds provided by the slave economy. And the history of the Catholic Church and Georgetown University is hardly unique, as the colonial-era Protestant churches similarly invested and profited from a thriving slave economy while building institutions of higher learning based upon American Indian and African slavery. Many American universities were also built with the use of slave labor, and enslaved people were instrumental in the maintenance and daily upkeep of American college campuses.

Slaves were a ubiquitous presence on college campuses. One Yale chronicler stated that "it was common custom of the times to own Negro and Indian slaves." Such slaves were used to attend the personal needs of the president, rectors, governors, faculty, students and campus grounds. College presidents, many of whom were also slave owners, used slaves as personal attendants and as house servants to maintain the president's mansion. Harvard president Increase Mather (from 1692–1701) used an enslaved man, gifted to him by his son Cotton Mather, "to run errands for the college." Harvard president Benjamin Wadsworth (1725–1737) brought his slave Titus, who lived with his family, to the college and "bought a Negro Wench" two days before arriving on campus. Benjamin Franklin, founder of the College of Philadelphia; the first eight presidents of the College of New Jersey (Princeton); and Georgetown presidents Fathers Louis William Valentin DuBourg (1796–1798) and Stephen L. Dubuisson (1825–1826), as Wilder's research highlights, all acquired and used slaves for their own personal service during their tenure as the top college administrator.

Some faculty and students had their own personal servants as well. When a group of Harvard scholars and students came together about a decade ago to research the university's historical involvement with slavery, they found that the Massachusetts school was home to many slaves during the 18th century, like Ciceely, a slave owned by Professor of Hebrew Judah Monis. Campus chores were in abundance and enslaved people were burdened with the most arduous tasks as according to Wilder:

> In the mornings, the professors and scholars needed wood for fires, water for washing, and breakfast after morning prayers in the chapel. As students ate, their rooms were cleaned, chamber pots emptied, and beds made. Multiple meals had to be produced every day in the kitchens. Ashes needed to be cleared from fireplaces and stoves, and floors needed sweeping. Clothes and shoes were cleaned and mended. Fires were lighted and maintained. Buildings wanted for repairs, and servants were impressed into small- and large-scale projects. There were countless errands for governors, professors, and students.

In many ways, campus life echoed life on the plantation, as excess workers would be hired out to college-town locals, as demonstrated by a Dec. 19, 1826, advertisement from Washington College (now Washington and Lee University) that read:

> **Negroes For Hire.** *WILL be hired out for the coming year on Saturday the 30th instant before the Court House door, in Lexington,* **Twenty Likely Negroes**, *belonging to Washington College: consisting of* **Men, Women, Boys and Girls**: *many of them very valuable. Bond with good security will be required, to bear interest from the date if not punctually paid. Terms more particularly made known on the day.* **Sam'l MD. Reid, John Alexander**, *committee.*[54]

(When hiring out slaves proved less profitable, Washington College, like Georgetown, sold slaves to recoup some of its losses.)

The enslaved population on college campuses also endured physical and emotional abuses. They were often conscripted into entertaining students or terrorized by them. For example, enslaved people at the University of North Carolina were often subjected to so-called pranks that in at least one case in 1811 involved students running wild while attacking their servants. They endured whippings, dismemberments, brandings, secret sales that disrupted family units and sexual assaults. This resulted in emotional trauma, leading some to commit suicide.

Slavery is a horrible and painful chapter of American history, the legacy of which continues to haunt the nation. While some would rather ignore it, we must no longer deny its reality or its effects. As DeGioia, speaking to the Georgetown University community stated, "we cannot do our best work if we refuse to take ownership of such a critical part of our history.... We must acknowledge it." Indeed, the full depth of slavery's contribution to early American academia must be openly acknowledged for truth and reconciliation to be fully achieved. ■

13

ALLIANCES BETWEEN AMERICA'S BLACK AND JEWISH ACTIVISTS HAVE LONG BEEN TROUBLED

TIME MAGAZINE, AUGUST 22, 2016

When the Movement for Black Lives released its long-anticipated policy platform earlier this month, attention quickly fell on the Invest-Divest section of the document, which called "for the U.S. government to divest from military expenditures and U.S. aid to the State of Israel." The authors of the section--Benjamin Ndugga-Kabuye, NYC Organizer for Black Alliance for Just Immigration and Rachel Gilmer, Chief of Strategy for Dream Defenders, who is Jewish--also chided the American government for being complicit in the Israel "apartheid" state and "genocide" of Palestinians.[55]

Though organizations such as the Jewish Voice for Peace and the Jews of Color Caucus have released statements supporting the platform, other prominent members of the Jewish community have repudiated Black Lives Matter. Attorney Alan Dershowitz in a recent Boston *Globe* article called the use of the term "genocide" anti-Semitic and admonished the organization to "remove this blood libel from its platform." Rabbi Dan Dorsch, writing for *Haaretz*, contended that the reference to "Apartheid Israel" and inserting the Israeli-Palestinian conflict "within the context of serious discussions of racial inequality in America" seemed to him "to be *chutzpahdik*, if not entirely out of bounds."[56]

This month also marks the 25th anniversary of another major clash between American Black and Jewish communities: the rioting that swept the Crown Heights neighborhood of Brooklyn between August 19 and August 21, 1991. As that conflict is remembered and today's is debated, it is worth remembering that, in fact, the alliance between those communities has been troubled for a long time — but it has nevertheless endured.[57]

As Ndugga-Kabuye stated in an interview with *The Times of Israel*, "Jewish reactions to the platform recalled the later years of the 1960s civil rights movement, when white and Black allies split over tactics and ideology." As Cheryl Lynn Greenberg notes in her book *Troubling The Water: Black-Jewish Relations in the American Century*, the 1965 iconic image of Rabbi Abraham Joshua Heschel and Dr. Martin Luther King Jr. marching together from Selma to Montgomery is representative of what many perceive as the heyday of Black-Jewish alliance, when the two fought side by side in the struggle for civil rights. The pairing made sense to many: though their pasts were vastly different, both populations had firsthand knowledge of 20th-century oppression. As Dr. King's confidante Andrew Young stated in an interview, "There has always been a natural kinship [among civil-rights leaders] with the Jewish community. ... I mean the movement was Jewish in the sense that our songs were 'Oh Pharaoh, Let My People Go,' 'Joshua Fit the Battle of Jericho.'"[58]

Greenberg, however, challenges this representation, contending that "cooperation and conflict coexisted throughout, with tensions caused by economic clashes, ideological disagreements, Jewish racism and Black anti-Semitism, as well as differences in class and the intensity of discrimination faced by each group."

As the movement toward Black Nationalism emerged, because of disillusionment with the slow gains of the Civil Rights Movement, organizations such as SNCC drew parallels between the black-liberation struggle and the larger international struggle against white colonialism. They argued that black ghettoes in the U.S. were similarly colonized. Regarding the Middle East, SNCC and other radical groups lambasted Israel as a "European-style oppressor of non-white Palestinians."

Black Nationalism would soon transform into a Black International consciousness.

Keith P. Feldman, in *A Shadow Over Palestine: The Imperial Life of Race in America,* correlates the emergence of Black Internationalism with what some believed to be "the 'tragic pro-Arab' wedge between American Jews and Black liberation struggles." In response to what many perceived as atrocities committed against Palestinians during the Six-Day War in June of 1967, the SNCC newsletter published in August featured a two-page article titled "The Third World Round-Up; The Palestine Problem: Test Your Knowledge" containing "documented facts" that contextualized the Black freedom struggle within an international framework "through a complex and sustained engagement with Palestine." SNCC spokesperson Ralph Featherstone well understood the risk of its publication, stating, "Some people might interpret what we say as Anti-Semitic."

Featherstone's prediction was correct. *The New York Times,* in a front-page article titled "S.N.C.C. Charges Israel Atrocities: Black Power Group Attacks Zionism as Conquering Arabs by 'Massacre,'" lambasted the organization by calling its rhetoric "hate filled" and mourning the passing of Black-Jewish cooperation. The then-general counsel of the Antidefamation League of B'nai B'rith, Arnold Forster, concurred. "It is a tragedy that the civil rights movement is being degraded by the injection of hatred and racism in reverse," he said. "This newsletter follows the pro-Arab, Soviet, and racist lines and smacks very heavily of anti-Semitism." Despite the repudiation SNCC received after that publication, from prominent civil rights leaders such as Dr. King and A. Philip Randolph of the Southern Christian Leadership Conference, and Whitney M. Young of the National Urban League, the rift between Black and Jewish activists seemed also irreparable.[59]

As Peniel Joseph stated in *Waiting 'Til the Midnight Hour: A Narrative History of Black Power in America*, "Palestine as a colony and its people as a community of color under siege, produced an uncomfortable stalemate in which representatives of the two longstanding minority groups attacked each other as racist and anti-Semitic."

The current controversy is a continuation of the challenge of Black-Jewish alliance as elements within both populations face an ideological impasse. While many are once again eulogizing the loss of solidarity, such sentiment appears premature. History is on the side of those who see an alliance continuing: whether in the 1960s or the 1990s, conflicts that have arisen in the past have never led to a complete fissure. African Americans and Jewish Americans still tend to share political affiliations, and the reasons they might share priorities are as pertinent as ever. Less than two weeks after BLM released its platform, *Mondoweiss*, a newsletter that focuses on the Middle East, reported on "the largest-ever Jewish demonstration for #BlackLivesMatter" which convened in Greenwich Village, New York City. When asked by reporter Wilson Dizard about the controversy, Jason Salmon, a leader in Jews for Racial & Economic Justice (JREJ) responded as he was led away by police for disorderly conduct, "Minority groups in this country have been pitted against each other since the beginning. Since the inception of this country. I've just had it."[60]

14

FORGET THE STAR-SPANGLED BANNER: WE HAVE OUR OWN NATIONAL ANTHEM

LA PROGRESSIVE, SEPTEMBER 21, 2016

We have come over a way that with tears has been watered; we have come, treading our path through the blood of the slaughtered. — James Weldon Johnson, "Lift Every Voice and Sing"/The Black National Anthem

By the time I was in the fourth grade at Mary E. Rodman Elementary School in West Baltimore, I hated "The Star-Spangled Banner." Not only was it an awkward, odious melodic nightmare, I also could not get past the opening phrase of the last sentence of the song: "O'er the land of the free..."

Hold up! What?

Slavery was not taught in school, even during what was then dubbed "Negro History Week." I learned about slavery while overhearing older relatives' conversations when they thought the kids were not listening. During a field trip to the Fort McHenry National Monument, the battle site which inspired Francis Scott Key's poem, I asked my teacher, "How could it be the land of the free when 'we' had slaves?" But when she and the tour guide, both white women, shot me the evil eye, I was too sorry I had asked. I do not blame them, though. I mean, we were at a replica of a battlefield. Indeed, American history is a battle, a never-ending power struggle over memory. As Maori scholar Linda Tuhiwai Smith states in her book, *Decolonizing Methodologies: Research and Indigenous Peoples*, "We believe that history is also about justice, that understanding history will enlighten our decisions about the future. Wrong. In fact, history is mostly about power .... It is because of this relationship with power that we have been excluded, marginalized, and 'Othered'."[61]

Of course, I had no idea about the politics of history then. Damn my nine-year-old brain and mouth. Since then, I have been estranged, and happily so, from that God-awful song with its glorification of war and schizophrenic musical arrangement. I do not mean to offend by appropriating schizophrenia which is a serious mental illness. But I cannot imagine a better term which captures the song's musicology and America's relationship to the anthem. Case in point, the histrionics over former 49ers quarterback Colin Kaepernick's refusal to stand during the anthem in protest of police brutality and racial inequality. Those who support Kaepernick believe his protest is justified by the continued reality of police overreach in Black communities and the racist underpinnings of the song, as the third stanza repudiates Blacks for having the gull to, of all things, side with the British in exchange for their freedom. Key wrote:

> And where is that band who so vauntingly swore,
> That the havoc of war and the battle's confusion
> A home and a Country should leave us no more?
> Their blood has wash'd out their foul footstep's pollution.
> **No refuge could save the hireling and slave**
> **From the terror of flight or the gloom of the grave,**
> And the star-spangled banner in triumph doth wave
> O'er the land of the free and the home of the brave.[62]

Those who oppose the quarterback, include Shirley Carole Isham, a great-great-great-granddaughter of Key who believes that Kaepernick's right to protest is irrelevant:

It just broke my heart to think that someone that gets so much money for playing a ballgame, who is half black, half white would do this ... . So many of his black race are oppressed, but it's not by the whites, it's by their own people. Look who their leaders are, and the president. Has (Barack Obama) done anything for these people? If he's not going to honor his country and his countrymen, he's dishonoring himself ... . This tells you an awful lot about him."[63]

I will not give Isham the dignity of a response except to say, "Girl bye!"

Anyway, we must also talk about the country's schizophrenia regarding how American authenticity is defined by who performs the national anthem and how it is performed. In 1968, Puerto Rican singer Jose Feliciano performed the national anthem at the World Series; he was booed, and the Baseball Commissioner received letters of complaint because the singer's added Latin flavor was viewed as un-American. It almost destroyed his career. The late, great Marvin Gaye rocked the 1983 NBA All-Star Game with his Motownesque cover of the song which was dubbed "National Healing," a play on his highly successful single "Sexual Healing;" as did Whitney Houston's Gospel inspired cover at the Super Bowl in 1990. Felicano's 2012 do over at the National League Championship Series received rave reviews which resulted in a new generation of fans; but the 2013 performance by San Antonio, Texas native, eleven-year-old Sebastian De La Cruz at Game 3 of the NBA Finals set social media ablaze. For many "a Mexican kid" singing the anthem mocked American patriotism. Lewie Groh tweeted, "Why is a foreigner singing the national anthem. I realize that's San Antonio but that still ain't Mexico." Fortunately, the response to the criticism drowned out the vitriol; De La Cruz was invited to Game 4 for an encore performance. President Obama tweeted his support: "Don't miss @selcharrodeoro's encore performance of the national anthem at the #NBAFinals in San Antonio tonight."

My friend, a middle-aged Puerto Rican woman, expressed shock that adults had so viciously attacked a child just for singing a song. "I don't understand why they would do that," she stated. "Do white people get angry when Black people sing it?"

"No," I responded, "and most Black folk wouldn't care because we have our own national anthem."

A look of surprise flashed across her face as she blurted out, "What, there's another national anthem?" Indeed.

"Lift Every Voice and Sing" began as a poem written by James Weldon Johnson which was set to music by his brother John Rosamond Johnson in 1899. In the book *Lift Every Voice and Sing: A Celebration of the Negro National Anthem: 100 Years, 100 Voices*, Weldon's creative process is captured in his own words:

> I got my first line—*Lift every voice and sing*. Not a startling line, but I worked along grinding out the next five. When, near the end of the first stanza, there came to me the lines *Sing a song full of the faith that the dark past has taught us; Sing a song full of the hope that the present has brought us*; the spirit of the poem had taken hold of me. I finished the stanza and turned it over to Rosamond. In composing the two other stanzas I did not use pen and paper. While my brother worked at his musical setting I paced back and forth on the front porch, repeating the lines over and over to myself, going through all of the agony and ecstasy of creating. As I worked through the opening and middle lines of the last stanza: *God of our weary years, God of our silent tears, Thou*

who hast brought us thus far on our way; Thou who hast by Thy might Led us into the light. Keep us forever in the path, we pray. Lest our feet stray from the places, our God, where we met Thee, Lest, our hearts, drunk with the wine of the world, we forget Thee ... I could not keep back the tears and made no effort to do so. I was experiencing the transports of the poet's ecstasy. Feverish ecstasy was followed by that contentment — that sense of serene joy — which makes artistic creation the most complete of all human experiences. When I had put the last stanza down on paper I at once recognized the Kiplingesque touch in the two longer lines quoted above; but I knew that in the stanza the American Negro was, historically and spiritually, immanent; and I decided to let it stand as it was written.[64]

The song was first publicly performed in 1900 in the Johnsons' hometown of Jacksonville, Florida. A choir of 500 Black school children sang out the lyrics during a program honoring Abraham Lincoln at Stanton "Colored" School, where Weldon was principal. The song grew in popularity and was quickly adopted as the "Negro (later Black) National Anthem."

Singing "The Star-Spangled Banner" followed by "Lift Every Voice and Sing" is a tradition at Black cultural events all over the country.

The Black National Anthem has been the focus of controversy in recent years. On July 1, 2008, just weeks before Obama was set to accept the Democratic nomination for President in Denver, Colorado, jazz singer René Marie performed a rendition of the anthem at a Denver state event which blended the music of "The Star-Spangled Banner" with the lyrics of "Lift Every Voice and Sing." Her performance was "denounced by state and local officials" with some calling the performance "a disgrace." Marie received a barrage of racist emails, phone calls, and death threats. Bridgette of the conservative blog Don't Get Me Started stated, "There is NO substitute for the national anthem and what this woman did was rude and in poor taste.

There should be no such thing as a 'black' national anthem." Some Blacks including then Senator Obama, concurred. "If she was asked to sing the national anthem, she should have sung that.... 'Lift Every Voice and Sing' is a beautiful song, but we only have one national anthem," Obama stated. Once again, patriotic provincialism underscored by political pandering, derailed a teaching moment by silencing Black progressive voices.[65]

The controversy resurfaced when civil rights legend Joseph Lowery invoked the words of the last stanza during his benediction at the 2009 presidential inauguration. Some accused Lowery of stoking racial tensions. But Marian Wright Edelman captured the sentiment of the moment for many African Americans when she stated:

The words made my deepest heartstrings throb. For all of us raised on those beloved words, the symbolism was overwhelming. For over a hundred years, every time it has been sung in a church hall, school auditorium or community meeting, it has enabled us Black folks to sing our own story about our faith in and struggle to make America's promise real.... For now, as part of the blessing of our nation and our new young, brilliant President who reflects the DNA of our nation and globe, the Negro National Anthem has become — at long last — part of the larger American hymn. As President Obama's name is added to the list that begins with George Washington, and his portrait becomes the face of America, the next chapters in Black and American history are being written together.[66]

Yet, as the backlash over Kaepernick's protest demonstrates, far too many Americans are only interested in writing a narrative which supports the white nationalistic sentiments expressed in Key's song. On the other hand, "Lift Every Voice and Sing" is an expression of an all-inclusive patriotism which embodies "the audacity of hope" for a brighter future while not forgetting the struggles of our past. Until structural inequality is dismantled in every segment of American society, Key's words "O say does that star-spangled banner yet waves o'ver the land of the free" remains an aspiration.

Indeed, a Black family in the White House has exacerbated rather than eased racial tensions in this country; and the blood of the slaughtered continues to run unabated in a nation of cowards, to borrow the words of former Attorney General Eric Holder. With some chanting, "We want 'our' country back" and the potential election of Donald Trump, who wants to "Make America Great [White] Again," it is clear that we remain a long way off from Dr. King's dream. The struggle continues. Therefore, in the words of the Black Nation Anthem, "Let us march on 'til victory is won."

#BlackLivesMatter!

15

WHETHER THE SECOND AMENDMENT APPLIES TO ALL CITIZENS IS NOT A NEW QUESTION

TIME MAGAZINE, SEPTEMBER 26, 2016

I t's been about 150 years since the ratification of the Fourteenth Amendment, which granted Black people the right to full citizenship, but some have recently questioned whether the Constitution applies equally to all citizens. Specifically, in the wake of the death of Keith Lamont Scott in Charlotte, North Carolina, some — like Eugene Robinson, writing in the *Washington Post* — have questioned whether "Second Amendment rights are for whites only," as the matter of whether he had a handgun ought to be made moot by North Carolina's being an open-carry state. This is not the first time the question has been asked in recent months: Erica Evans asked the same question in the *Los Angeles Times* in July, after the police-shooting deaths of Alton Sterling and Philando Castile. But, while the question has recently returned to headlines, it is in fact as old as the country itself.[67]

Gun restrictions in America date back to the colonial era when the settler class, engaged in violent conflicts with the indigenous population, initiated laws in 1611 against American Indians owning guns. By 1640 gun restrictions were expanded to include "Negroes and mulattoes." After the American Revolution, the fear of disarmament was widespread, particularly among southern whites who feared they would be left vulnerable in a slaveholding South. As constitutional law expert Carl T. Bogus has argued, James Madison wrote the amendment as a guarantee to his constituents in Virginia and to the south at large "that Congress could not use its newly-acquired powers to indirectly undermine the slave system by disarming the militia, on which the South relied for slave control."[68]

To the contrary, the founders justified the forced disarmament of slaves, freed Blacks and mulattoes for fear of insurrections. Slave codes were enacted and enforced by slave patrols, which comprised armed militias, to ease white fears of Black violence. As Bogus noted, "Slavery was not only an economic and industrial system, but more than that, it was a gigantic police system." Notwithstanding, Virginia passed a law in 1806 allowing free Negroes and mulattoes to own guns with the approval of local officials; but in the aftermath of the 1831 Nat Turner rebellion, the Commonwealth repealed the law and prohibited the sale of guns to free Blacks.

During the 1840s and 1850s, abolitionists such as Lysander Spooner of Massachusetts, Joel Tiffany of Ohio, and Rev. Henry Ward Beecher (the brother of Harriet Beecher Stowe) of New York supported gun ownership for Blacks for the purpose of self-defense against southern tyranny. Beecher, who believed the gun rather than the Bible would overturn slavery, expressed in the New York *Tribune* in 1856, "You might just as well read the Bible to Buffaloes" as those who support slavery only revere "the logic that is embodied in Sharp's rifles." Soon after, however, the Supreme Court stepped in.

In his March 1857 opinion in *Dred Scott v. Sandford*, Supreme Court Chief Justice Roger B. Taney stated that Blacks are "so far inferior that they had no rights which the white man was bound to respect." These are the most quoted words from this infamous decision, which determined that Blacks, even if free, were not citizens of the United States and therefore not entitled to equal protection under the law. Taney maintained that Black people were governed by "the operation of a special set of laws" and "police regulations … necessary for their own safety." As such they were denied Constitutional rights like freedom of speech, freedom of movement, the freedom to assemble — and the right to bear arms. To put it bluntly, the Second Amendment (and the entire Constitution) did *not* apply to Black Americans except when it justified their oppression.

After the Civil War, Radical Republicans in 1866 passed the Freedmen's Bureau Act and the Civil Rights Act, guaranteeing the right of freedmen to bear arms for self-defense. Yet, the fight to keep guns out of the hands of Blacks continued. As historian Gerald Horne has claimed, after the Civil War "a good deal of the battles of the bloody reconstruction period, circa 1865 going forward, [were] about keeping arms out of the hands of black people." Leading the charge to disarm the freedmen was the Ku Klux Klan, organized in Tennessee that same year. The group's primary objective was gun control. Chapters of this vigilante group soon emerged all over the South to assume the role of the former slave patrols in maintaining law and order (i.e. white supremacy). The goal of the Klan was to completely disarm Blacks of all guns and ammunition acquired during the war. The Klan's reign of terror persisted throughout the Jim Crow era.[69]

While the South spent a century in its effort to keep Blacks unarmed, another campaign to accomplish the same aim began in California in the 1960s. By 1963, as many Blacks grew disillusioned with the unfulfilled promises of the Civil Rights Movement, paramilitary organizations such as the Black Panther Party for Self Defense emerged in Oakland, to resist the terror of police brutality which was a daily reality in Black communities throughout the nation. The Panthers turned urban policing on its head with the mantra "policing the police." They strolled through the streets dressed in black attire accessorized by bandoliers and rifles observing police arrest from a legal distance to ensure that an arrestee's legal rights were not violated. In those days, California was an open-carry state. Though carrying loaded weapons in public was legal, Negroes With Guns, to borrow the title of Robert F. Williams's 1962 autobiography on armed resistance against the Klan, still set the state and the nation's teeth on edge. In response to this open display of militancy, California passed the Mulford Act, named for its sponsor, Republican Don Mulford, with the support of Governor Ronald Reagan and the NRA.

The debate for individual gun rights was thrust onto the national stage when on May 2, 1967, 30 fully armed members of the Panthers appeared at the California Statehouse in Sacramento to protest the Mulford Act. The Black Panther Party (not the NRA) was at the vanguard for the Second Amendment debate on individual gun rights and pioneered the modern pro-gun movement. FBI Director J. Edgar Hoover dubbed the group "the greatest threat to national security."[70]

For certain, the question of the right of African Americans to bear arms is an old one. No matter which side of the battle over the Second Amendment one agrees with, the effort to ensure that the Constitution applies to each citizen equally is a battle we must all continue to fight — together. ◼

16

AN OLD PHENOMENON: THE VICTIM AS CRIMINAL

TIME MAGAZINE, SEPTEMBER 29, 2016

t is a sad truth that videos of the killings of Black people by police officers have become what one writer for *The Guardian* called "America's new TV violence." The tapes are almost ubiquitous in mainstream and social media, as the use of body cams and camera phones has resulted in a proliferation of recordings of fatal encounters. But, even as these videos may appear to offer an objective perspective on what has happened, it's become clear that these filmed deaths are still subject to interpretation. As *Al Jazeera* noted, news outlets often highlight criminal activity, whether real or imagined, of those who are killed by police and engage in speculation over the character of the victim. This manner of reporting reinforces "tropes about black criminality that have long tainted media coverage of instances of police violence," contends *Media Matters*.[71]

Consequently, family members and community organizations such as The Center for Racial Justice Innovation find it necessary to challenge media reports that put Black victims on trial before all of the facts are known. But this mass circulation of images of the killings of Black victims, like this conversation about the narratives that accompany them, has been the focus of debate since the late 19th century. The current iconography and textual representations of brutalized Black citizens is reminiscent of late-19th to mid-20th century representations and narratives regarding lynching victims. As *Salon* writer Chauncey DeVega has put it, the videos can be seen as "a new digital-era version of lynching postcards." Those "lynching postcards" were a phenomenon of the years following the invention of the Kodak camera in 1888. The new technology allowed lynchings to be captured in real time, and images of those crimes to be distributed nationwide.[72]

Without Sanctuary: Lynching Photography in America by James Allen, et al., is a photo documentary of the horrors of that system, as documented by southerner whites, who made a point to capture these public events. As Allen observes, "Hundreds of Kodaks clicked all morning at the scene of the lynching. . . Picture card photographers installed a portable printing plant . . . and reaped a harvest in selling postcards." Postcards of lynched victims were sold as souvenirs and mailed to friends and relatives as gifts. They were also sent to those, particularly northern whites, who opposed these crimes as a form of intimidation. As Allen notes, newspapers often advertised public lynchings in advance, and afterwards provided gruesome details of the event. Sensationalized headlines such as "Five White Men Take Negro Into Woods; Kill Him: Had Been Charged with Associating with White Women," wired by the *Associated Press* about a lynching in Louisiana, are representative of how the press often cited the alleged crimes of the victim in order to justify such executions without due process.[73]

But in 2015, The Equal Justice Initiative released a report on the history of lynching in the U.S., starting during the immediate post-Civil War era— and historians now concur that lynching, as Bryan Stevenson, Executive Director of EJI told the *New York Times*, was less about crime and more about "executing people for violating the racial hierarchy." In other words, whether the person killed had committed a crime was irrelevant to the punishment meted out.[74]

The criminalization of lynching victims, made popular by the national press, did not go unchallenged. Frederick Douglass provided a counter narrative in an 1895 article, "Why is the Negro Lynched?," in which he proposed to give "a coloured man's view" of a subject that had thus far been debated in public mostly by white speakers. Douglass recounts that after emancipation, "scores of Negroes" were killed for alleged conspiracies such as "schemes to kill all white people, plots to burn the town, and commit violence in general." Such accusations were played out "in glaring headlines in the columns of nearly all our newspapers." By the 1890s, those earlier justifications for lynching were largely replaced by the trope of the Black male rapist who lusted for the purity of white womanhood. This pernicious campaign resulted in an immediate increase in Black male lynching, which lasted from the 1890s to the 1930s. Douglass denounced the accusation as fear mongering.[75]

Civil rights feminist Ida B. Wells-Barnett concurred, adding that the southern definition of rape went well beyond that of the courts; the mere proximity of a Black man to a white woman constituted rape. As an investigative journalist and newspaper editor, Wells-Barnett traveled all over the nation investigating individual cases of lynching and their justifications. She was inspired to do so after two Black male acquaintances, who owned a store directly across from a white shop owner's business, were accused of rape and were lynched. She compiled her findings in a pamphlet titled *The Red Record: Tabulated Statistics and Alleged Causes of Lynching in the United States*. Wells-Barnett learned that in most cases the justification for lynching was based on trumped up-charges leveled against local Black business owners who posed an economic threat to competing white businesses. She compiled a laundry list of offenses that justified lynching, which included "anything or nothing." Compiling factual information for the "red record" continued into the 1920s, with the NAACP purchasing full ads in newspapers and issuing broadsides that challenged mainstream stereotypes of black criminality in an attempt to garner support for a federal anti-lynching bill. This effort continued into the 1930s, but Congress failed to pass any legislation in support of the anti-lynching cause.

One of the unique ways Blacks sought to counter negative stereotypes promoted by the press was though theatrical representations that aimed to humanize Black victims of vigilante violence, a genre known as "lynching plays." Ohio State University Associate Professor of English Koritha Mitchell, in her book *Living with Lynching: African American Lynching Plays, Performance and Citizenship, 1890-1930*, notes the development of the concept, which emerged during the turn of the century. Playwrights moved beyond the brutalized images produced by photographers and circulated by the mass media. As Mitchell notes, "their scripts spotlighted instead the black home and the impact that the mob's outdoor activities have on the family."

These past efforts by civic leaders and dramatists augur the current movement to counter media narratives that transform Black victims into perps. Countering such stereotypes, by focusing on victims' family and community relations, maintains the humanity of the fallen and serves as a coping tool for those who live with the clear and present danger of imminent violence.

POSTSCRIPT: In 2018, Senators Kamala Harris (D), Cory Booker (D), and Tim Scott (R), the only African Americans serving in the Senate, sponsored a bill "To amend title 18, United States Code, to specify lynching as a deprivation of civil rights, and for other purposes." For a century, between the years 1882 and 1986, 200 attempts were made to get federal anti-lynching legislation passed. Every attempt failed. Unfortunately, the 201st time was not the charm as the bill was blocked by Senator Rand Paul (R). Although the bill passed the House, in 2020 Paul insisted on amendments which he argued would strengthen the bill. But Senator Harris (now Vice President Harris) and Booker disagreed countering that their Republican colleague's amendments weakened rather than strengthened the legislation. ■

17

THE TRAGIC HISTORY BEHIND MICHAEL JORDAN'S STATEMENT ON POLICE SHOOTINGS

TIME MAGAZINE, JULY 26, 2016

In 1990, during a heated North Carolina Senate contest between the incumbent, ultra-conservative Republican Jesse Helms, and Harvey Gantt, the African American Mayor of Charlotte, Gantt's campaign approached NBA superstar Michael Jordan for an endorsement. Jordan declined to endorse, allegedly quipping that "Republicans buy sneakers too."[76]

Jordan's refusal to endorse drew the ire of many in the African American community — and 25 years later, he still had not lived down that infamous moment. In a 2015 interview, athlete-author-activist Kareem Abdul-Jabbar chided his colleague stating, "You can't be afraid of losing shoe sales if you're worried about your civil and human rights. He took commerce over conscience. It's unfortunate for him, but he's gotta live with it."[77]

This week, in light of the continued violence plaguing the nation, Jordan decided he could "no longer stay silent."

On Monday, in an exclusive statement published by *The Undefeated*, a blog focused on the intersections of sports and race, Jordan described his reaction to recent police shootings, and the ways in which his own experience has made him both appreciative of law enforcement and concerned about the injustices experienced by people of color. "As a proud American, a father who lost his own dad in a senseless act of violence, and a black man, I have been deeply troubled by the deaths of African Americans at the hands of law enforcement and angered by the cowardly and hateful targeting and killing of police officers," he wrote. "I grieve with the families who have lost loved ones, as I know their pain all too well."[78]

Indeed, on August 4, 1993, the corpse of James Jordan, Michael Jordan's father, was found among the branches in Gum Swamp just across the South Carolina border from Robeson County. Two weeks prior, on July 23, 1993, the elder Jordan, who resided about 120 miles southwest in Charlotte, North Carolina, was returning home from attending the funeral of a friend in Wilmington. He parked his cherry-red Lexus Coupe alongside the road at a country store off U.S. highway 74 to rest.

Carjacking was on the rise during that time. Whether in urban, suburban, or rural America, and no matter the make of the car, no one was exempt. Carjacking was up 25% in 1992, from the previous year, wrote TIME's now-Editor Nancy Gibbs in a story that summer. "Car crime is no longer a matter of stealing parts but of taking lives," the story noted.

James Jordan being fast asleep at a closed business on a lonely country road made him an easy victim.

And the Jordan family's suffering didn't stop there: At the same time that they learned of the murder of their loved one, they also learned that Marlboro County, South Carolina coroner Tom Brown, citing lack of space, had ordered the body autopsied and cremated within three days. Dental records received a week later positively identified the John Doe as James Jordan.

Years later, boyhood friends Daniel Andre Green and Larry Martin Demery were both sentenced to life in prison for the murder, after trials that revealed that the two had come upon the Lexus and shot the elder Jordan point blank in the chest with a .38 caliber handgun. He died instantly. It had not been hard for the police to identify the killers. The pair had videotaped themselves with a watch, golf shoes and a replica NBA championship ring from the Bulls' 1990-1991 season, all items that belonged to the deceased. In addition, the two had placed calls from the car cell phone, which was a major clue in helping police in their capture.

Jordan's personal experience not only motivated him to make an historic statement, but he has also pledged $1 million each to the International Association of Chiefs of Police's newly established Institute for Community-Police Relations and the NAACP Legal Defense Fund. "Although I know these contributions alone are not enough to solve the problem," Jordan stated, "I hope the resources will help both organizations make a positive difference."

POSTSCRIPT: The Memorial Day 2020 murder of George Floyd by Officer Derek Chauvin (see essay #40) transformed Michael Jordan into a full-scale social justice activist as he joined other high-profile athletes in affirming #BlackLivesMatter. In an interview with ESPN, Jordan stated, "I am deeply saddened, truly pained and plain angry. I stand with those who are calling out the ingrained racism and violence toward people of color in our country. We have had enough." While Jordan may have put "commerce over conscience" in his early career, Jordan and the Nike Jordan Brand put out a statement on his commitment to the Black community. "*Black lives matter,*" *Jordan stated, "This isn't a controversial statement. Until the ingrained racism that allows our country's institutions to fail is completely eradicated, we will remain committed to protecting and improving the lives of Black people. Today, we are announcing that Michael Jordan and Jordan Brand will be donating*

$100 million over the next 10 years to organizations dedicated to ensuring racial equality, social justice, and greater access to education." It was the largest corporate donation made in response to Floyd's demise. ■

18

A PERSONAL TRIBUTE TO GWEN IFILL

HISTORY NEWS NETWORK, NOVEMBER 15, 2016

I read the news Monday afternoon of Gwen Ifill's passing and immediately burst into tears. I have always admired her. With so few women of color in the national media, it was inspiring to turn on the television and see this beautiful "well-educated-chocolate-skinned" (words she used to describe Michelle Obama) daughter of Caribbean immigrants, moderate *Washington Week* and co-anchor *The PBS News Hour* with colleague Judy Woodruff.

I had the pleasure of meeting Ifill when she came to Delaware in 2009 as a part of her *Break-Through: Politics and Race in the Age of Obama* book tour. As one can imagine, the line for the book signing was quite long, but she took the time to look each person in the eye and engage them in a brief conservation while providing an autograph that was at once personal and exquisite.

Needless to say, I was star struck when she and I were finally face to face. I tried not to appear awkward and nervous when she asked about my work. I gave her my well-practiced elevator speech and expressed my gratitude for her continued inspiration to Black women and little Black girls everywhere.

Then the unexpected happened. When I told her that her book release came just in time for me to incorporate it into my course Contemporary African American Issues, her smile widened as she came out of her seat and hugged me. "Thanks for teaching the book," she said. She inscribed those same words under her signature. That Black Girl Magic moment we shared made me feel a special connection with her every time I tuned in to watch.

Today as I mourn her enormous loss and celebrate her inspiring life, I would be remiss not to acknowledge the ways in which the race and gender politics she reported on and wrote about also defined her career. Ifill captured this brilliantly in the opening sentences of *Breakthrough* recalling:

I LEARNED HOW TO COVER RACE RIOTS BY TELEPHONE THEY DIDN'T pay me enough at my first newspaper job to venture onto the grounds of South Boston High School when bricks were being thrown. Instead, I would telephone the headmaster and ask him to tell me the number of broken chairs in the cafeteria each day. A white colleague dispatched to the scene would fill in the details for me.

According to a *New York Times* obituary, Ifill's dream of becoming a journalist began at age 9. She blazed the trail for Black women in journalism and covered national politics on the White House, Congress, and national campaigns for the *Washington Post*, *NBC*, and *PBS* in an illustrious career which spanned three decades. In a 2011 interview with the Archive of American Television, Ifill reminisced, "I was very conscious of the world being this very crazed place that demanded explanation." She was also aware that her race and gender posed a specific challenge to her entry into television journalism:

> I didn't see a whole lot of people who looked like me doing [journalism] on television … but you get used to being underestimated. I got my first job by exceeding expectations … This is the way it is. How do I get around it, get through it, surprise them?[79]

Indeed, as many women are often reminded, credentials and experience do not make one immune to racialized and gendered notions of presumed incompetence which was blatantly displayed in the days leading up to the Biden-Palin 2008 Vice-Presidential debate moderated by Ifill. Her integrity as a journalist was viciously attacked by conservative media pundits who believed her race and "left leaning" politics would influence her to favor Biden, Obama's choice for vice president. Many also pushed for her to recuse herself arguing that her book "about Obama," which in fact was about black politics in the post-Civil Rights era, demonstrated a blatant conflict of political and financial interest. Yet, despite the vitriol and a broken ankle, Ifill defied her critics and soldiered on.

Laurel Thatcher Ulrich stated, "Well-behaved women seldom make history." Ifill seemed to concur confronting political candidates and even her colleagues on issues pertinent to Black women often ignored by mainstream media. During the 2004 Cheney-Edwards Vice Presidential Debate, prior to providing national statistics on the health disparity faced by Black women with HIV/AIDS, Ifill announced, "I want to talk to you about AIDS — and not about AIDS in China or Africa — but AIDS right here in this country." She asked each candidate to explain what he believed the proper role of government should be in addressing the epidemic. Again in 2007, on *Meet the Press*, Ifill called out the late moderator Tim Russert and her *PBS* colleague, conservative commentator David Brooks, due to their silence about Don Imus referring to Black women on the Rutgers University Basketball team as "nappy headed hoes and jjggaboos" contending "Tim, we didn't hear from you. David, we didn't hear from you."

This was classic Ifill; professional, yet direct.[80]

Trailblazer and torch bearer, Ifill's untimely death is a tremendous loss to American journalism. I will certainly miss what for me was the embodiment of Black female journalistic excellence who gave voice to Black women's issues where there was none.

Rest in peace Gwendolyn L. Ifill. You shall always be an American treasure.

XO,
Arica

PS. Thanks for writing a book worthy of teaching! ■

19

HOW THE STORY OF BLACK HISTORY MONTH PARALLELS THE FIGHT FOR A BLACK HISTORY MUSEUM

TIME MAGAZINE, JANUARY 21, 2017

When Black History Month begins on Wednesday, the annual observance will come, for the first time, with a new way for Americans to learn about that history: the National Museum of African American History and Culture (NMAAHC), which opened in September. It's an important milestone, as the fight to create such a museum actually dates back to before Black History Month was conceived. As *TIME* has explained, Carter G. Woodson established Negro History Week, the precursor to Black History Month, in 1926, as an initiative to make African American achievements a permanent part of American public history. When the observance was formally declared on a national level in 1976, it was characterized by President Gerald Ford as "the opportunity to honor the too-often neglected accomplishments of black Americans in every area of endeavor throughout our history."[81]

Ironically, 1976 was the eighth consecutive year that legislation to create the NMAAHC had failed in Congress. Robert L. Wilkins, who chaired the NMAAHC Presidential Commission under George W. Bush, detailed the history of the museum in his book *Long Road to Hard Truth: The 100 year*

Mission to Create the National Museum of African American History and Culture, which began with a simple question, "Why don't we have a museum to tell all of those stories?"

Wilkins found the answer in a complicated narrative that began in 1915, the year of the 50th anniversary of the Union's Civil War victory. The Committee of Colored Citizens, which had raised funds and organized social activities for black veterans visiting the nation's capital — but which had been barred from social activities organized by the Grand Army of the Republic, which according to Wilkins was "the preeminent organization of Union veterans" — decided to use the leftover funds as seed money for "a monument in this city to the memory of the colored soldiers and sailors who fought in the wars in our country." The following year, Black leaders organized the National Memorial Association and embarked on a nationwide fundraising campaign to support the effort. Missouri Republican Leonida Dyer sponsored HR 18721, the first of many bills in support of the memorial. But America's entry into World War I in 1917 brought the project to a standstill.

But the NMA did not give up. By 1920, the group had broadened its vision beyond commemorating Black military achievements to also include "Negro achievement in business, education, politics, the arts and every other aspect of American life." On March 4, 1929, President Calvin Coolidge, on his final day in office, signed Public Resolution No. 107, which authorized the NMA to plan a building in Washington that would be "a tribute to the Negro's contributions to the achievements of America." The association, however, was required to raise $500,000 in private contributions before the Treasury would pitch in to help make the plan a reality. That October, the stock market crashed, the Great Depression began, and the hope of a national memorial was once again deferred.

The post-World War II Civil Rights Movement gave rise to the Black Museum Movement which, according to *From Storefront to Monument: Tracing the Public History of the Black Museum Movement* by Andrea A. Burns, resulted in the establishment of several groundbreaking local museums during the 1960s and '70s, including the DuSable Museum of African American History in Chicago in 1961; The Charles H. Wright Museum of African American History (formerly the International Afro-American Museum) in Detroit in 1965; the Smithsonian Anacostia Community Museum (formerly the Anacostia Neighborhood Museum in Washington, D.C.) in 1967; and the African American Museum in Philadelphia in 1976. As noted by the African American Museum Association, founded in 1978, the "community" museum "may be identified both in terms of the physical — that is the predominately African American neighborhoods that typically surrounded these early museums — and the global community that comprises the African Diaspora." While the Black Museum Movement was successful on the local level, during this period, all efforts to gain federal support for the creation of a national museum failed.

As Wilkins has noted, just days after the assassination of Dr. Martin Luther King Jr., Rep. Clarence Brown proposed legislation that would create a national museum of Black history and culture in his home district in Ohio — a place called Wilberforce, which had been founded by manumitted Blacks and had served as a stop on the Underground Railroad. But, though several pieces of legislation were proposed over the next few years to build a national museum at Wilberforce, the idea never gained congressional support, partially due to the idea (supported by the National Park Service) that any national museum of that sort ought to be operated by the Smithsonian Institute, and not in Wilberforce. But at that time the Smithsonian declined to endorse the project. By 1989, however, the

Institute accepted a recommendation from "An African American Institutional Study" to create the NMAAHC. During the 1990s the NMAAHC faced political opposition in both the House and the Senate, but bipartisan support gradually grew, thanks to the work of Rep. John Lewis and others. On Dec. 16, 2003, President George W. Bush signed H.R. 3491, which formally authorized the creation of the National Museum of African American History and Culture within the Smithsonian.

This year the NMAAHC will have its first of many annual Black History Month celebrations, at a site that for decades to come will stand as a shrine to the thousands whom Wilkins aptly characterized as "brave and visionary souls," who — like Woodson — maintained that Black achievement should be acknowledged and celebrated not just for one week, or for one month, but all year long, every year. ■

20

WHEN AMERICAN SOLDIERS BECOME AMERICAN VIGILANTES

THE CRISIS MAGAZINE, FEBRUARY 15, 2017

"To be a Negro in this Country and to be relatively conscious is to be in a rage all the time."

—*James Baldwin*

The early days of July 2016 were the bloodiest in recent history involving Black citizens and police officers. It began on Tuesday, July 5th with the shooting death of Alton Sterling in Baton Rouge, Louisiana by Officers Blane Salamoni and Howie Lake as he laid pinned to the ground with his hands secured behind him. By Wednesday morning, an amateur video of his killing went viral with Blacks vocalizing outrage and grief over another senseless killing of a Black man from police overreach.

At 9 p.m., while the nation was still grappling with the Sterling killing, Diamond Lavish Reynolds livestreamed on Facebook the aftermath of the shooting of her boyfriend Philando Castile by Officer Jeronimo Yanez during a routine traffic stop in Falcon Heights, Minnesota. Yanez fired into the car hitting Castile multiple times. He died twenty minutes later.

The two deaths sparked a nationwide protest from Boston to Los Angeles. But the bloodshed was not over.

On Thursday, July 7th, as a peaceful protest concluded in Dallas, Texas a single gunman, 25-year-old veteran Army reservist Micah Xavier Johnson of Mesquite, Texas, opened fire on police officers killing five and wounding seven. Dallas police killed Johnson while he was holed up in a garage by using a bomb-disposal robot with an explosive device on its manipulator arm.

The protest against police brutality continued; so too did the vigilante violence.

On Sunday, July 17th in Baton Rouge, Louisiana, veteran Marine Sergeant Gavin Eugene Long of *Kansas City*, Missouri, ambushed police, killing three and wounding three. Long was shot dead during the ambush. It was his 29th birthday.

The killings of police officers were widely condemned. President Obama denounced the acts as "a vicious, calculated and despicable attack on law enforcement." While empathizing with Black America's "sense of helplessness, of uncertainty and of fear," Attorney General Loretta Lynch also admonished, "But the answer must not be violence. The answer is never violence."[82]

The blanket condemnation of Johnson and Long, while convenient, drowned out the broader conversation on the continued neglect of the mental health needs of veterans by the federal government. These men were American soldiers who took an oath to defend this country from enemies both foreign and domestic; but something changed. What was the impetus which transformed these men from American soldiers to American vigilantes? Close relatives believed each man suffered from Post-Traumatic

Stress Syndrome. Could PTSD, exacerbated by what some psychologists call Race-Based Traumatic Injury, have driven these men to embark on a murder/suicide mission? The aim here is not to phish for excuses, but rather to recognize that racism, despite the resilience of Black people, is taking a mental toll on many in our community.

Before exploring these questions, it is fitting to recall a similar tragedy which happened forty-three years ago in New Orleans.

Mark James Robert Essex (1949-1973) grew up in Emporia, Kansas. According to Leonard M. Moore, author of *Black Rage in New Orleans: Police Brutality and African American Activism from World War II to Hurricane Katrina*, his father, Mark Essex Sr., a World War II Army veteran, was a foreman at Fanestil Meat Packing Company; his mother, Nellie Essex, held a Master's degree in Education and worked at a local Head Start Program. Essex Jr. was described by neighbors, acquaintances, and teachers as "a happy-go-lucky, congenial, and well-liked youth." After graduating from Emporia High School in 1967, Essex enrolled in college, but later dropped out and enlisted in the Navy on January 13, 1969. According to a January 22, 1973, *Time Magazine* article, his mother contended that her son's troubles "all started in the Navy. He was all right when he left here," she said.

Essex enlisted in the Navy on his father's advice that it was less racially biased than the Army. Yet, as Ben Fleury-Steiner demonstrates in his book *Disposable Heroes: The Betrayal of African American Veterans*, racism was/is prevalent in every branch of the military. Essex soon realized that he indeed was not in Kansas anymore where the racism was far more subtle than the overt racism he daily experienced on the naval base in San Diego, California. His sister described his military experience to *Time Magazine* as "his own private hell." In October 1970, Essex went AWOL (absent without leave) for 28 days. According to Moore, Essex expressed a deep resentment towards white people at his court martial stating, "I had to talk to some black people because I had begun to hate all white people. I was tired of going to white people and telling them my problems and not getting anything done about it."

Almost two years after he was granted a general discharge for "'unsuitability' based on character and 'behavior disorder,'" Essex moved in with a friend in New Orleans. Distressed by the November 16, 1972, killings of Leonard Brown and Denver Smith by state troopers during a protest at Southern University at Baton Rouge, Essex killed two police officers with a Ruger .44 Magnum Deer Slayer rifle on New Year's Eve. A week later on January 7, 1973, he continued his killing spree at a local Howard Johnson Hotel which took the lives of 6 people including 3 police officers. After an eleven-hour standoff, Essex died in a hail of bullets. He was 23 years old.

The late poet-musician Gil Scott-Heron wrote about Essex as a revolutionary martyr rather than a cold-blooded killer in a poem called "The Siege of New Orleans": "Did you ever hear about Mark Essex and the things that made him choose to fight the inner city blues?" Scott-Heron stated in a 1982 interview with *Nihl Magazine* that the poem was "a comment on what was happening to our veterans ... A lot of confusion, a lot of questions about what this society was turning our young folks into." As Nellie Essex told *Time Magazine*, "I do think Jimmy was driven to this ... [He] was trying to make white America sit up and be aware of what is happening to us."

Micah Johnson's mother, Delphine Johnson echoed a similar sentiment in a recent interview with the news site *The Blaze* stating, "The military was not what Micah thought it would be.... . He was very disappointed, very disappointed. But it may be that the ideal that he thought of our government what he thought the military represented, it just didn't live up to his expectations." According to Mrs. Johnson, her extrovert son returned from Afghanistan a hermit.[83]

Johnson's troubles, however, began prior to his tour in Afghanistan. According to documents published by the *Dallas Morning News* on July 29, 2016, Johnson came to the Mesquite police headquarters in January 2011, just a year into his reserve duty, "visibly upset and bouncing from side to side. . . . He had felt like this in the past," he said, "but not as bad." He was upset because a female friend had lied to him so he came to the station seeking help because he did not have any place else to go. Officers determined that Johnson posed no danger to himself and others; he was released into the custody of a fellow Army reservist from his unit who promised to report the incident to the NCO.[84]

Yet, Johnson remained in the reserves and was assigned to support Operation Enduring Freedom in Afghanistan from November 2013 to July 2014; but his assignment was cut short due to a sexual harassment charge made by a female soldier and close friend. As reported by *The Military Times* on July 8, 2016, his JAG lawyer Branford Glendening stated Johnson "never made any remarks that were threatening to me or that he wanted to seek retaliation with the Army." According to Dallas Police Chief David O. Brown, Johnson said during the standoff that he was upset by the two recent high-profile shootings of Sterling and Castile and "wanted to kill whites, especially police officers."[85]

The Falcon Heights and Baton Rouge killings were also the tipping point for Gavin Long who according to his mother, Corine Woodley, a psychiatric nurse, became increasingly agitated with each police killing of a Black citizen. Long served in the Marines from 2005-2010. Beginning in 2008 after his deployment in Iraq, he sought help on numerous occasions for PTSD. According to a document obtained by the *Tavis Smiley Show*, the VA refused Long treatment believing his trauma was unrelated to his military service because he had not seen combat. Yet, like Johnson, Long worked with an engineering unit near the combat zone where the sound of active fire and exposure to raining debris were a daily reality. After his honorable discharge, Long refused to discuss his military experience with family members. His mother told Smiley her son showed signs of paranoia. "He believed he was being followed by the CIA," she stated. Long spent two years in Africa but returned to the U.S. because he believed he was being tracked by the government while overseas. After returning stateside, he declared himself a sovereign citizen, assumed the name Cosmo Ausar Setepenra, and took to social media contending that protest had run its course. "Violence is not The answer (it's a answer)," he tweeted. In his final tweet hours before the rampage Long stated, "Just bc you wake up every morning doesn't mean that you're living. And just bc you shed your physical body doesn't mean that you're dead."[86]

Essex, Johnson and Long were all veterans in their twenties; each expressed disillusionment with the government, embraced an Afrocentric worldview post-military service, and cited recent killings of Black men by law enforcement as their motivation for retaliating against police officers. Regardless of when their mental health issues began, these veterans' military experience contributed in some way to their mental health deterioration.

Psychologist Dr. Monica T. Williams argues in a 2015 article for *Psychology Today* that racism can also cause or further compound PTSD. Williams recounts the story of a Colorado veteran who told her "the bullets he faced in combat were nothing compared to the mistreatment he experienced at the hands of his fellow soldiers in arms. When he searched for treatment for his resulting mental health issues, the VA system could not find a qualified therapist to help him." In addition to direct trauma, Williams discusses "vicarious traumatization" which for example can result from seeing "clips on the nightly news featuring unarmed African Americans being killed on the street." Because trauma "alters one's perception of safety in society," notes Williams, "Black people with PTSD ... held more negative perceptions of the world, appearing more skeptical and mistrustful."[87]

This certainly appears to be the case of these veterans whom the government trained to kill in the name of freedom; but feeling betrayed and disposed of, they turned their weapons against the same government they once swore an oath to protect, when it failed to protect them and us. ■

21

JAMES BALDWIN DOCUMENTARY
I AM NOT YOUR NEGRO IS
THE PRODUCT OF A SPECIFIC
MOMENT IN HISTORY

TIME MAGAZINE, FEBRUARY 24, 2017

Though the Oscar-nominated documentary *I Am Not Your Negro* is a brand new movie, by filmmaker Raoul Peck, it is also a historical document: the narration, delivered in the film by Samuel L. Jackson, was written by James Baldwin, one of America's foremost public intellectuals of the 20th century, who died in 1987. The main source material was a 30-page packet of letters obtained by Peck from Baldwin's youngest sister, Gloria, that were notes for a book project called *Remember This House*, which Baldwin began to propose in the late 1970s but never got to write.

Remember This House was to be Baldwin's magnum opus, a critique of American society from the viewpoint of the assassination of his friends Medgar Evers, Malcolm X and Martin Luther King Jr. As Peck aptly notes in the introduction to the film's companion book, what these activists had in common had less to do with race and each man's approach to the Black Liberation Movement, but rather that all three were "deemed dangerous" and "disposable." So, though the film provides a provocative analysis of American race relations up to the present day, as a testament to Baldwin's continued relevance, an understanding of the moment when Baldwin began the project can add another layer to the movie's meaning.

Baldwin's straight-no-chaser style of criticism, as captured in his essay collection *The Fire Next Time,* had made him a household name more than a decade earlier. As a 1963 *TIME* cover story about the author and activist noted, "in the U.S. today there is not another writer — white or black — who expresses with such poignancy and abrasiveness the dark realities of the racial ferment in North and South." At the heart of Baldwin's argument was the question of who is responsible for the problem of racism, a point the film makes with Baldwin's use of language. Never one to mince words, he wrote and spoke what Toni Morrison called in a 1987 remembrance of her friend the "undecorated truth" about the American illusion, which juxtaposed whiteness as American innocence with blackness as sullying American purity hence, "the Negro Problem."[88]

Such an illusion was based on what Jabari Asim in his book *The N Word: Who Can Say It, Who Shouldn't ,and Why* dubbed one of America's "founding fictions," the invention of a specific term to define Blacks as subhuman and to lend credence to notions of white supremacy. As Asim notes, "From the outset, the British and their colonial counterparts relied on language to maximize the idea of difference between themselves and their African captives." Yet it was far more than just a word. Asim demonstrated how over the centuries the N word became the ideological justification that codified American society and its institutions.

One of the most striking moments in *I Am Not Your Negro* comes from a 1963 PBS interview between Baldwin and the esteemed psychologist Kenneth Clark, whose research — produced with his research partner and wife Mamie Phipps Clark — had influenced the Supreme Court decision in *Brown v. the Board of Education.* Baldwin, rejecting America's founding fiction quipped, "I am not a 'nigger,' I am a man!" He asserted that "the future of the country" depended on white people's ability to ask themselves "why it was necessary to have a 'nigger' in the first place" and why they would have invented that idea. Despite his harsh criticism, Baldwin remained optimistic that American equality was achievable. The passage of the Civil Rights Act of 1964 and the Voting Rights Act of 1965 had brought a renewed sense of hope.

But though Baldwin's message would essentially remain the same for the rest of his life, the world changed around him. The assassination of King in 1968 was the death knell of that period's Civil Rights Movement, and, in the decade that followed, the assassination did not spur any great movement among white Americans to reconsider. Instead, as Carol Anderson has demonstrated in her book *White Rage: The Unspoken Truth of Our Racial Divide*, a political backlash against civil rights had ensued, and politicians like Richard Nixon and Ronald Reagan would capitalize on opposition to civil rights victories in order to win elections. Meanwhile, Baldwin was being tracked by the FBI; as his FBI file, which spanned the years 1958-1974, attests, he was under continued surveillance. The film captures Baldwin's sentiments during this time with Jackson narrating, "What can I do? Well I'm tired."

When Baldwin began work on *Remember This House*, he had resolved, as he stated in a 1979 speech at Berkeley, to communicate that, despite the legislative achievements of the Civil Rights Movement, Blacks remained ruled by slave codes and that his fallen companions were carrying out a "modern day insurrection." In other words, though the three assassinated men at the center of *I Am Not Your Negro* had given their lives to their own visions of black liberation, the film comes not from a place of simple celebration of the legacy of Evers, X and King, but from a moment when Baldwin saw, as much as ever, the need to point out to white audiences that the work those men had done had *not* achieved its aim, and that it was their job — white Americans — to make things better. As he once put it, "You always told me 'It takes time.' It's taken my father's time, my mother's time, my uncle's time, my brothers' and my sisters' time. How much time do you want for your progress?"[89]

Despite his disillusionment and his view that it was not the responsibility of Blacks to fix things, Baldwin continued to use his writing and his voice throughout the 1970s and much of the 1980s as a vehicle for social change — though the world to which he spoke was a new one. On December 10, 1986, almost a year before his death, Baldwin, during a Q&A session after a National Press Club lecture, insisted that the country institute "a white history week; and I'm not joking," focused on dispelling the illusions that kept the nation in a constant state of peril. "History is not the past," stated Baldwin, "It is the present. We carry our history with us. We are our history." ◼

22

EXACTLY ONE YEAR BEFORE HIS DEATH DR. KING DENOUNCED THE VIETNAM WAR

HISTORY NEWS NETWORK, APRIL 4, 2017

I am sure that since you have been engaged in one of the hardest struggles for equality and human rights, you are among those who understand fully, and who share with all their heart, the indescribable suffering of the Vietnamese people. The world's greatest humanists would not remain silent. You yourself cannot remain silent.
    —*Letter from Thich Nhat Hanh to Dr. Martin Luther King Jr., 1965.*

On April 4, 1967, Dr. Martin Luther King Jr. stood before a crowd of 3,000 expectant listeners gathered at the Riverside Church in the City of New York. King was no stranger to Riverside Church, known for its national and global activism since opening its doors in 1930. For almost a decade, the civil rights leader's visits to the Neo-Gothic edifice was an annual event; but this evening was different, as King's message was a departure from domestic issues about race and economic inequality. Instead he addressed the most pressing foreign policy issue of the day: the war in Vietnam.

The even toned eloquence of King's voice echoed throughout the heightened cathedral as he patiently laid out his case against "my own government" which he characterized as "the greatest purveyor of violence in the world today." Using the platform of the Clergy and Laymen Concerned About Vietnam (CAlCAV), an interfaith organization created in October 1965, and the sponsor of the Riverside Church event, King admonished his audience, "Silence is betrayal." Hence, "For the sake of those oppressed in the [American] ghettoes, for the sake of this government, for the sake of the hundreds of thousands trembling under our violence, I cannot be silent."[90]

King's nearly hour-long speech, "A Time to Break Silence: Beyond Vietnam," was a scathing rebuke of the American government for its role in the escalating violence in the small Southeast Asian country riven by civil war. The official platform was that U.S. intervention was necessary to prevent what officials characterized as a "domino effect" for the potential spread of communism. But King challenged this assertion by recounting a laundry list of U.S. overreach in Vietnam spanning two decades which included the financial backing of France's post–WWII effort to recolonize the peninsula (1946-1954); its disregard for the Geneva Agreement; its support of dictator Ngo Dinh Diem (1955-1963); its deployment (beginning in March 1965) of an estimated 400,000 American troops— disproportionately Black and/or poor — to the region thus "testing out our latest weapons [Napalm] on them just as the Germans tested out new medicine and new tortures in the concentration camps of Europe"; and engaging in human rights atrocities with impunity "destroying families and villages." The esteemed orator concluded that rather than a war against communism, the Vietnam War was a war of imperialism.

That historic evening served as a capstone of what had been a two year journey of King's move "to break the betrayal of my own silences," which began not with his membership in the CALCAV, but rather with a letter from a young Buddhist monk in Saigon named Thich Nhat Hanh.[91]

A prolific author, calligraphy artist, social activist, and humanitarian, Thich Nhat Hanh was born in Central Vietnam in 1926; he was ordained a Buddhist monk in 1949 and established the Phuong Boi (Fragrant Palm Leaves) Meditation Center in 1955. Hanh came to the United States in 1961 to study and teach at Princeton and Columbia Universities, but returned to his "fatherland" in 1963 after several monks self-immolated in order to bring international attention to the ruthless policies of the Diem regime which included government raids on Buddhist temples.

In his June 1, 1965, letter to King, "In Search of the Enemy of Man"— written three months after the U.S. campaign Operation Rolling Thunder began in Vietnam— Hanh began by refuting Western interpretations of self-immolation as mere suicide which is caused by, among other things, "a lack of courage to live and cope with life's circumstances," which "is considered by Buddhism one of the most serious crimes." But to sacrifice one's self—as the Buddha had done in *Jakata: Or Stories of the Buddha's Former Births* when he allowed a starving lioness to devour him instead of her cubs— the monks and nuns believed they were "demonstrating a willingness to protect the people" by "practicing the doctrine of highest compassion by sacrificing [themselves]in order to call the attention of, and to seek help from, the people of the world." Hanh reminded King of the most recent self-immolation which occurred on April 20, 1965, when "a Buddhist monk named Thich Giac Thanh burned himself." These were acts of a desperate people continually victimized by the atrocities of war with no end in sight. As Hanh emphatically stated to King, "Nobody here wants the war. What is the war for, then? And whose is the war?"[92]

The Buddhist monk compared the long struggle for an independent Vietnam to the Civil Rights Movement, identifying the enemies of man as not man himself, but rather in the case of Vietnam "intolerance, fanaticism, dictatorship, cupidity, hatred, and discrimination;" and in the case of the U.S., "intolerance, hatred, and discrimination." All were a condition of the heart which could only be cured by divine intervention via the activism of communities of faith. Hence, Hanh implored the prominent Black southern preacher stating, "You cannot be silent since you have already been in action and you are in action because, in you, God is in action — too." Hanh's letter awakened King's conscience and he began immediately to speak out against the war; however, due to strong opposition from those within his inner circle who feared that his anti-war stance was counterproductive to the Civil Rights Movement, King tempered his public criticism and agreed that it would be more prudent, at least for the moment, to use his influence behind the scenes.[93]

King and Hanh met in Chicago in 1966 during the monk's three-month international tour as a representative of the people, particularly the Vietnam village peasant population who were pleading for an end to the war. At a June press conference in Washington, D.C. Hanh stated "that the war kills far more innocent peasants than it does Viet Cong." He reiterated this point in his book, *Vietnam: Lotus in a Sea of Fire — A Buddhist Proposal for Peace,* stating that the masses cared little about ideology and did not support the South Vietnamese-U.S coalition or the National Liberation Front. "The first problem of the Vietnamese peasant" Hanh asserted was "How to survive in the midst of all the forces that threaten him; how to cling to life itself."

King was so impressed with Hanh that in January 1967, he wrote a letter to the Nobel Institute nominating the peace activist for that year's Nobel Peace Prize stating, "I do not personally know of any one more worthy of the Nobel Peace Prize than this gentle Buddhist monk ... Here is an apostle of peace and non-violence." King also echoed the views of his Buddhist colleague and friend in his Riverside speech, quoting directly from his peace proposal:

This is the message of the great Buddhist leaders of Vietnam. Recently one of them wrote these words, and I quote: Each day the war goes on the hatred increases in the heart of the Vietnamese and in the hearts of those of humanitarian instinct. The Americans are forcing even their friends into becoming their enemies. It is curious that the Americans, who calculate so carefully on the possibilities of military victory, do not realize that in the process they are incurring deep psychological and political defeat. The image of America will never again be the image of revolution, freedom, and democracy, but the image of violence and militarism (unquote).[94]

In other words, the U. S. presence in Vietnam guaranteed a Viet Cong victory. The following month King and Hanh met again in Geneva, Switzerland, at the *Pacem in Terris* ("Peace in the World") Conference sponsored by the World Council of Churches; they would meet for the final time in Atlanta, Georgia, in late February of 1968. By this time Hanh —having been assured that he faced certain assassination if he returned to Vietnam for his peace activism — was living in exile in the South of France. As was customary, the two men spoke about their common goal for peace and their longing to create Beloved Communities built on compassion and mutual respect for all of humanity.

On April 4, 1968, on the anniversary of his historic speech, King was shot dead by an assassin's bullet. The long night's war in Vietnam persisted for an additional seven years.

In the poem "Our Green Garden" from his collection of poems on Vietnam, Hanh reflected on the tragedy of war stating,

Here is my breast. Aim your gun at it, brother, shoot!
Destroy me if you will

And build from my carrion whatever it is you are dreaming of.
Who will be left to celebrate a victory made of blood and fire?[95]

Indeed. On April 30, 1975, King and Hanh's prophetic words were
fulfilled as the red and blue flag of the Viet Cong was raised over the
presidential palace in Saigon. The last of the troops headed home to an
America awash in bitterness and disillusion. ▪

POSTSCRIPT: After 39 years in exile, Hanh made his first subsequent visit
to Vietnam in 2005. According to a statement released by the Plum Village
Practice Center in southern France dated September 18, 2020, Thich Nhat
Hanh, the beloved Buddhist Zen Master affectionately called Thây by his
students, turned 94 years old on October 11, 2020. "Since October 2018,"
the statement reads, "Thây has been residing at Tù Hiêu Temple Huê,
[Vietnam]." Despite fair health, "He has been able to make frequent visits
to the familiar temple grounds, join the monastic community for walking
meditations, ceremonies, and festivals, and interact with his students and
well-wishers coming from all over the world to pay their respects. Since the
coronavirus pandemic emerged, the temple has been closed, and precautions
put in place to protect Thây's health.

23

POLLUTION HURTS SOME PEOPLE MORE THAN OTHERS. THAT'S BEEN TRUE FOR CENTURIES

TIME MAGAZINE, APRIL 21, 2017

When communities around the world mark Earth Day on Saturday, the issues that will be highlighted are ones that, by definition, affect everyone on the planet. And yet, over the centuries during which people have inflicted harm on the environment, the very harm that led activists to create Earth Day in the first place, it has not been the case that those problems affected everyone equally.

This fact was recently highlighted by former Environmental Protection Agency (EPA) official Mustafa Santiago Ali, who helped found the agency's Office of Environmental Justice under President George H.W. Bush and in March resigned in protest of the EPA budget cuts called for in the Trump Administration's recent budget proposal. "Communities of color, low-income communities, and indigenous populations are still struggling to receive equal protection under the law. These communities both urban and rural," Ali stated in his letter to EPA head Scott Pruitt, "often live in areas with toxic levels of air pollution, crumbling or non-existent water and sewer infrastructure, lead in their drinking water, brownfields from vacant and former industrial and commercial sites, Superfund and other hazardous waste sites," and exposure to a host of other pollutants. Ali believed the deep budget cuts will put vulnerable communities at greater risk.

The disproportionate impact of pollution on the vulnerable is certainly not new. Concerns regarding a lack of adequate sanitation to combat pollution date back to the mid-19th century, yet it wasn't until the late 20th century that environmental protection emerged as a nationwide grassroots effort to address what activists have identified as environmental racism. According to Carl A. Zimring in his book *Clean and White: A History of Environmental Racism in the United States*, this phenomenon — defined by former NAACP President Benjamin Chavis in 1992 as "the deliberate targeting of people of color communities for toxic waste facilities, the official sanctioning of the life threatening presence of poisons and pollutants in our communities" — was part and parcel to the construction of race during the post-Civil War era.

In the late 19th century, some subscribed to notions of hygiene that claimed, as Zimring puts it, that "whites were cleaner than non-whites." Industrialization and migration to urban centers during the period led to overcrowding in northern cities, suffocating pollution and widespread epidemics. Nativists, particularly among the elite class, blamed the problem on the moral depravity of southern and eastern European immigrants, who were considered "less than white." Yet, some politicians and civic leaders disagreed and focused on developing a sufficient sanitation infrastructure to address waste management, a public health campaign underscored by notions of hygiene to combat disease, and the creation of jobs in sanitation to lower unemployment. As Zimring notes, the U. S. census shows that between 1870 and 1930 street sanitation work, also known as "dirty work," was performed primarily by first- and second-generation eastern and southern European immigrants and Blacks. Some of these foreign-born individuals, categorized during the early decades of the 20th century as white ethnics (to distinguish them from the native-born Anglo Saxon Protestants), went into the waste-management business while others obtained "cleaner occupations" and left sanitation altogether. With white ethnic categories eliminated from the census after WWII and assistance from the 1944 GI Bill, those occupying the margins of whiteness were granted full integration into white American society, fleeing "dirty jobs and dirty cities" for the clean and white life of suburban America.

In a world of de jure and de facto segregation, this situation meant that Blacks, Hispanics and American Indian communities were left to bear much of the environmental burden of the 20th century. As one Chicago lawyer put it, according to Zimring, "Gentlemen, in every great city there must be a part of that city segregated for unpleasant things." Segregated employment also justified relegating non-white workers to performing the most hazardous jobs in the worst unsanitary conditions, an issue that became central to the civils rights movement during the latter years of the 1960s.

The 1968 Memphis sanitation strike is a case in point. The Public Works Department employed 1,300 sanitation workers, most of whom were Black. These workers were subjected to long hours, low wages, and exposure to extreme hazardous conditions, resulting in health deterioration and sometimes injury or death. In fact, the strike was launched when two men were killed on the job in early February of that year. The strike gained national attention when Martin Luther King Jr. and local civic leaders organized the Poor People's March, which was led by Coretta Scott King on April 8, four days after her husband's assassination. The Memphis strike integrated issues of economic and environmental justice into the movement for civil rights. That relationship has underscored the Environmental Justice Movement (EJM) for the past three decades.

According to Dorceta E. Taylor in her book *Toxic Communities: Environmental Racism, Industrial Politics and Residential Mobility*, during the 1960s and 1970s "minority activists became more deliberate in their environmental activism," linking the "environment with racial and other kinds of social inequalities" and demanding the right "to safe and healthy environments." In the decades that followed, high-profile cases helped expand the EJM movement, as citizens saw how predominately Black areas — like the rural towns of Triana, Ala., and Warren County, N.C., and the urban areas of northern New Jersey and southern Louisiana, which were dubbed "Cancer Alley" by the *Washington Post* in 1978 and 1987 respectively — were often the places that had their lands and waterways contaminated by the manufacturing of insecticides, the dumping of PCB-laced fluids in landfills and the operation of petrochemical factories.

A 1987 report by the Commission for Racial Justice, titled *Toxic Waste and Race in the United States*, found that while "socio-economic status appeared to play an important role in the location of commercial hazardous waste facilities, race still proved to be more significant." For example, the facilities that "accounted for 40% of the total estimated landfill capacity in the United States" were located in three Black and Hispanic communities in Alabama, Louisiana and California, which had an average minority population of 85%. A follow up report published in 2007 confirmed that this pattern remained unchanged during this 20-year period.[96]

For certain, the protest against the Dakota Access Pipeline at Standing Rock and the water crisis in Flint, Mich., demonstrate that the fight for liberty and environmental justice for all remains a formidable one. Despite the odds, let us on this Earth Day hold fast to our resolve to protect our planet against the exploitation that endangers us all. ■

24

DEAR BLACK PEOPLE: AN OPEN LETTER TO BLACK AMERICA

LA PROGRESSIVE, MAY 27, 2017

Just like the lotus flower, we too have the ability to rise from the mud, bloom out of the darkness, and radiate into the world.

— *Siddhartha Gautama (Buddha)*

Dear Black People,

Well, I guess that's a start. I know who I want to write to but finding the language to articulate precisely what I want to convey is difficult, perhaps even impossible. But I've set my manuscript work aside anyway because I feel the need to write something about the recent killing of Bowie State University senior and U.S. Army 2nd Lieutenant Richard Collins, III, who was stabbed to death on May 18th by white nationalist Sean Christopher Urbanski. It is uncanny that Collins was murdered on the same day that white female Tulsa officer Betty Jo Shelby was found not guilty of the murder of Terence Crutcher. As a writer and a "race" historian, I am supposed to be able to, at least in theory, critically analyze tragic events such as these and help readers make sense of the senseless.

I do not think my difficulty writing this piece stems from the fact that I have chosen to write an open letter to us instead of an article about us. Perhaps my dilemma has to do with the fact that I do not have anything to say or at least anything new. As Cord Jefferson asserted in his article "The Racism Beat: What It's Like to Write About Hate Over, and Over, and Over," "racial trauma is widespread . . . writing anything would be to listlessly participate in the carousel ride: an inciting incident, 1,000 angry think pieces, 1,000 tweeted links, and back to where we started, until next time."[97]

I certainly do not need to remind you of the painful reality that there is going to be a next time: today, tomorrow, next week, next month, and next year. The renowned law professor Derrick Bell was right when he argued in his book *Faces At the Bottom of the Well: The Permanence of Racism*, "racism is an integral, permanent, and indestructible component of this society." Indeed, it is woven into the very foundation of this country despite the lofty rhetoric of "liberty and justice for all." And it is the elusive promise of that rhetoric which is at the center of Black American rage. As James Baldwin stated, "To be a Negro in this country and to be relatively conscious is to be in a rage almost all the time." His predecessor W. E. B. Du Bois first captured this sentiment in his book *The Souls of Black Folk* when he stated:

> It is a peculiar sensation, this double-consciousness, this sense of always looking at one's self through the eyes of others, of measuring one's soul by the tape of a world that looks on in amused contempt and pity. One ever feels his two-ness, an American, a Negro; two souls, two thoughts, two unreconciled strivings; two warring ideals in one dark body, whose dogged strength alone keeps it from being torn asunder.

Keeping ourselves from being torn asunder is, to use the words of Ralph Ellison, "a tricky magic." I would go so far to call it a miracle. How have we survived so much for so long? The physical and psychological brutality of the Maafa, slavery, Jim Crow, beatings, lynchings, rapes, bombings, medical experimentations, and murders; and the centuries of racialized disparagement via science, politics, and popular culture all sanctioned by a predatory oppressor whose very sense of superiority, in fact, whose very existence relies upon our denigration and dehumanization. America has worked overtime to convince itself and us of our "innate inferiority."

Yet, at the same time it unabashedly and unapologetically appropriates (read: steals, copyrights, trademarks, patents, and markets) our inventions, biological cells, mannerisms, language, music, styles of dress, hairstyles, lips, and even our asses. Why? Because the white psyche assumes that it owns everything and everybody and thus can take freely without acknowledgment or compensation. Truth is, white folk commodify and profit from our rhythm and our blues. The writer Ralph Ellison once quipped, "What would America be without Blacks?" The answer is culturally and financially broke!

But despite the Black wealth which has been central to the enrichment of this country, our contributions continue to be denied and in fact, hidden. As Dr. Carol Anderson highlights in her book *White Rage: The Unspoken Truth of Our Racial Divide*, America has employed numerous strategies to undermined Black advancement and achievement since Reconstruction. The Thirteenth Amendment is evidence that we were never intended to be a free people. As the 2016 celebrity filled video titled *23 Ways You Could Be Killed If You Are Black in America* demonstrates, to be Black and free is an oxymoron. Now once again we find ourselves in collective mourning due to justice denied and another senseless killing. It seems the more emphatic we are that "Black Lives Matter," America's response is, "No they don't!"

Today we are bearing witness to what Dr. King identified fifty years ago in his speech against the Vietnam War (see essay #22) as "a symptom(s) of a far deeper malady within the American spirit." In his book *Columbus and*

Other Cannibals, the late American Indian scholar Jack D. Forbes called this malady "cannibal psychosis" in which "the 'cult of aggression and violence' reigns supreme," and is characterized by:

> The aggression against other living things and more precisely, the consuming of other creatures' lives and possessions .… Brutality knows no boundaries. Greed knows no limits. Perversion knows no borders. Arrogance knows no frontiers. Deceit knows no edges. These characteristics all tend to push towards an extreme, always moving forward once the initial infection sets in. From the raping of a woman, to the raping of a country, to the raping of the world. Acts of aggression, of hate, of conquest, of empire-building.

For certain, this disease has been around for thousands of years. But as Forbes contends, cannibal psychosis is like any disease that goes untreated or has no vaccine. It gets worse with time; and has now become a global crisis of epic proportions as "exploitation thrives. The exploitation of children, of love, of women, of old people, of the weak, of the poor, and of course, the intentional commercial exploitation of every conceivable thing."

What is most unfortunate is that many of our community leaders, elected and self -appointed, have this disease or are enablers of it. I will not name names. You know who you are —on second thought I will just name a few: Clarence Thomas, David Cameron, Vernon Jones, Diamond and Silk, Omarosa Newman, Jay-Z, Ice Cube, Candice Owens, Kanye West, and my former department chair Dr. Carol E. Henderson.

Make no mistake, America is an empire. Its culture and policy have always supported and continue to support, an imperialist agenda despite the "sacred" rhetoric and founding documents touting democracy or promises of reform made by politicians during election season. As Bryant Gumbel aptly stated in a 2015 interview with Charlie Rose on American racism, "My son was arrested for walking while black . . . .You can't pay, dress or educate your way out of this." Indeed, nor can we march, sing, boycott, sit-in, petition or vote our way out of this. We live in a society whose very culture, as Gumbel further stated, "is to denigrate people of color." In June 2020 Gumbel once again pointedly articulated in a closing commentary for his show *Real Sports* the daily cost of being Black in America describing what is known as "the Black Tax." "It's not an IRS thing," Gumbel stated.

It's the added burden that comes with being Black in America. And it's routinely paid no matter how much education you have, how much money you make, or how much success you've earned. It's about the day in and day out fatigue of trying to explain the obvious to the clueless. It's about being asked to overlook blue failings and white failings so they can be conveniently viewed as Black issues. It's about being asked by so many what they should do or say about race when the easy answer lies in the privacy of each person's heart. It's the "Black tax" … it's paid daily by me and every person of color in this country, and frankly, it's exhausting.

Bryant concluded his powerful commentary on a more personal note which echoed the late twentieth century sentiments of James Baldwin. "I've been paying the 'Black tax' for almost 72 years," he stated. "Long enough that I shouldn't have to ask others to simply accept one very basic reality. . . that our Black lives matter,"[98]

The eradication of racism has never been a part of the American agenda. I know this is of little solace in this time of unabated grief and fear; but the fierce urgency of now demands that we face this inconvenient truth and devise new strategies for healing and liberation for the sake of our own survival, and that of our children. This is what it means to "Be Woke." But first you must get woke!

Let's start by dissing the "Dear White People" and "Dear White America," appeals. White people are not as ignorant about racism as they pretend to be. Case in point, when anti-racism activist Jane Elliott asked a room full of white people to stand up if they wanted to be treated like Blacks are in this society, the gaze from the audience and the fact that everybody remained seated tells us as Elliott stated, "you know what's happening; you know you don't want it for you. I want to know why you are so willing to accept it and allow it to happen to others."[99]

The answer in a word is privilege. The hard truth is white people, even our staunchest allies, love their privilege. Acknowledging privilege, as many white liberals and progressives do, is one thing; letting go of it is another matter altogether. But our freedom cannot wait! As Zen priest Rev. Angel Kyodo Williams contends, "Our healing cannot wait until the structures [of oppression] acquiesce, are dismantled, or come undone." [100]

How then can liberation possibly be achieved? I do not know the answer to that question; but you and I must work smarter, not harder for our individual and collective freedom. It is quite evident that we must go back to the drawing board. As Bell admonished, "If we are to seek new goals for our struggles, we must first reassess the worth of the racial assumptions on which, without careful thought, we have presumed too much and relied on too long."

Okay, I think I will stop there. I know I have not told you anything new or said anything you have not already heard. I just wanted to write this open letter of love and support to My people, or as poet Margaret Walker put it, "For My People." I close with her meditation of lovingkindness — and pray it becomes our guiding light for the difficult road ahead:

For my people standing, staring, trying to fashion a better way
From confusion, from hypocrisy and misunderstanding,

trying to fashion a world that will hold all the people . . .
let a people loving freedom come to growth. Let a beauty full of
healing and a strength of final clenching be the pulsing
in our spirits and our blood. Let the martial songs
be written, let the dirges disappear. Let a race of men [women and
children] now
rise and take control.

Love you much,
Arica

25

HOW THE COURT ANSWERED A FORGOTTEN QUESTION ON SLAVERY'S LEGACY

TIME MAGAZINE, SEPTEMBER 11, 2017

In recent weeks, as Americans across the country have engaged in debates about how the Civil War period is publicly commemorated, a quieter battle over a related question was finally put to rest. On Aug. 30, 2017, Senior United States District Judge Thomas F. Hogan answered an old question for Cherokee Freedmen — the descendants of people who were enslaved by members of the Cherokee Nation of Oklahoma — who have been fighting for their tribal citizenship since the early 1980s.

In the case of *The Cherokee Nation v. Nash, et al.* Judge Hogan looked at whether an 1866 Treaty — which stated that people who had been emancipated by the Cherokee would, along with their descendants, "have all the rights of native Cherokees" — ensured continuing citizenship rights for the people whose ancestors were freedmen included on the Dawes Roll (the U.S. government's official list of tribal citizens) between 1898 and 1914. In the case, the Cherokee Nation had held that their revised constitution, which had expelled the Freedmen from the tribe in 1983 on the premise that they were not "blood" Cherokee (though many of them are of Black-Cherokee ancestry), held more legal weight than the 1866 treaty. However, the judge ruled that the revised constitution does not negate the Freedmen's treaty rights granted to their forebears at the end of the Civil War. In other words, Cherokee Freedmen *are* Cherokee.

While the case of the Cherokee Freedmen has continually made headlines during the past decade, the story of American Indians as enslaved people and slave owners remains a relatively unknown aspect of American history. Slavery was a reality of indigenous life in the Americas prior to the arrival of Africans and Europeans. As Christina Snyder explains in her book *Slavery in Indian Country: The Changing Face of Captivity in Early America*, "captivity" was "widespread, and it took many forms." But, as Snyder explains in tracing the history of Southern Indian captivity to the pre-Columbian era, the advent of European colonialism meant that Indians found themselves thrust into a global economy underscored by a racialized system of human trafficking for profit. "Slavery was not peculiar to indigenous societies," where captives were prisoners of war obtained from enemy tribes, Snyder notes, but "the [commodified] form that slavery took in the antebellum South and elsewhere in the colonial Americas" was very much new.

With the introduction of a rigid slave system to North America, which exploited both Indian and African bodies as human commodity, indigenous people became part of that economy, on both sides of the transaction. For example, in his book *The Westo Indians: Slave Traders of the Early Colonial South*, Erin E. Browne describes how the Westo Indians from the Northeast captured enemy tribes to trade to the English Virginians for guns, ammunition, metal tools and other goods. And in the west, as highlighted by the scholar Andrés Reséndez in his book *The Other Slavery*, the buying and selling of Indians—even though it was illegal and California entered the Union as a free state—was "common practice" in the years after the Mexican-American War. While the myth that African slavery replaced Indian slavery continues to persist in our society, "Indian slavery never went away," contends Reséndez, "but rather coexisted with African slavery from the sixteenth all the way through to the late nineteenth century."

The Five Tribes — whose original homeland was located in the southern interior, in an area bounded by the Cumberland River to the north and the Mississippi valley to the west, and who included the Cherokee — adopted racialized chattel slavery in the late 18th century. Southern whites urged them to participate in the enslaving of Black people as a part of the Federal Government's Indian "civilization" effort. Hence, the name "The Five Civilized Tribes." The Cherokee Nation exceeded their counterparts in embracing white southern slave culture and profited the most from slave ownership. By 1809, there were 600 enslaved Blacks living in the Cherokee Nation; by 1835, the number increased to 1,600.

In her book *The House on Diamond Hill: A Cherokee Plantation Story*, historian Tiya Miles tells the intriguing story of The Chief Vann House, located on a vast plantation in northeast Georgia. It was named Diamond Hill in 1801 by its owner James Vann, the wealthiest and "reportedly cruelest of Cherokee slave owners," who owned at least 100 slaves. Diamond Hill later fell into disarray as a consequence of Andrew Jackson's forced Indian removal, but the Vann family continued to prosper, as slavery in the Indian Territory (now the state of Oklahoma) proved far more profitable to the tribes than it had been in the Southeast. By 1860 there were 4,000 enslaved Blacks living in the Cherokee Nation alone.

Although the Cherokee Nation had resolved to remain neutral at the outset of the Civil War in April 1861, by October they entered a treaty to join the Confederate cause. The reason, they argued in that document, was that the "Cherokee people had its origin in the South; its institutions are similar to those of the Southern States, and their interests identical with theirs." In addition, they painted the war as one of "Northern cupidity and fanaticism against the institution of African servitude; against the commercial freedom of the South, and against the political freedom of the States."[101]

But by the following fall, with the Nation sorely divided as thousands of Cherokees fled to Union lines, the Cherokee Council abrogated its treaty alliance with the Confederacy. On Feb. 19, 1863 — shortly after Lincoln's Emancipation Proclamation went into effect — the Cherokee Nation issued An Act Providing for the Abolition of Slavery in the Cherokee Nation, which called for "the immediate emancipation of all Slaves in the Cherokee Nation." In a treaty ratified on July 27, 1866, the Cherokee Nation declared that those Freedmen "and their descendants, shall have all the rights of native Cherokees."

It is these words the Freedmen held onto during their long legal battle. Marilyn Vann, a descendant of the James Vann family and one of the plaintiffs in the lawsuit, expressed that idea to *NPR* after the decision was issued. "All we ever wanted," she said, "was the rights promised us."[103]

POSTSCRIPT: On November 9, 2020, Cherokee Nation Principle Chief, Chuck Hoskin Jr. announced a new plan to explore the history, culture, and contributions of Cherokee Freedmen to the Cherokee Nation. Hoskin also signed an executive order "on equality, reiterating Cherokee Nation's commitment to equal protection and equal opportunity under Cherokee law" for all of its citizens. The Cherokee Freedmen Art and History Project, slated to begin in January 2021 "will include comprehensive research for historical materials, references, documents and images, as well as an assessment of current interpretations at all tribal sites. Cherokee Nation will utilize the assessment to identify gaps in its representation and storytelling and develop new content that shares the Freedmen perspective throughout tribal history." A feature exhibit at the Cherokee National History Museum slated for 2022 will educate the tribe and general public about how Cherokee Freedmen history contributes to the overall history of the Cherokee Nation. ▪

26
YOUR DEEPEST FEAR

LA PROGRESSIVE, SEPTEMBER 13, 2017

For my daughter Julienne and Black women everywhere

In her poem "Our Deepest Fear" Marianne Williamson opens with these words, "Our deepest fear is not that we are inadequate. Our deepest fear is that we are powerful beyond measure. It is our light, not our darkness, that most frightens us."[104]

I serendipitously encountered these words today after a telephone conversation with a white male associate which left me feeling, in a word, exhausted. The long and short of the conversation can be summed up in his assertion that "People don't like Black women like you Arica. Your intelligence, confidence, and assertiveness is unappealing." While he agreed that this attitude reflected classic discrimination, he nonetheless placed the onus upon me to "tone it down for your own sake."

While I had often found solace, inspiration and affirmation in Williamson's words, the poem at once took on a different meaning. It was no longer an affirmation, a reminder of unrealized potential, but rather an erasure of my own reality, and that of numerous Black women in America and indeed the world. "Our" deepest fear? No! My deepest fear is that I live in a society which presumes I am incompetent and punishes self-actualized Black women like me who refuse to remain "in their place," and due to this hostile environment I will be robbed of opportunities to provide my gifts to a world that is in such desperate need of them. As I wrestled with Williamson's words, I soon realized as legendary activist Angela Y. Davis said, rather than "accept the things I cannot change," as the "Serenity Prayer" suggest, I can "change the things I cannot accept." So rather than abandon the poem altogether, I decided to modify it to reflect my own truth.

America your deepest fear is not that I, a Black woman, am inadequate. Your deepest fear is that I am powerful beyond measure. It is my light, not my darkness (which you use to justify your dehumanization of me), that most frightens you.

"Who are you to be brilliant, gorgeous, talented, and fabulous," you ask?

Who are I not to be?!

I am a child of God! A daughter of the original peoples of this earth, radiating phenomenal beauty and wisdom embodied in this feminine form which has been French kissed by the sun.

My mother is Maya who taught me that the sassiness, haughtiness, and sexiness of Black women is the envy of the ages; and that despite all of your lies, Still I rise. My other mother is Nikki who taught me that *Ego Tripping* can make me "fly high like a bird in the sky" above the centuries of stereotypes and disfigured images of Black womanhood. Each morning when I rise, I celebrate that "I am perfect, divine, ethereal, and surreal," drinking in my goddess beauty declaring, "Mirror, mirror on the wall, I am bad! I mean damn, I am one badaaaazz Sistah!"

American, I know you like to play ignorant; but you know who I be. It's a pity that your unjustified fear of my divine magnificence makes you think that by playing me small somehow serves you. Well, it does not serve you or the world. Despite what the seventeenth century European philosophers thought, there is nothing enlightened or enlightening about shrinking my importance so that you will not feel insecure around me. But your fear and ignorance does not change my destiny. As Zora once quipped, "I am not tragically colored!" And I damn sure ain't tragically female! I am born to make manifest the glory of God, the Divine Feminine that is within me. But it is not just in me; it's in everyone, even in you. But we must each choose our own path, fear or liberation. You do not need my permission; and I certainly do not need yours. I have chosen to let my own light shine and to liberate my own self. ■

27

BLAMING "BAD DUDES" MASKS THE ROLE OF WOMEN IN THE HISTORY OF WHITE NATIONALISM

TIME MAGAZINE, SEPTEMBER 18, 2017

The "Unite the Right" Rally last month in Charlottesville, Va., continues to dominate headlines, with President Trump reigniting controversy last week by reiterating his belief that both sides are to blame for the violent fallout between protesters and counter-protesters. "You have some pretty bad dudes on the other side also," the President said. The president's choice of words — the idea that there are "bad dudes" out there — is significant, as it sheds light on an aspect of the controversy that has largely been ignored, which is the role of women in the white nationalist movement. The images that have dominated the Charlottesville narrative in its aftermath have likewise tended to have one thing in common: the white nationalists they portray are men.[105]

Yet, despite the absence of white women from public displays of white nationalism this month, women have played an important role in the ugly history of racism in America. These days, as Seyward Darby explained in a recent *NPR* interview, women's participation in contemporary white nationalism takes place primarily online "in the underbelly of the Internet." The women involved in that world in many cases contend that they reject feminism and embrace traditional gender roles, which are part of the regressive worldview of those movements. Yet some of the most famous of them also champion women as central to the success of the white nationalist movement. They are viewed as Alt-Feminist, women who struggle for gender equality within the context of white supremacy. Consequently, such women have faced backlash from male counterparts who complain of their transgression of gender boundaries.[106]

The contention over gender roles within white nationalist organizations is nothing new, as evidenced by the Ku Klux Klan's foremost female "leader" Elizabeth Tyler, and the rise of the Women's Ku Klux Klan (WKKK) during the 1920s. As related by Kathleen M. Blee in her book *Women of the Klan: Racism and Gender in the 1920s,* Tyler and her male business partner Edward Clarke founded the Southern Publicity Association, which in 1920 contracted with the KKK "to create a Propaganda Department to publicize and recruit for the Klan." Expanding the Klan's enemy list from Blacks to also include "Catholics, Jews, nonwhites, Bolsheviks, and immigrants" and utilizing "the modern marketing and advertising techniques of the twentieth-century capital consumerism" proved an effective strategy in increasing the organization's membership and revenue.

As Blee notes, however, Tyler's gender became a vexing issue for some within the upper echelons of the Klan who feared that their fraternity had been coopted by a woman. Although there were some who appreciated her effective organizing and promotion skills, not to mention her dedication to the Klan, many others viewed her as a seductress and attributed her successes to her ability to cater "to [men's] appetite and vices." The controversy over Tyler's leadership role in the Klan resulted in a 1921 Congressional investigation that came to the exaggerated conclusion that "an ostensibly all-male Klan" was indeed under the leadership of a woman. Despite Tyler's appointment to oversee the development of a women's organization that she contended, "would not be a 'dependent auxiliary of the Knights of the

Ku Klux Klan' but would be on par with the men's organization," she was pushed out.

The WKKK was officially chartered on June 10, 1923, and headquartered in Little Rock, Ark. (Tyler died the next year). The distance from the Knights of the Ku Klux Klan's headquarters in Atlanta symbolized the independence of the WKKK from its male counterpart. It was billed, Blee notes as "an organization by women, for women, and of women [that] no man is exploiting for his individual gain." The WKKK grew rapidly. Within two years, membership was estimated at 500,000 with chapters in every state of the Union.

The recruitment philosophy of the WKKK was underscored by feminist notions that rejected patriarchy and urged women, whether at home or in business, to "put her efforts behind a movement for 100 percent American womanhood." Women had won the right to vote. Their duty was not only a racial one "to ever be true to the maintenance of White Supremacy" as outlined in the *Kloran* or Ritual of the Women of the Ku Klux Klan, but also a political one in which the struggle for gender equality would be central to the movement. While Klansmen exploited symbols that underscored patriarchy and relished in the supposed superiority of white American male Protestantism, Klanswomen rejected the notion of female vulnerability and complained of their historical and contemporary exclusion from American politics. To them, the supposed superiority of white Americans extended to white women, too. As Blee puts it, "Klanswomen embraced the KKK's racist, anti-Catholic, and anti-Semitic agenda and symbols of American womanhood but they used these to argue as well for equality for white Protestant women."

But the heyday of the WKKK was short lived. By the end of the 1920s as the Klan declined due to internal conflicts over leadership, corruption and gender—as well as public outcry over its mounting atrocities—the women's order was completely dismantled, and unlike its male counterpart, it failed to reemerge. This, however, did not end women's involvement in the white nationalist movement. During the 1930s and 1940s, women's participation in white nationalism continued, as they served as auxiliaries in such organizations as the pro-Nazi German American Bund and numerous women's patriotic societies. Much as is the case today, these women tended to articulate their activism within the context of safeguarding traditional gender roles. They worked behind the scenes as subordinates to the public activism of their male counterparts. Yet when they emerged in public, their impact could be great.

For example, during the 1950s, as Toni Morrison observed in her article "What the Black Woman Thinks About Women's Lib," white women who viewed themselves as protectors of public education became the public face of anti-integration. One could hardly forget the "faces of those white women hovering behind that black girl in Little Rock in 1957," Morrison wrote. White nationalist movements that reemerged in the 1980s have now once again overtaken the streets of America with angry white men as their public face. Yet, regardless of the role they have chosen, quiet traditionalist or outspoken alt-feminist, the women of white nationalism have always been there, standing by their men.[107]

POSTSCRIPT: After his biting October 11, 2020, opening monologue on SNL highlighting the hypocrisy of white women who had "hijacked the woke movement" which was supposed to be about "people of color," Bill Burr found himself in hot water for telling the unadulterated truth. "Generals around the world should be analyzing this," he quipped. "The woke movement was supposed to be about people of color not getting opportunities that they deserve," a moment Burr said lasted only "eight seconds." Then Burr went all in. "Then somehow," he stated, "white women swung their Gucci booted feet over the fence of oppression and stuck themselves at the front of the line. I don't know how they did it. I've never heard so much complaining in my life from white women." Next the comedian went straight for the jugular vein. "The nerve of you white women," he continued, "you guys stood by us toxic white males through centuries of our crimes against humanity. You rolled around in the blood money, and occasionally, when you wanted to sneak off and hook up with a Black dude, if you got caught, you said it wasn't consensual. Yeah, that's what you did! So, why don't you shut up, sit down next to me, and take your talking to?" Burr's sketch was labeled by some as controversial and misogynist. Yet, George Bernard Shaw once stated, "If you want to tell people the truth, you had better make them laugh, or they will kill you." But in this so-called time of racial reckoning, it seems that many whites who consider themselves "woke" aren't ready for that level of truth. Perhaps Burr should beef up his security. ■

28

FROM THE 'POCAHONTAS EXCEPTION' TO A 'HISTORICAL WRONG': THE HIDDEN COST OF FORMAL RECOGNITION FOR AMERICAN INDIAN TRIBES

TIME MAGAZINE, FEBRUARY 9, 2018

For a Native American tribe, federal recognition comes with a host of benefits, including housing, health, and education funding. But the process of achieving that recognition from the Bureau of Indian Affairs (BIA) can be difficult — particularly because the BIA requires tribes to demonstrate continuous existence as an Indian entity from colonial times to the present. That's a standard that, as recent news shows, doesn't match up with the reality of American history.

On Jan. 30, President Trump signed H.R. 984, the Thomasina E. Jordan Indian Tribes of Virginia Federal Recognition Act of 2017, which granted federal recognition to six Virginia state-recognized Native American tribes via a special act of Congress rather than through the usual BIA process. The recognition means that members of the six tribes have achieved sovereign (albeit limited) status. Virginia Senators Tim Kaine and Mark Warner hailed the bill as having "righted a historical wrong." Yet the story of federal recognition for those six tribes—the Chickahominy, the Eastern Chickahominy, the Upper Mattaponi, the Rappahannock, the Monacan, and the Nansemond—also shows that at least one particular "historical wrong" remains unaddressed. In fact, their story illuminates a central problem with the way Indian recognition is managed on both the state and federal levels, as it is based on a problematic idea of racial purity.

The history behind that idea — that racial purity specifically requires the demonstrable absence of African-American ancestry — goes back to none other than Thomas Jefferson. His blood politics became the cornerstone of Virginia (and later federal) Indian policy, which poisoned Black-Indian relations and divided the families of those who struggled to maintain an Indian identity by seeking formal recognition.

As I demonstrate in my book *That the Blood Stay Pure: African Americans, Native Americans and the Predicament of Race and Identity in Virginia,* interracial intimacy between people of African descent and American Indians dates back to the early colonial era in Virginia. The Virginia General Assembly enacted its first proscriptions against interracial marriage in 1691, but this law only applied to intimacies between whites and non-whites. And, as noted by Jack D. Forbes in his book *Africans and Native Americans: The Language of Race and the Evolution of Red-Black Peoples,* by the end of the colonial period, enslaved Indians were classified as Negro along with their black enslaved counterparts.

By the late 18th century, in adherence to the idea that "one drop" of African blood defined a person as Black, white settlers advocated for the state to stop recognizing Indian identity (and tribal land ownership) on the idea that the Native American identity had been lost due to intimacy with Black Virginians. To wit, free Native Americans were classified on the census not as Indian but as free people of color or mulattoes.

By the end of the 19th century, the remnants of the state's Powhatan people began to push back against the state-sanctioned reclassification of their identity with a dogged resolve. To do so, they embraced an identity not based on who they were, but rather on who they were not: Black.

While complicated definitions of racial categories were not unique to Virginia, the state's residents had another factor to deal with. Among the state's most elite families were many that claimed descent from John Rolfe and Pocahontas. They were proud of their Native American heritage, but they were also adamant that they were white, and had to reconcile that idea with the widespread desire among the Virginia elite for the Commonwealth to be the nation's leading example of racial purity. So, when the state enacted its Racial Integrity Act in 1924, it defined whiteness using the "Pocahontas Exception," which spared those families from being forced to identify as colored, and thus subjected to Jim Crow.

But this raised the specter for the act's backers that the Virginia Indian community would subvert the law to marry white people and "contaminate" the white gene pool. So, in the aftermath of the law's passage, Walter Plecker, Virginia's Vital Statistics Registrar, declared war on the Virginia Indian community. Plecker, who called Indians "Negroes in feathers," sought to obliterate the Virginia Indians using what many have called "pencil genocide," disallowing the use of the term *Indian* as a racial designation on government documents.

In the same period, the Virginia Indians found a steadfast ally in anthropologist Frank Speck of the University of Pennsylvania. Speck spent three decades among the Powhatan Tribes and became a fierce advocate for their formal recognition. In his monographs about the Powhatan Tribes, he significantly downplayed the historical kinship ties between Blacks and Indians. In this view, these tribes were distinct from other Indian tribes and the state's Black population, because they had only intermarried with whites for nearly two centuries. Hence, Speck certified that the Powhatan Indians were racially pure.

During the 1930s and 1940s, Speck lobbied the Federal Census Bureau to classify members of the Powhatan Tribes as Indian, despite Plecker's strong opposition. The 1940 battle was a draw, as the bureau decided that the designation would be permitted, but with an asterisk to indicate racial uncertainty. Also at this time, prominent citizens began lobbying state and federal officials with petitions that "certified" that the Powhatan Tribes were of white-Indian only ancestry. The resistance continued during World War II as three Caroline County residents were jailed for refusing to enlist in the Military as colored. One draftee of the Rappahannock Tribe expressed that he would rather go to jail than "go down in history as a negro."

Resistance to the "colored" classification also affected Powhatan Indian education; Indian schools only went to eighth grade. Because Virginia Indian children could not attend white schools and Powhatan parents refused to send them to colored schools, many Powhatan children did not attend high school. Others, after Speck's lobbying, completed high school at Federal Indian residential schools in North Carolina, Kansas and Oklahoma. Even after Virginia's schools were "integrated" after the *Brown* Supreme Court decision, the fallout from Speck's campaign continued.

First, during the 1980s the Virginia Council on Indians (VCI) was established and eight tribes, seven of which were descendants of the former Powhatan Confederacy, received state recognition by a special act of the Virginia General Assembly. Second, tribal leaders and their anthropologist advocate Dr. Helen Rountree, professor emerita of Anthropology at Old Dominion University in Norfolk, Virginia, were appointed to the council to oversee Indian Affairs throughout the Commonwealth and to make recommendations to the VGA for tribes seeking state recognition. Third, in 1998, six of the eight state-recognized tribes began their efforts toward seeking federal recognition.

Yet, by 1990, the VCI established state recognition criteria based on the same BIA criteria for which tribal leaders sought and have now received exemption: the idea of continuous existence as a purely Indian entity. Hence, once the standard was adopted, the VCI did not grant a single additional Virginia Tribe a favorable recommendation for state recognition.

Even after last week's historic signing, Plecker's, Speck's, and Rountree's legacies are alive and well, in the idea that intimacy with Blacks invalidates Indian identity. Broken friendships, disrupted kinship relations, and deep-seated animosities testify to the damage wrought by these people. Yet, as Lynette Allston, Chief of the Nottoway Tribe, told me just prior to submitting the tribe's petition for state recognition, "We are Indian people of white and Black ancestry, and we won't deny any part of who we are." ■

29

THERE'S A TRUE STORY BEHIND BLACK PANTHER'S STRONG WOMEN. HERE'S WHY THAT MATTERS

TIME MAGAZINE, FEBRUARY 22, 2018

In Loving Memory of Chadwick Boseman (1973 – 2020)

When *Black Panther* opened last weekend to record-breaking box office success, many of the viewers driving the film to that achievement were female moviegoers, who made up 45% of the audience. Though that number may defy conventional wisdom about superhero movies, it's not so surprising given the actual plot of the movie. After all, as the University of Pennsylvania's Salamishah Tillet noted for *The Hollywood Reporter*, the movie doesn't just pass the Bechdel test — a measure of the substantiality of a film's female characters — but "those scenes in which two or more women are talking to, disagreeing with, or fighting alongside each other without a man present are some of the movie's most riveting ones." But the strong women of *Black Panther* are more than just a potential inspiration to women in the audience today. They're also a window into a true, if oft-forgotten, piece of history.[108]

In the film, the fictional Dora Milaje — "adored ones," an all-female military group that protects the King and the fictional nation of Wakanda

— are perhaps the most obvious example of female strength. The Dora Milaje were introduced in the *Black Panther* comic by Christopher Priest, who took over as lead writer of the series in 1998; since the series' relaunch in 2016, they've become much more central to the plot. (The title character, who was Marvel's first African American superhero, was created in 1966). In their initial appearance, Priest's narrator describes the female bodyguards as "Deadly Amazonian high school karate chicks," who were also the King's "wives-in training." While many have speculated about the inspiration behind these warriors, it is clear that their main antecedent included the famous all-female African military corps of Dahomey, West Africa (now The Republic of Benin), whom the French dubbed "Dahomey Amazons" after female warriors in Greek mythology.

Some experts believe that the first such regiment, which emerged sometime in the 17th century, comprised hunters called *gbeto*, while others contend they were recruited from among the King's many wives. As Sylvia Serbin describes in *The Women Soldiers of Dahomey*, these warriors can be difficult to categorize, as their names were based on a woman's weapons expertise and unit to which she was assigned. Whatever their origin, the King was always surrounded by armed women in public and private life. By the end of the 19th century an estimated 4,000 women, many of whom began their training as teens, were among the Dahomey military ranks. In times of war, during the transatlantic slave trade and in the fight against French colonialism, Dahomey female warriors "were the last line of defense between the enemy and the King," writes Serbin, "and were prepared to sacrifice their lives to protect him."[109]

Not only is this history clearly reflected in the fictionalized Wakanda, where *Black Panther* is set, but so is the idea of a political system wherein men and women control political institutions jointly. Though the nation has a King, he depends on the central female characters, played by Angela Bassett (mother/adviser to the King), Letitia Wright (Princess/lead scientist),

Lupita Nyong'o (spy/insurrectionist), and Danai Gurira (adviser to the King/General of Dora Milaje). As numerous Africianist historians have attested, this system also shows up in the true history of pre-colonial African reality. For example, John Henrik Clarke explained in his essay on African Warrior Queens in *Black Women of Antiquity*, in the years before colonialism, "Africans had produced a way of life where men were secure enough to let women advance as far as their talents would take them."

European societies of the time were constructed differently, and men believed women were not intellectually capable of making political decisions. Even so, European women were viewed as virtuously superior to their foreign female counterparts. Consequently, notions of Black female innate inferiority led to the creation of stereotypes — what scholars Patricia Morton and Patricia Hill Collins have called "disfigured images" and "controlling images," respectively — that were used to justify oppression.

From slavery to the present, Black women have had to contend with four major stereotypes, which Collins identified in her classic book *Black Feminist Thought*. First, the Jezebel, the hyper-sexual woman who sought to corrupt the good morals of white men. Second, the Mammy, the dutiful caretaker who insured that everyone, white and Black, adhered to the tenets of white supremacy. Third, the Matriarch, an ultra-domineering woman who terrorized her children and castrated her male partner. And fourth, the Welfare Mother (an update of the Jezebel), a woman with no work ethic or sexual morals, who has multiple children just to receive government assistance.

Notably absent among those stereotypes is the idea of the righteous warrior.

The Dora Milaje aren't the only way in which *Black Panther* brings pre-colonial African ideas into modernity. As Nathan Connolly has written for

The Hollywood Reporter, the movie contends with five centuries of imagining a world without a history of "environmental degradation, colonialism, cultural genocide or the elevation of white aesthetics to the exclusion of all else." Part of the real work of creating such a world must begin with moving Black women, in the words of bell hooks, "from margin to center," and creating an aesthetics that challenges, refutes, and destroys those stereotypical concepts of Black womanhood.[110]

The importance of this achievement cannot be overstated. For Black women and girls, the world over, Wakanda represents a fictional world in which their natural beauty and intelligence are accepted norms of a society that values and affirms both their femininity and humanity. How much more significant, then, to know that this vision is based on reality. ■

30

BILL COSBY PLAYED RESPECTABILITY POLITICS. IT BLEW UP IN HIS FACE

WASHINGTON POST, AUGUST 28, 2018

Bill Cosby's luck finally ran out.

On Thursday, a jury convicted the 80-year-old on three counts of aggravated indecent assault: penetration with lack of consent, penetration while unconscious and penetration after administering an intoxicant. Though the conviction only covered the case of Andrea Constand, she served as a proxy for the more than 50 women who have accused Cosby of drugging and raping them. So, the moment has finally come: "America's favorite dad" has been convicted of rape. While few people lament the verdict, some worry that Cosby's criminal actions will invalidate the good that he has done for Black America. But Cosby was not good for Black America. And, in fact, it was his betrayal of Black America, as well as his devotion to the politics of respectability, that ultimately led to his downfall.

Bill Cosby first made history in 1965 when he became the first African American to co-star in a major network television drama — "I Spy" — and again in 1966 when he won an Emmy Award, the first of nine Emmys and

Grammys (for best comedy album) that decade. In the 1970s, Cosby became the first African American to star in his own eponymous comedy series, "The Bill Cosby Show," which ran for two seasons, and he began working in children's educational programming. He even earned a doctorate in urban education in 1977. By the 1980s, Cosby's infectious comedy had endeared him to parents and children alike. He was the educated, respectable, funny man; a master storyteller whose family stories affirmed the humanity and culture of everyday Black folk. He taught them that it was okay to laugh at themselves and to love themselves, and they laughed and loved him for it. He was Black America's most celebrated entertainer, its pride and joy.

But apparently there was a hidden, darker side to Cosby: Even as he publicly appeared to be a wholesome hero for Black Americans, Cosby was drugging and raping women — women who were silenced by his stature. As Jewel Allison — who says she was assaulted by Cosby during this time — explained, "I didn't want to let black America down." The idea that coming forward would reinforce stereotypes of Black men as sexually violent "sent chills" through Allison's body. She feared that she would not just bring Cosby down, she would "undermine the entire African American community."[111]

In the 1980s and 1990s, "The Cosby Show" and the spinoff "A Different World" were two of NBC's biggest hits, bringing the upper-middle-class Huxtables and black college students into living rooms across America. These shows not only paved the way for other sitcoms centered on middle-class Black families, but more important, they helped spike enrollment at historically Black colleges and universities by 24.6 percent. The success of "The Cosby Show" catapulted Cosby to new heights. He projected an image of wholesomeness, refraining from swearing, memorably shilling for Jell-O with kids, while also emerging as a major philanthropic force.

In the 2000s, however, Cosby moved to use his fame to advance his politics, which transformed him from a much-celebrated actor into a deeply controversial figure. Black America loved Cosby because his success had not caused him to forget the poor community which raised and nurtured him. But his politics stirred up intense debates as he reinforced a white supremacist value system that told Black youth that their own creative imagination was of no value. His politics of respectability and black conservatism reinforced stereotypes of black pathology — criminality, anti-intellectualism, hypersexuality, family dysfunction — that gave America a reason to once again deny its culpability in maintaining the Black underclass. This assault on Black America would prove to be Cosby's undoing.

Cosby launched his controversial political career with the infamous "Pound Cake Speech," which he delivered at the 2004 NAACP Image Awards. He justified the killing of an unarmed youth for stealing "a piece of pound cake." He criticized those who dared to challenge an excessive use of force, stating, "But what the hell was he doing with the pound cake?" Cosby took his Pound Cake Black Conservative Show on the road, constantly chiding young Black men to "pull up your pants" (advice he should have adhered to himself). He never gave voice to issues of racism, sexism, the failed public school system, health and economic disparities, mass incarceration or police brutality. Instead, he spent over a decade disparaging Black folk to the delight of white conservatives. While Cosby's philanthropy benefited historically Black colleges and universities such as Spelman College and the Morehouse Medical School, he was largely an agent of oppression, ignoring systematic racism and dismissing the problems of the Black urban underclass as self-inflicted, rather than structural.[112]

Cosby's turn to the politics of respectability, however, eroded the invincibility he once had in Black America. In 2007 at the Miami

International Book Fair, the legendary Black Arts poet Nikki Giovanni reprimanded the comedian. Chiding him for his betrayal of the community that had elevated him as the "Great Black Hope," Giovanni said, "We ate that Jell-O and that mighty fine pudding, whatever he was doing with that. We would go in to have our pictures made and demand Kodak paper to try to help that Negro and then he's going to turn around and tell me I'm a bad mother? Uh-uh, I'm not buying that."[113]

Giovanni wasn't the only Cosby critic. Professor and political commentator Michael Eric Dyson lambasted the comedian in his 2006 book *Is Bill Cosby Right or Has the Black Middle Class Lost Its Mind?* — a scathing commentary on the hypocrisy of Cosby's Pound Cake Speech. Dyson continued his criticism of Cosby after sexual assault allegations against him surfaced publicly: "He's throwing rocks, and he's living in a glass house, so that contradiction will always get you sunk."[114]

Even as Cosby became deeply controversial in the Black community, his aura of respectability remained intact until comedian Hannibal Buress shattered it in 2014, a pivotal moment that ended Cosby's status as an untouchable star. During a performance in Philadelphia (Cosby's hometown), Burress directly connected Cosby's respectability politics and his history of — at that point unprosecuted — sexual assault. Burress recounted that he hated the smugness with which Cosby lectured, "Pull your pants up, black people, I was on TV in the '80s. I can talk down to you because I had a successful sitcom. Yeah," Burress shot back, "but you raped women, Bill Cosby." Burress took an open secret and made it a front-page story. Within a few days, video of the set went viral, unleashing the media firestorm that Cosby had eluded for almost two decades. Given his denigration of the Black underclass, especially young Black men, this was poetic justice: Cosby's demise delivered on his home turf by a young Black male comedian.[115]

The following year, the courts, too, decided that Cosby's public role was justification for revealing his secrets. U.S. District Judge Eduardo Robreno unsealed a sworn 2005 deposition, in which Cosby admitted to acquiring prescriptions of Quaaludes to give to women for the purpose of sex. He reasoned that Cosby could not claim a broad right to privacy because he "has donned the mantle of public moralist and mounted the proverbial electronic or print soap box to volunteer his views on, among other things, child rearing, family life, education and crime. To the extent that Defendant has freely entered the public square and 'thrust himself into the vortex of [these public issues],' he has voluntarily narrowed the zone of privacy that he is entitled to claim." In other words, Cosby paved the way for his own prosecution when he voluntarily anointed himself the moral scold of Black America.[116]

For certain, Cosby's downfall is a tragic one. He was not only America's favorite dad, but an elder statesman of Black America whose philanthropy has helped many. In this desperate moment when merely breathing while Black is a crime, this is the last thing Black America needs. But we must face the inconvenient truth that Cosby was living a double life of reprehensible proportions. A 20 million dollar gift to a prestigious Black women's college will never be enough to atone for the sins committed against the countless women who say he victimized them; millions donated to Black museums will not undo the damage done by his respectability politics. There is some justness, though, in the knowledge that those same politics helped pave the way for this week's verdict, and for justice, however delayed.

POSTSCRIPT: In September 2016 following his rape conviction, 81-year-old Cosby was sentenced to 3 to 10 years and is now incarcerated at the State Correctional Institution – Phoenix in Pennsylvania. In December 2019 judges in the Pennsylvania Superior Court unanimously rejected Cosby's appeal which sought to overturn his rape conviction on the basis that he had not received a fair trial. In April 2020 Pennsylvania Gov. Tom Wolf ordered the temporary release of the inmates considered to be "non-violent and who otherwise would be eligible for release within the next nine months or who are considered at high risk for complications of coronavirus and are within 12 months of their release." Based on the governor's guidelines, Cosby was ineligible for early release. ■

31

BIAS TRAINING AT STARBUCKS IS A REMINDER THAT THE HISTORY OF RACISM IS ABOUT WHO BELONGS WHERE

TIME MAGAZINE, MAY 29, 2018

When Starbucks closes 8,000 stores nationwide on Tuesday, the coffee chain's employees will receive a day of anti-bias training. Though this is just one day — and, as many have argued, a single day seems insufficient to deal with racial bias that is inculcated in the American psyche — the event exposes a complicated but important factor at play in centuries of American history. The Starbucks move comes in response to an incident that took place last month at a Philadelphia store, in which two Black male entrepreneurs who were waiting for a business partner to arrive were arrested after the manager called police because the men had not made a purchase. They were charged with "deliberate trespassing" and held in custody for hours. They were finally released when the district attorney, amid public pressure, announced he would not pursue charges.

Since then, there has been a surge in media reports of similar incidents in which white people have called the police on Blacks — and, in one instance, two American Indian brothers — merely for their presence in public spaces. Implicit in these recent incidents of Black bodies — which have been inscribed by history to be read as inferior and even criminal —

"trespassing" in perceived "white spaces" are the legacies of de jure and de facto segregation, in which race and geography collide. The response given by police when a white female graduate student at Yale University called law enforcement on a Black female graduate student who was napping in a common room was telling: an officer who demanded that the second student show them her university ID explained that "we need to make sure that you belong here."

The question of who belongs where is a central component of the history of racism, and many scholars have theorized that this collision of race and space helps to codify the constructs of difference and the Other. For example, in her book *Demonic Grounds: Black Women and the Cartographies of Struggle*, Katherine McKittick demonstrates the intersections of geography and race stating, "Black Matters are spatial matters." Her work challenges the notion that geography is apolitical. In other words, the history of racial bias in the United States is a history of geography underscored by settler-colonialism that, as McKittick observes, reifies a racial hierarchy that promotes ideas "that some bodies belong, some bodies do not belong and some bodies are out of place."

Rashad Shabazz also explores issues of spatialized difference in his book *Spatializing Blackness: Architectures of Confinement and Black Masculinity in Chicago*. He argues that space has become racialized and gendered via constraints "built into architecture, urban planning, and systems of control that functioned through policing and the establishment of borders literally and figuratively create[ing] a prison like environment." In few places is this tension clearer than in Philadelphia, right in the neighborhood where the Starbucks incident took place.

At the turn of the 20th century, W. E. B. Du Bois's seminal study *The Philadelphia Negro* explored the city's Seventh Ward, which "stretched along a narrow strip west from Seventh and Lombard streets to the Schuylkill

River, bordered by Spruce Street to the north and South Street to the south"; it was the hotbed of Black life and culture. Although the area had a reputation for "filth, poverty, and crime," Du Bois found a nuanced and complex community of African Americans, some locally born and others southern transplants trying to eke out a living. While some Blacks beat the odds, becoming doctors, lawyers, businessmen, teachers, barbers, and caterers, "a fresh wave of immigration from Europe would arrive and undermine the Black middle class as it was emerging." As Du Bois noted, these immigrants also displaced the coveted domestic positions held by Blacks on Rittenhouse Square.

The federal "urban renewal" program of the 1950s and 1960s opened urban areas such as the Seventh Ward to developers, which in turn increased its real estate values as the Black population sank from 30% to 7%. As displaced Blacks relocated to other areas of the city, the general area once known as the Seventh Ward was divided into three sections, a portion of which incorporated the surrounding area of the park — and includes 18th and Spruce Streets, the home of the Rittenhouse Square Starbucks. It "is now an upper-middle-class community" stated sociologist Elijah Anderson in the foreword to the 2010 edition of DuBois' book, "comprised of assimilated white ethnics" where "a strong caste line still exists." It is an area that Blacks pass through but where they seldom linger.

In other words, though the neighborhood has a long history as a home to the city's African American population, it has become one of the places where they do not "belong."

Likewise, Craig Steven Wilder, in his book *Ebony and Ivy: Race Slavery, and the Troubled History of America's Universities,* noted that Yale University founded in 1701 relied on a slave-worked plantation. In 1834, though he was only allowed to audit classes, James Pennington, a fugitive slave, became the first African American to study at Yale Divinity School. Yale enrolled its first Black student at the medical school in the 1850s; the first Black student to enroll in Yale College was in 1870. It was nearly a century before Yale increased its efforts towards the admission of African Americans in any substantial way. By 2016, the proportion of African Americans at Yale reached 7.1 %. This is a space founded on whiteness.

Similarly, Colorado State University, where two Mohawk students were recently detained by police during a campus tour, was founded in 1870 during the period of intensified attacks on the tribes of Colorado. The university is less than 300 miles from the Southern Ute Tribe reservation, established in 1881. Indians reservations are an extreme example of the way geography and race intersect, as they became the legal means to spatialize indigeneity, based on the doctrine of Manifest Destiny, which justified the further expansion of American territory on the bases of race and religion. While most American Indians currently live in urban and suburban areas, their being "off the reservation" can subject them to both micro- and macroaggressions like the CSU incident. As American Indian Michelle Lot stated during an interview with *The Guardian*, "I can't find a spot that the government tells me I'm not trespassing on."

Race and geography are twin forces that have shaped American culture since the colonial era, long before "white only-colored only" signs dotted the South. The impact of those forces continues to this day and will take more than one day's training at one company to uproot and dismantle. Indeed, it will require the sustained effort of an entire nation. ◼

32

HERE'S WHY ROSEANNE'S TWEET WAS A RACIST SLUR, NOT A BOTCHED JOKE

WASHINGTON POST, MAY 31, 2018

Comedian and former ABC sitcom star Roseanne Barr became the latest social media casualty when the network canceled her show "Roseanne" after a tweet about Valerie Jarrett, who was a senior adviser to President Barack Obama, in which Barr compared Jarrett to a blend of the Muslim Brotherhood and the film "Planet of the Apes." Nor was it the first time Barr referred to a Black woman using the ape trope — in 2013, she wrote a similar tweet about Obama's national security adviser Susan E. Rice. As president and first lady, Barack and Michelle Obama were subject to similar insults. While Barr and others dismiss their association of people of African descent and apes as a mere joke, this racist trope has been used for centuries to condone slavery, segregation, and eugenics. The trope has its roots in 16th- and 17th-century European and American thought, when it was used to argue that Africans were subhuman, thereby justifying the enslavement and much later the second-class citizen status of African peoples.

The dehumanization of African peoples is rooted in what scholar Anne McClintock has dubbed "the porno-tropic tradition." For centuries, Europeans saw Africa as a site of sexual vice. European lore abounded with tales of the "monstrous sexuality of far-off lands where, as legend had it, men sported gigantic penises and women consorted with apes." From the second century on, such figures as Ptolemy, Leo Africanus, Francis Bacon, John Ogilby and Edward Long envisioned the inhabitants of Africa as the most sexually promiscuous beings to inhabit the earth. Englishmen began incursions into West Africa in the late 15th century. These first explorers were informed by literary myths like those from the medieval era, which portrayed bestiaries of strange creatures who resembled humans.

In 1607, for instance, "The Historie of Foure-Footed Beastes" by Edward Topsell explicitly described the lustful disposition of apes, connecting them to devils, associations that would become common in England. The English began propagating their own myths based on supposed correlations between Africans and tailless apes called orang-outang. As historian Winthrop Jordan contended, characterizations about apes "revolved around evil and sexual sin; and rather tenuously connected apes with blackness." While some 17th-century commentators suggested Africans were descended from apes or that apes were descended from "blacks and some unknown African beast," the notion that apes were fond of African women and inclined to rape them became widespread. Eighteenth-century Enlightenment thinkers such as John Atkins lent credence to these ideas, writing that "the Negroes have been suspected of Bestiality with them, apes and monkeys, and by the Boldness and Affection they are known under some circumstances to express to our females."

These racist ideas were not limited to England. In "Notes on the State of Virginia," Thomas Jefferson argued that Black men were a "lower species" lusting after white women. He expressed hyper anxiety about interracial relationships — though he would later have children with Sally Hemings, an enslaved woman — by equating sexual desire with a preference to maintain one's superior race traits (that is, their whiteness). "Are not the fine mixture of red (blushing) and white the expression of every passion by greater or less suffussions of colour in the one, preferable to that eternal monotony … the immoveable veil of black which covers all the emotions of the other race?" Jefferson wrote. He then invoked the timeworn myth of Black women engaging in bestial relations, arguing, "Their own judgment in favor of the whites, declared by preferences of them, as uniformly as is preference of the Oranootan for the Black woman over his own species." In other words, Jefferson believed Black men were filled with lust for the superiority of the white female body to elevate themselves, just as an orangutan lusted after the bodies of Black women to elevate itself. In both scenarios, Black people were viewed as subhuman and inferior to whites.

By the 19th century, the racist notion of blackness as bestial was burned into the European and American psyche, justifying the centuries-long enslavement of African peoples who were chained and herded like cattle onto slave ships to be sold at auction to the highest bidder. Reduced from human beings to chattel, slaves endured speculators prodding and picking at their potential commodity to ensure the quality and production in labor. For women, their childbearing potential as "breeders" to reproduce the slave labor force was a premium. The inspection included the public examination of teeth, limbs, and private parts. Such indiscretion was viewed as natural because of their status as property rather than people. Blacks were characterized as brutes who needed to be under the authority of whites so as to keep their bestial nature in check. Free Blacks were always viewed as a threat to white society, an anxiety heightened during the post-Civil War era as white fears of a nation of newly freed slaves gave rise to the theory of retrogression, which contended that freedom would cause Blacks to revert to their lowest type, unleashing crime and violence, particularly Black male sexual violence against white women. These sentiments underscored Jim Crow segregation, a doctrine of separate and unequal.

To reinforce the racial hierarchy which placed whites at the top of the human food chain, Africans were placed on exhibit in monkey cages such as the Zoological Park in Bronx, New York as detailed in Pamela Newkirk's heart wrenching book *Spectacle: The Astonishing Life of Ota Benga*. On September 9, 1906, the *New York Times* carried a featured article about a teen named Ota Benga, who was captured from his home in the Congo by former missionary and professor Samuel Phillips Verner, brought to the United States, and "handed over to the New York Zoological Society for care and keeping." The headline proclaimed, "BUSHMAN SHARES A CAGE WITH BRONX PARK APES!" Benga, a 4'11" and 103 lbs. human being, who was first exhibited at the World's Fair held in Louisiana in 1904, was housed two years later in an iron cage at the zoo's Monkey House. "It is probably a good thing," the article noted" that Benga doesn't think very deeply. If he did it isn't likely that he was very produ [sic] of himself when he woke in the morning and found himself under the same roof with the orang-outangs and monkeys." Approximately a quarter of a million people flocked to the zoo in the following weeks to see the human spectacle which garnered headlines all over the world. But even those most amused by the spectacle "turned away with an expression on their faces such as one sees after a play with a sad ending or a book in which the hero or heroine is poorly rewarded," the paper reported. "Something about it that I don't like," stated one observer. Notwithstanding, the *New York Times* defended the human exhibit stating:

> Ota Benga, according to our information, is a normal specimen of his race or tribe, with a brain as much developed as are those of its other members. Whether they are held to be illustrations of arrested development, and really closer to the anthropoid apes than the other African savages, or whether they are viewed as the degenerate descendants of ordinary negroes, they are of equal interest to the student of ethnology, **and can be studied with profit** (emphasis mine).[117]

Yet, as public pressure mounted, Benga was released to the care of his staunchest advocate Rev. James H. Gordon who ran the Howard Colored

Orphan Asylum in the Brooklyn Weeksville section. For the next 10 years Benga tried to put the horrible episode behind him and move on with his life. But the psychological damage had been done. On March 19, 1916, Benga died by suicide. He shot one bullet through his broken heart.

The racist ideology of the ape trope is no joke. It has had devastating effects on Black people globally. Its continued use reinforces notions of Blacks as inferior, subhuman and bestial. This results in the continued justification of their subjection and quasi-citizenship both nationally and globally as Jarrett stated on "Everyday Racism in America," a town hall hosted on Tuesday by MSNBC. "I see this as a teaching moment," she stated. "I am fine. I worry about those people without friends and followers who come right to their defense," and "those ordinary examples of racism that happen every single day." If we are to become a society where Black lives, rather than race, matters, these teaching moments must also become learning moments.

POSTSCRIPT: On June 19, 2020, The Wildlife Conservation Society which runs the Bronx Zoo issued an apology for the imprisonment of Ota Benga in a statement which reads in part:

"As the United States confronts its legacy of racism and the brutal killings that have led to mass protests around the world, this, too, is an important moment in history to reflect on WCS's own history, and the persistence of racism in our institution and in human society.

First, we condemn the treatment of a young man from Central Africa's Mbuti people named Ota Benga, who lived at the Bronx Zoo for a month and was displayed in the Monkey House for several days during the week of September 8, 1906. Ota Benga would tragically take his own life in 1916 in Virginia, a victim of the racism that robbed him of his humanity.

Today, we apologize for our organization's role in these injustices. We deeply regret that many people and generations have been hurt and betrayed by these actions. We recognize that overt and systemic anti-Black racism persists, and our institution must play a greater role in recognizing this fact and doing more to overcome these challenges." ▪

33

THE COMPLICATED HISTORY BEHIND BEYONCÉ'S DISCOVERY ABOUT THE "LOVE" BETWEEN HER SLAVE-OWNING AND ENSLAVED ANCESTORS

TIME MAGAZINE, AUGUST 10, 2018

With Beyoncé's appearance on the cover of the September issue of *Vogue,* the magazine highlights three facets of the superstar's character for particular focus: "Her Life, Her Body, Her Heritage." The words she shares are deeply personal, and that last component also offers a window into a complicated and misunderstood dynamic that affects all of American history. While opening up about her family's long history of dysfunctional marital relationships, she hints at an antebellum relationship that defies that pattern: "I researched my ancestry recently," she stated, "and learned that I come from a slave owner who fell in love with and married a slave." She doesn't elaborate on how she made the discovery or what is known about those individuals, but fans will know that Beyoncé Knowles-Carter is a native of Houston whose maternal and paternal forbears hailed from Louisiana and Alabama, respectively. Her characterization of her heritage stands out because those states, like others across the South, had stringent laws and penalties against interracial marriage. In fact, throughout the colonial and antebellum eras, interracial marriage would have been the exception — even though interracial sex was the rule.[118]

Within the context of America's slave society, such relations as that described by the star — and the larger system of cohabitation and concubinage, or involuntary monogamous sexual relations, in which they existed — have been the subject of much study by historians. After much debate, the consensus amongst scholars of American slavery is that sex within the master-slave relationship brings into question issues of power, agency and choice that problematize notions of love and romance even in cases where there appears to be mutual consent. As Joshua Rothman, in his book *Notorious in the Neighborhood: Sex and Families Across the Color Line In Virginia, 1787-1861,* observed about history's most famous such relationship, that between Thomas Jefferson and Sally Hemings, "Whatever reciprocal caring there may have ever been between them, fundamentally their lives together would always be founded more on a deal and a wary trust than on romance."

Indeed. In a 2013 article in the *Journal of African American History* entitled "What's Love Got to Do With It: Concubinage and Enslaved Women and Girls in the Antebellum South," historian Brenda E. Stevenson highlighted the complexity of interracial sexual liaisons in American slave society with regard to consent. Slaveowners propositioned enslaved girls in their early teens who at that age were "naïve, vulnerable, and certainly frightened." Promises of material gain and freedom for the enslaved woman and her family were enticements often used to gain sexual loyalties. As Stevenson observed, "Some concubinage relationships obviously developed overtime and could mimic a marriage in some significant ways such as emotional attachment; financial support; better food, clothing, and furnishings; and sometimes freedom for the woman and her children."[119]

Annette Gordon-Reed noted in her book *The Hemingses of Monticello: An American Family* the unusual case of Mary Hemings, Sally's oldest sister, whom Jefferson leased to local businessman Thomas Bell. Not long after Mary began working for Bell, the two developed a sexual relationship, which resulted in two children. Jefferson later, at her request, sold Mary and the children to Bell, though her four older children remained the property of Jefferson. She took Bell's last name and remained with him until his death in 1800. "Bell and Hemings, who adopted the last name of her master/lover," Gordon-Reed wrote, "lived as husband and wife for the rest of Bell's life." In most cases, however, young girls were forced into concubinage, not marriage.

That more common story is told by the historian Tiya Miles in her book *The Ties That Bind: The Story of a Afro-Cherokee Family in Slavery and Freedom*. Shoe Boots was a Cherokee warrior who had married, according to Cherokee custom, a young white female who was captured during an Indian raid in Kentucky in 1792. Also, during this time Shoe Boots purchased a young girl named Doll in South Carolina; she was placed under the supervision of his white wife as a domestic servant. When his wife and children abandoned him after an arranged family visit to Kentucky in 1804, Shoe Boots took 16-year-old Doll as his concubine. In a letter he dictated to the Cherokee Council two decades later, Shoe Boots described what happened as "I debased myself and took one of my black women" in response to being upset at losing his white wife. One can only imagine the years of physical and psychological trauma Doll endured to console her master's grief.

And, while much attention has focused on sexual relations between slaveowners and enslaved women, enslaved men could also be coerced or sexually exploited. In her 1861 autobiography *Incidents in the Life of a Slave Girl*, Harriet Jacobs told the chilling story of a male slave named Luke who was kept chained at his bedridden master's bedside so that he would be constantly available to tend to his physical needs, which included sexual favors. In veiled language so as not to offend the sensibilities of 19th-century polite society, Jacobs reported that most days Luke was only allowed to wear a shirt so that he could be easily flogged if he committed an infraction such as resisting his master's sexual advances.

And in a 2011 *Journal of the History of Sexuality* article, the scholar
Thomas Foster contended that enslaved Black men regularly were sexually
exploited by both white men and white women, which "took a variety of
forms, including outright physical penetrative assault, forced reproduction,
sexual coercion and manipulation, and psychic abuse." In one example
provided by Foster, a man named Lewis Bourne filed for divorce in 1824
due to his wife's longtime sexual liaison and continued pursuit of a male
slave named Edmond from their community. Foster contended that such
pursuits "could enable white women to enact radical fantasies of domination
over white men" while at the same time subjecting the Black enslaved
male to her control. Foster also contended that such pursuits were not
uncommon, as demonstrated by testimonies from The American Freedmen's
Inquiry Commission established by the secretary of war in 1863, which took
depositions from abolitionists and slaves regarding the realities of slave life.
Such depositions included stories of sexual liaisons between enslaved men
and their mistresses. Abolitionist Robert Hinton stated, "I have never found
yet a bright looking colored man who has not told me of instances where he
has been compelled, either by his mistress, or by white women of the same
class, to have connection with them." Foster further concurs with scholars
who argue that rape can serve as a metaphor for both enslaved women
and men: "The vulnerability of all enslaved black persons to nearly every
conceivable violation produced a collective 'rape' subjectivity."[120]

For certain, interracial sexual liaisons between the slave-owning class and
the enslaved is a well-established reality of American history. But caution
must be used when describing relationships that appear consensual using
the language of love and romance. We cannot know what was in the hearts
of Beyoncé's ancestors, or any person who does not leave a record of their
emotions, but we can know about the society in which they lived. Complex
dynamics of power are at work when we talk about sex within slavery, and
the enslaved negotiated those forces daily in order to survive. ■

34

THE DOCTOR AND THE SAINT: WHAT MARTIN LUTHER KING OVERLOOKED ABOUT GANDHI

HISTORY NEWS NETWORK, AUGUST 15, 2018

Today marks the 72nd anniversary of India's independence from Britain, which occurred on August 15, 1947. Twelve years later in 1959 Dr. Martin Luther King visited "the land of Gandhi" touring the subcontinent and meeting dignitaries, relatives, and friends of the man honored as "the Father of India." The month-long trip not only solidified King's commitment to the Gandhian concept "Satyagraha," meaning "truth force or love force," but it also deepened his admiration for his intellectual idol so much so that King's Palm Sunday sermon, delivered two weeks after his return to Montgomery, Alabama, centered on Gandhi. King's view of his revolutionary forbear echoed early twentieth century Christian theologians, who believed the Mahatama (Great Soul) was an avatar of Christ, the embodiment of Jesus's Sermon on the Mount. "Christ furnished the spirit and motivation," King stated, "while Gandhi furnished the method. And isn't it significant that he died on the same day as Christ died?"[121]

Yet, for the past decade scholars have taken a closer and more critical look at the life and words of India's beloved founding father, deconstructing a saintly image steeped in a mythology that had captured the imagination of millions of admirers, including arguably his most devoted American disciple, MLK. In fact, the early Civil Rights Movement demonstrates that King's philosophy was based on an uncritical acceptance of the Gandhi myth, a construct of the Mahatama's devoted followers; but during the latter years of his tenure, King, while maintaining devotion to the philosophy of nonviolence, unwittingly transformed his philosophy to reflect the viewpoint of his idol's ideological opponent, Dr. Bhimrao Ramji Ambedkar.

King had only a cursory knowledge of Gandhi when he heard a lecture by Howard University President Mordecai Johnson in 1950, just three years after India acquired independence from Britain. King, an impressionable twenty-one-year-old graduate student of Theology, "left the meeting" so inspired that he "bought a half-dozen books on Gandhi's life and works." Before studying Gandhi, King believed that war and even violence was a necessary evil; but he changed his mind, as he stated in his autobiography. "But after reading Gandhi, I saw how utterly mistaken I was. Gandhi was probably the first person in history to lift the love ethic of Jesus above mere interaction between individuals to a powerful and effective social force on a large scale." King initiated the Gandhian philosophy in the Civil Rights Movement during the 1955-56 Montgomery, Alabama Bus Boycott. King stated that "India's Gandhi was our guiding light ... We spoke of him often." Once the victory of bus desegregation was won, King was determined to visit India.

In a lengthy article written for *Ebony Magazine*, King called his visit to the subcontinent "the most concentrated and eye-opening experience" of his life. The thirty-year old civil rights leader believed India represented the alternative to violence, which in its aftermath only yielded bitterness and hatred. To the contrary, "Gandhi followed the way of love and nonviolence," the aftermath of which was "the creation of a beloved community so that when the battle is over ... a new love ... new understanding ... and new relationship comes into being between the oppressor and the oppressed." Yet,

King's theory of beloved communities did not consider the complexity of post-revolution realities for oppressed peoples. Case in point, King inflated India's love for the British people stating, "If you ask the Indian People who they love more, they will say to you immediately . . . the British people. But who were "the Indian people" King spoke about? King treated the violent death of his Indian Hindu hero by a Hindu fundamentalist as an isolated incident while ignoring the post-independence violence and riots that led to the deaths and displacement of millions of Indians when Britain partitioned the subcontinent into Hindu India and Muslim Pakistan. While neither the gross poverty of the country nor the troublesome issue of caste was not lost on King, his view of these issues was distorted by the propaganda machine of India's elite. King believed that the Indian government demonstrated a firmer commitment to eradicate casteism than America's commitment to eradicate racism; and he credited Gandhi's leadership on the issue. "He not only spoke against the caste system, but he acted against it."[122]

But Ambedkar, an Untouchable and fierce opponent of Gandhi, would have disagreed. As writer-activist Arundhati Roy stated in her seminal book, *The Doctor and the Saint*, Ambedkar challenged the Mahatama "politically, intellectually, and morally" due to his support for policies which embraced rather than eradicated caste.

As demonstrated by Ashwin Desai and Goolem Vahed in their book, *The South African Gandhi: Stretcher-Bearer of Empire*, Gandhi's caste problem appeared very early in his activism. During his years in South Africa from 1893 to 1914, Gandhi a Vaishya of the privileged caste of Hindu traders, completed a law degree in London and afterwards received a one-year contract with a legal firm in southern Africa. Gandhi's political awakening occurred when he was thrown off a train in Pietermaritzburg for riding in a first class "whites only" car. Outraged that "passenger Indians," those of the privileged merchant class, were treated on a par with Africans, whom he referred to using the pejorative "raw Kaffirs," Gandhi organized the Natal

Indian Congress (NIC) in order to pressure the British government to adhere to Queen Victoria's 1858 proclamation, which granted equality to all Imperial subjects.

Gandhi secured the NIC's first victory when his request for a third entrance to the post office for Indians was granted. His petition was based on the idea that the European and the Indian "came from the same stock, called the Indo-Aryan." He further demonstrated his support for segregation when he decried being placed in a jail cell with a "Kaffir." "They as a rule are uncivilized," he stated, "the convicts even more so. They are troublesome, very dirty and live almost like animals." Gandhi's activism in South Africa was underscored by caste and racial segregation; and rather than agitating to eradicate the system, it seems that he sought to make friends with it; despite his work among the "Depressed Classes" including denouncing "untouchability" when he returned to India permanently in 1915, Gandhi, as Desai and Vahed persuasively argued, never denounced caste.

Untouchability, which was outlawed in 1917, referred to those within the Untouchable (Dalit) caste, whose movements were restricted due to the belief that any physical contact with them, including their shadow, would cause others to be contaminated. Hence, they were relegated to segregated settlements. They were forbidden to use the same public roads as the privilege-caste; and were also barred from public wells, Hindu temples, and privilege-caste schools. While Gandhi spoke out against "untouchability" he continued to support the caste system calling it "the genius of Indian society." He believed that the hierarchy of caste should be eradicated, but that the hereditary principle of caste, which designated a person's life occupation, should remain, otherwise India would descend into chaos.

Yet Ambedkar, lawyer, politician and Untouchable, countered Gandhi, contending that "the outcaste is a bye-product of the caste system.... Nothing can emancipate the outcaste except the destruction of the caste system." For three decades Ambedkar fiercely opposed Gandhi, contending that his views were steeped in Hindu orthodoxy, which underscored the notion of caste sanctioned by the Hindu Shastra (sacred text). He argued in his essay "The Annihilation of Caste" that merely "holding inter-caste dinners and celebrating inter-caste marriages" was a "futile method." Those who supported "Mahatma Gandhi," failed to see that "the removal of untouchability will not change their [people's] conduct." In other words, the problem was not people's behavior, but the system of discrimination, which informed social relations. Less than a year before his assassination, King came to a similar conclusion. [123]

When King returned from his triumphant visit to India, he took on the entire South and the entire country with nonviolent marches, acts of civil disobedience, and a speech about a dream that shook the core of a democratic nation founded upon undemocratic principles (to borrow the words of Ambedkar). But three and a half years later, the spark that lit that dream had faded. On May 8, 1967, a visibly wary King told *NBC News* correspondent Sander Vanocur that the dream he had on the day of the famous March on Washington for Jobs and Freedom, "has in many points turned into a nightmare." King stated that deep "soul-searching" and "agonizing moments" forced him to realize "some of the old optimism was a little superficial and now it must be tempered with a solid realism." The realism that King spoke of unwittingly echoed the sentiments Ambedkar had expressed thirty years prior. King stated, "It's much easier to integrate a bus than it is to eradicate slums. It is much easier to guarantee the right to vote than it is to guarantee an annual income. It is much easier to integrate a public park than it is to create jobs." Perhaps King revisited his trip to India and realized that he had been fed, as Arundhati Roy stated, "a diet of Gandhi hagiographies," only to realize that there can be no revolution without social reform.[124]

A still young yet more sober King envisioned that 'there are difficult days ahead" as the movement pivoted to combat what he viewed as the three evils of society— racism, economic exploitation, and militarism. Social reform would require no less than the transformation of the soul of America, a radical social change which India and the United States still now desperately need to achieve genuine equality.

POSTSCRIPT: In June 2016 a statute of Gandhi was installed at the University of Ghana in Accra which immediately stirred unrest amongst students and faculty who viewed the statue as an insult not only because the campus did not have statues of African notables, but also because of Gandhi's racist views of African peoples. While Ghana's ministry of Foreign Affairs resisted calls for the removal of the statue for two years contending "that the 'unfortunate verbal attack' against Gandhi could potentially 'create disaffection not only at the level of Government relations, but also between people not only in our country but all over the world,'" in December 2018 the statue was removed during the night to an undisclosed location — a decision many believed resulted from internal actions taken by the university. ■

35
SEPTEMBER 11, 2001: WHERE WAS I?

LA PROGRESSIVE, SEPTEMBER 11, 2018

I was at home that tragic morning. It was my day off from teaching. My husband was at work and my children were in school. I was going to sleep in and be up by mid-morning to begin grading a set of essays my freshman composition students had recently handed in. At least that was the plan. Then the phone rang. It was my husband Tracy.

"Wake up Rick!," he hollered though the phone. "Ricky, Ricky you wake!," he continued before I could respond.

"Yes, I am now," I responded with irritation.

"Turn on the TV," he stated. "We're being attacked!"

I immediately leaped out of bed, hurriedly put on my robe and slippers than rushed downstairs to the family room to turn on the only TV we had in the house with these words flying out of my mouth, "GOOD GRIEF, WHO IN THE HELL HAVE WE PISSED OFF NOW!"

I never thought the attack was unprovoked. I figured it was payback for our arrogant display at the World Conference on Racism and Xenophobia in Durham, South Africa which occurred a week prior to the attack. On September 3, 2001, the U.S. government literally told the world to kiss its ass when it abruptly withdrew from the conference. Or I thought that MLK's prophetic word that the U.S. would reap terrorism if we did not change our vicious foreign policy had finally come to pass. As Coretta Scott King reminded us in a 2005 interview, "If Martin's philosophy had been lived out in Iraq we wouldn't have had Bin Laden."[125]

Osama Bin Laden, the mastermind behind the 9/11 attack was once a friend of the U.S. government.

By the time I turned on the TV the first tower was already hit, and black smoke was filling the sky. The nightmare continued as a plane sliced through the second tower. Then the towers collapsed. I stood before the TV completely paralyzed. I simultaneously felt everything and nothing.

The phone rang again. It was my oldest brother Tony Wade this time. He and his family were living in Queens, New York. He called to say they were all safe. He had witnessed the towers fall from the rooftop where he worked.

My heart ached for the thousands who died and would not be able to make that phone call, and for those who would not receive it. Businesses and schools closed early that day. By that afternoon, my family and I were safe at home, watching news footage of the horror that had happened in New York, Washington, D.C, and Pennsylvania. We had not been directly affected by the enormous tragedy of the day. We were some of the lucky ones.

The following day I deviated from my syllabus and allowed my students to express their shock, anger, and fear of the unspeakable events we were all still trying to process. Many of them expressed outrage of rumors that there were some parts of the world dancing in celebration of the attack. I emphasized that no one deserved what had happened the previous day and if there were some celebrating, we should ask ourselves why? I told them of King's prophecy, the Conference in South Africa, and that Afghanistan had already been bombed back to the Middle Ages more than once. I concluded the class urging them to "Question everything. What you see is most often not the complete picture."

I went straight to my office after class. I had barely crossed the threshold when I heard a small knock on the door. It was a South Korean exchange student who for the sake of privacy I will simply call Kim. I smiled and waved for her to come in. She asked if it was okay to shut the door. I usually meet with students with the door at least halfway open but made an exception in this case.

Kim began by apologizing for not speaking up in class as I encourage students to do but stated that she was afraid to express her views openly for fear of backlash. She thanked me for what I said in class particularly about the lack of knowledge American citizens have regarding our government's foreign policy. She talked about what it meant to be a South Korean national living under U.S. imperialism. According to Kim, South Koreans hated the U.S. and military presence in their country and wanted us out. They also hated that U.S. military personnel are seldom punished for the crimes they commit against South Korean citizens. Kim was especially indignant about how issues of sexual harassment and rape of South Korean women by American men went unaddressed by both governments.

The hour of conversation interspersed with tears and laughter was good for both of our souls. We parted ways that day hoping that the silver lining of the previous day would be that the U.S. upon deep reflection would lead the world in demonstrating that there are alternative responses to violence. But the drums of war were already loudly beating in the nation's capital and reverberating throughout every region in the nation. With George W. Bush's "Shock and Awe" military campaign in Iraq — a country which had nothing to do with the horror of 9/11 — we used terror to initiate our so-called "War on Terror," unleashing an orgy of violence which persists to this day with no end in sight.

On September 20, 2001, President Bush admonished the leaders of the world, "You're either with us or you're with the terrorist." Yet, as a Black citizen of this nation whose ancestors and contemporaries were/are subjected to continued racialized terrorism in this country, 43's statement smacked of reductionism and historical amnesia. "I am with those who advocate for peace not war," was my response then; and now. ■

36

ELIZABETH WARREN'S DNA TEST AND THE DIFFICULT HISTORY OF LOOKING FOR ANSWERS IN BLOOD

TIME MAGAZINE, OCTOBER 20, 2018

If Massachusetts Senator Elizabeth Warren hoped that releasing the results of a DNA test would settle the issue of her claim to Cherokee heritage, she was quickly proved wrong. In a video highlighting her family heritage, which she released on Monday, Stanford University geneticist Carlos Bustamante states on camera that "the facts suggest that you absolutely have a Native American ancestor in your pedigree"; in later tweets, Warren explained that she released the test results as a response to the "racism" of President Donald Trump's repeated mockery of that part of her background.

In the days that followed, the release reignited debate regarding not only the reliability of commercial DNA tests, but also the very meaning of DNA when it comes to questions of race and heritage. In Warren's case, the Cherokee Nation quickly responded that "a DNA test is useless to determine tribal citizenship" and that using such a test to claim a connection "is inappropriate and wrong." (Warren herself acknowledged that the results said nothing about tribal citizenship). But the problem with trying to use a DNA test to claim *any* racial identity goes far beyond this one example.

In fact, the uproar over Warren's case is part of a long American history of trying, and failing, to use science or pseudoscience to categorize people.[126]

At the heart of the debate is the matter of science as a social institution informed by societal norms — not a separate, apolitical enterprise based on objective observation.

Geneticist R. C. Lewontin, in his classic book *Biology as Ideology: The Doctrine of DNA,* traces the connection between the history of DNA and the rise of Western secularism in the 19th century. Lewontin argues that science is a social institution that—despite its claims of objectivity—"reflects and reinforces the dominant values and views of society at each historical epoch." During the Middle Ages and the Renaissance, the science of the period held a holistic view of nature that mirrored religious notions of the way the world worked. Later, science shifted to reflect a new idea that to understand the whole required analyzing individual bits and pieces (such as atoms, molecules, cells, and genes). "Our genes and the DNA molecules that make them up are the modern form of grace," Lewontin writes. In this new thinking, which Lewontin calls the "ideology of biological determinism," those biological components tell people who they are and where they fit in society.

The mid-19th century, as I describe in my book *That the Blood Stay Pure,* saw the rise of the American School of anthropology, which used theories of scientific racism to support pro-slavery ideology and the doctrine of Manifest Destiny — with its destruction of Native American communities — on the basis of what W. E. B. Du Bois later called "the grosser physical difference of hair, skin, and bone." Scientific findings validated societal notions of human difference in which Europeans occupied a higher rung on the hierarchy of humanity, with Indians below them and Africans at the bottom.

But among the many problems with the idea was one of racial categorization based on science. If you believed that some races were better than others, it mattered a lot who fell into which category. The followers of this theory, whose findings *appeared* to be scientific, were in fact using ideas appropriated from old European notions of blood and purity based on religion to answer their questions about who was white, who was Black and who was Native American.

By the late 19th century, the ideology of biological determinism had made its way into American law, where the politics of blood reigned. People of African descent were defined by the law of hypodescent, meaning that one drop of black "blood" made one Black, despite any other ancestry. Meanwhile, a competing concept called blood quantum, requiring much more than one drop, defined American Indian identity. The discrepancy of racial definitions was captured by author Karen Blu in her book *The Lumbee Problem: The Making of An American Indian People.* "It may only take one drop of black blood to make a person a Negro, but it takes a lot of Indian blood to make a person a 'real' Indian," she stated.

Society's definitions of race — and the attendant social ramifications of those categories — did not map directly with biology. Even so, such ideas were on the rise.

In 1904, Francis Galton, a cousin of Charles Darwin, delivered a lecture before the Sociological Society in London on the science of eugenics, a theory he began to develop in the 1880s that, in his words, "deals with all influences that improve the inborn qualities of a race." Galton's ideas were instrumental in spreading what would become one of the most insidious pseudoscientific falsities of the 20th century: the idea that some races are biologically better than others, and that human beings can be bred for improvement. He thus set the stage for a pernicious racial campaign that contributed to everything from stricter anti-miscegenation laws and the rise of involuntary sterilization to the philosophy of Hitler and the Third Reich.[127]

But thinkers on the other side were already countering these ideas. In 1942, as Americans crossed the Atlantic to fight in WWII, anthropologist Ashley Montagu—a student of Franz Boas who opposed eugenics and the scientific racism of the previous century – published his influential book *Man's Most Dangerous Myth: The Fallacy of Race,* in which he attacked biological determinism on the premise that the concept of race had no genetic basis. Individual physical appearance, individual intelligence and "the ability of the group to which the individual belongs to achieve a high civilization" could not be scientifically determined.

His work was the side that stood the test of time. In 1998, the American Anthropological Association released "A Statement on Race" that debunked the ideology of biological determinism and the concept of race as scientific fact. In other words, race is politics not biology. Still, old myths die hard. Even today, many people rely on racial definitions of who is Black and who is Indian that can easily be traced back to the old ideas of the one-drop rule and blood quantum.[128]

Meanwhile, with the question of race as a social construct considered settled by a large swath of the scientific community, genetic science pressed full speed ahead. In the late 20th century, as James Shreeve details in his 2006 *National Geographic* article "Reading Secrets of the Blood," two separate genomic projects were launched. The most popular was the Human Genome Project, an international scientific collaboration that aimed to provide an entire blueprint of a human being by sequencing the estimated 25,000 genes in the nucleus of the human cell known as DNA. In summer 2000, when scientists Francis Collins and Craig Venter stood with President Bill Clinton at an international press conference to present the first draft of the mapping and sequencing of human DNA, one aspect of the presentation that drew particular media attention was the unequivocal assertion that racial classifications made no biological sense.

Advances in genetic science have also allowed home DNA tests to grow as a business, offering people a chance to see what their blood could tell them. But with that possibility came the danger of sliding back into a history that many hoped had been left behind. For example, the 2006 *PBS* special *African American Lives,* hosted by Harvard scholar Henry Louis Gates, used DNA tests to trace the supposed lineage of the eight guests to their African countries of origin as well as to calculate their percentage of American Indian heritage. Gates was taken to task for the weight he placed on DNA results, but the gates were already open: many Americans were convinced that DNA tests could provide perfect and complete proof of ancestral lineage.

But in fact, as the scholar Kim TallBear, author of *Native American DNA: Tribal Belonging and the False Promise of Genetic Science*, has stated on numerous occasions, "People think there is a DNA test to prove you're Native American. There isn't."

Reliance on DNA reinforces old notions of separate biological races and lends credence to archaic ideas of racial purity, which are now being appropriated by white supremacists. That Sen. Warren would look to DNA to prove her point is not surprising; for more than a century, Americans and others have accepted the notion that race is blood in the search for those answers. But what people have found instead, time and again, are more questions.[129]

Today science is as sacred as religion. Its claimed authoritative validity has mostly gone unquestioned. But just as the age of science resulted in what Lewontin called "a reasonable skepticism" of the overarching claims of the institution of the Church, we must also question the sweeping claims of the doctrine of science if we intend to truly know who we are. ■

37

GREEN BOOK GETS DON SHIRLEY ALL WRONG!

HOLLYWOOD PROGRESSIVE, NOVEMBER 20, 2018

reen Book is a tour de force of revisionist history. Riddled with racial clichés and indulging in gross embellishments, it achieves historical erasure of epic proportions as even the book from which it takes its title is treated with insignificance.

This movie is loosely based on the true story of Dr. Don Shirley, a African American pianist extraordinaire and his Italian American chauffeur/body guard, previously a nightclub bouncer who was hired by Shirley's record label to accompany him on a 1962 tour which included gigs in the Deep South. *Green Book* privileges the racist imagination of its Hollywood creators and their interpretation of Shirley as a Black man whose redemption lies in his restoration to Black culture and Black people by a white savior; but it is based entirely on fiction. In fact, *Green Book* is the 21st century version of the movie *Driving Miss Daisy* (1989), except that Daisy Werthan would have never taken the wheel from her exhausted African American driver Hoke Colburn so he can make it home to his family in time for Christmas.

Contrary to the Hollywood character, Dr. Donald Walbridge Shirley was a brilliant virtuoso who loved and was loved in the African American community. His ability to infuse numerous musical styles including classical, jazz, and blues as well as Negro spirituals defied the limits of music convention and inspired him to create a genre all his own. Currently, there is no biography of Donald W. Shirley, hence his life prior to joining Cadence Records in 1955 is sketchy. What is known of his early years has been gleaned from album liner notes and informal sources.

Shirley was born on January 29, 1927, in Pensacola, Florida of Jamaican parents who migrated to the American South in 1914. Shirley's father, Edwin Samuel Shirley was an Episcopal priest, and his mother, Stella Gertrude Young was a teacher who first taught her son to play the piano. Shirley had three brothers (and a sister from his father's second marriage) who were similarly gifted. Two of his brothers became medical doctors and the other a sociologist. His youngest brother, Edwin Jr., was close friends with civil rights icons Martin and Coretta King and often vacationed with them.

Just six months after his first lesson, Shirley gave his first public performance at age 3. In 1936, the year his mother died, Shirley was invited to study theory with Mittolovski at the prestigious Leningrad Conservatory of Music. He later studied with the famous organist Conrad Bernier who, in addition to Dr. Thaddeus Jones at Catholic University of America in Washington D. C., taught him advanced composition.

On June 25, 1945, at age 18, Shirley made his concert debut with the Boston Pops. His first major composition was performed by the London Philharmonic Orchestra in l946. In 1949 he was invited by the Haitian government to play at the Exposition International du Bi-Centenaire De Port-au-Prince, and he gave a repeat performance the following week at the request of President Léon Dumarsais Estimé.

By the early 1950s, Shirley had left the music scene and was practicing psychology in Chicago having obtained doctorates in Music, Psychology, and the Liturgical Arts. In 1955 when Shirley resumed his music career, he met music great Duke Ellington. A lasting friendship developed between the two virtuosos with Shirley performing with Ellington's orchestra for the premier of Duke's Piano Concerto at Carnegie Hall with the NBC Symphony of the Air. It is alleged that Ellington stated of Shirley, "He is the only pianist for whom I would give up my bench."

There is much more. Shirley also performed as a guest soloist for the Alvin Ailey Dance Ensemble playing Gershwin's Concerto in F at the Metropolitan Opera House.

Historian Adele Logan Alexander who grew up in New York City recalled that "the [upscale] Carlyle Hotel on Madison Ave was really Shirley's 'home base.' He performed there for several stretches every year for well-dressed, well-heeled audiences that included both Blacks and whites."

While Shirley would have been resentful of the racism within classical music that derailed his career as a concert pianist, his friendship with Ellington would have certainly inspired him to move beyond musical boundaries. Hence, rather than despise the music for which he was popular, as the movie insisted, Shirley embraced his own ability to defy convention and create his own music genre. As Cadence Records President Archie Bleyer highlighted on the back cover of Shirley's 1961 album titled *Don Shirley Trio*, "He has the same admiration for Odetta [African American folk singer and civil rights activist] and Ellington that he has for Rachmaninoff and Debussy. All these influences — plus many more — create the uniqueness of his musical expression. The first song from this album, "Water Boy," the trio's most popular song and the only song to hit the charts, was a "famous old prison song" which was adopted "from Odetta's interpretation." The album also featured a tribute to Shirley's friend the late Billie Holiday in which he selected four songs he believed perfectly reflected Holiday's life: "Traveling Light," "Don't Explain," "Easy Living," and "God Bless the Child."

In 1962, the same year Shirley met Vallelonga/Tony Lip, he released an album titled *Don Shirley Presents Martha Flowers*. Flowers was a world renowned African American mezzo-soprano who Shirley described as "first and foremost a musician; she can sing anything and sing it well, from a Schubert lieder to a tune from a Broadway show." Shirley selected the songs for this album "that clearly demonstrate her flexibility, her dramatic talent, and above all her musicianship." Indeed, Shirley's focus was musicianship rather than remaining true to mainstream musical categories. As Bleyer noted:

> Don Shirley does not fit any of the "pigeon-hole" categories into which Show Business likes to put people. Although he makes use of the jazz idiom, he cannot be called a "jazz pianist." Although he makes use of the blues idiom, he cannot be called a "blues pianist." Because he makes use of the jazz, blues, and classical idioms—and often develops thematic material in the manner of a serious composer—he cannot be called a "popular pianist." Because he devotes his performing and creative talent to "music of the people"—folk songs, blues, spirituals, and so-called "popular songs"—he cannot be called a "classical pianist." What is he then? I say he is a uniquely talented creative artist-perhaps a genius—who brings an extraordinary musical experience to anyone who listens to him with an open mind and an open heart.

In a June 27, 2000, email to his fans, Shirley confessed that it was his refusal to be pigeonholed that proved most challenging to his music career. He also apologized for not answering each individual email. "Please accept my apologies. I don't like to write," he stated. "I am not good at it, and often cannot find the right words to compose the answers you deserve."

*N*onetheless, Shirley found the right words to articulate a sense of triumph. "But there is also a feeling of vindication," he stated. "My music has always been hard to place because it does not adhere to any particular style or school." Nor did his life adhere to the narrow societal definition of blackness. Clearly, the movie *Green Book* has robbed this brilliant man of vindication.

POSTSCRIPT: Despite the controversy surrounding the limitations of the movie due to its misrepresentation of Don Shirley and his family relations, *Green Book* won five Academy Awards including Best Picture. It was called the "worst Oscar best picture win since '*Crash*.'" Hollywood was also criticized for snubbing the groundbreaking and record shattering masterpiece *Black Panther* which grossed over one billion dollars worldwide that same year. The Hollywood establishment's choice to validate white mediocrity at the expense of Black excellence demonstrated that indeed, to borrow the words of Marianne Williamson, America's deepest fear is that Black people are powerful beyond measure.

38

THE HOUSE HEARING ON SLAVERY REPARATIONS IS PART OF A LONG HISTORY: HERE IS WHAT TO KNOW ON THE EARLY ADVOCATES OF THIS IDEA

TIME MAGAZINE, JUNE 18, 2019

On Wednesday, the issue of reparations for slavery will be a topic of discussion on Capitol Hill during a hearing scheduled by the Subcommittee on the Constitution, Civil Rights and Civil Liberties "to examine, through open and constructive discourse, the legacy of the Trans-Atlantic Slave Trade, its continuing impact on the [African America] community and the path to restorative justice." This round of hearings is a follow-up to the 2007 hearings led by former Michigan Congressman John Conyers, who from 1989 to 2017 sponsored House Resolution 40, calling for a congressional study of reparations. Conyers (who passed away in 2019) contended that raising the topic was not meant to be divisive or controversial but rather that it was necessary. "Slavery is a blemish on this nation's history," he stated, "and until it is addressed, our country's story will remain marked." With the publication of Randall Robinson's bestselling book *The Debt: What America Owes Blacks* in 2000, the compelling 2014 article "The Case for Reparations" by Ta-Nehisi Coates (who will testify at the hearing), and its injection into the 2020 Presidential election, some in Congress believe the moment has come to accept the invitation to debate the issue.[130]

Yet the debate about reparations for slavery is not a new one — and the history of the idea shows just how many roadblocks there are to a meaningful conversation about the topic. In fact, around the turn of the 20th century, the federal government exercised its power to silence the voices of thousands of formerly enslaved African Americans who sought restitution for their two and a half centuries of legalized enslavement.

While the 13th Amendment abolished chattel slavery in the United States in 1865, it made no provision for restitution to the surviving formerly enslaved population, which numbered approximately four million. The policy popularly referred to as "40 acres and a mule," a promise by the federal government to redistribute land to former slaves that had been confiscated from Confederate rebels during the Civil War, was immediately overturned by Lincoln's successor Andrew Johnson, who reestablished white Southern rule. With the end of government support for land going to freedpeople, a sharecropping system arose in its place, leaving them economically destitute.

In a letter to Democratic politician Walter R. Vaughan of Iowa in 1890, Frederick Douglass marveled that the American government had failed to compensate Black people for 250 years of unpaid labor, which included building the Capitol and White House. "The Egyptian bondsmen went out with the spoils of his master, and the Russian serf was provided with farming tools and three acres of land upon which to begin life," Douglass wrote, "but the Negro has neither spoils, implements nor lands, and today he is practically a slave on the very plantation where formerly he was driven to toil under the lash."

During this time the first iteration of what became known as the "Ex-Slave Pension Bill" (H.R.11119) was introduced in Congress at Vaughan's request. The concept of an ex-slave pension was based on the post-Civil War program for disabled veterans (including Blacks) established by the Bureau of Pensions. Vaughan articulated his pro-reparations views in a pamphlet titled *Vaughan's Freedmen's Pension Bill. Being an Appeal in Behalf of Men Released from Slavery,* in which he argued that reparations were equally beneficial to Blacks and whites because the system would provide economic justice to former slaves and their spending would help boost the Southern economy.

Vaughan's advocacy for ex-slave pensions fueled the national debate on reparations and gave rise to numerous organizations during the last decade of the 19th century, none more prominent than the National Ex-Slave Mutual Relief, Bounty, and Pension Association (MRB&PA), which historian Mary Frances Berry has called "one of the largest grassroots movements in African American history." That movement was led by a woman.

In her book *My Face Is Black Is True: Callie House and the Struggle for Ex-Slave Reparations,* Berry tells the remarkable story of Callie House, a seamstress-washerwoman, widow, mother of five and former slave turned activist, who co-founded the MRB&PA in 1898. The association aimed to provide mutual aid and burial expenses, and to lobby Congress to enact legislation that would compensate the formerly enslaved, especially the elderly, for their unpaid years of labor. "If the Government had the right to free us," House stated, "she [the U.S.] had a right to make some provision for us and since she did not make it soon after Emancipation she ought to make it now." House's passion and ability as a grassroots organizer were unmatched as she crisscrossed the nation urging Blacks to exercise their Constitutional rights. In 1899, the first bill introduced on behalf of the association in both houses of Congress (S. 1176) was simply titled "A Bill to provide pensions for freedmen and so forth." By the early 20th century, according to government figures, the MRB&PA had an estimated 300,000 members, all "demanding a law ordering reparations for slavery."

But the federal government was not amused. In fact, House became
a target. The Post Office Department used its anti-fraud powers against
the movement, especially against the MRB&PA, issuing a fraud order
against House in September 1899. House fought back, but the harassment
continued, as notices were issued to local post offices ordering them to
deny any money orders made out to the association or any of its officials.
Association literature and letters, or anything addressed to the association
officers, were not allowed to be distributed. The campaign to stop House,
"thirty-three-year-old former slave, seamstress and laundress with no right to
vote," as Berry highlights, continued for almost two decades.

Yet, despite the government's relentless character-assassination campaign,
which tarnished her reputation even among African Americans, in 1915
House's group sued the federal government.

The historic case *Johnson v. McAdoo* is the first documented federal
litigation for reparations for slavery. The class-action suit started from the
idea that $68,073,388.99 that had been taken as a cotton tax was actually
owed to the people who had produced that cotton. The District Court in
the nation's capital, and the U.S. Supreme Court on appeal held that the
U.S. was safeguarded against such suits. And after House had the audacity to
bring her suit, in 1917 the MRB&PA leader was arrested, convicted of mail
fraud and jailed. Despite her conviction, ex-slaves continued to petition the
federal government. The reparations movement remained on life support
until 1922 when the federal government finally succeeded in shutting it
down.

In 1995, the *Johnson v. McAdoo* rationalization was repeated when African
American plaintiffs, under the collective name "Cato," attempted to sue the
United States for reparations in the U.S. District Court for the Northern
District of California. Again, a judge claimed U.S. immunity. As historian
Ana Lucia Araujo writes in her book *Reparations for Slavery and the Slave*

Trade, "Because the government of the United States must agree to be prosecuted, a successful outcome for these lawsuits is 'nearly impossible.'"

Nearly a century after the original lawsuit, and more than 150 years after the end of slavery, that logic remains difficult to get around — but they who feel that Callie House's logic also holds are clearly not done fighting. ■

39

THE ROSEBUD CHARITY CLUB: A HISTORY OF BLACK WOMEN'S CHARITY WORK IN BALTIMORE

THE NORTH STAR, MARCH 31, 2019

THE ROSEBUD CHARITY CLUB receives NAACP Lifetime Membership Award at Wayland Baptist Church, 1966 (Courtesy of Mrs. Frances L. James). Photo from left to right: (front) Rev. John Tilley, Mrs. Frances L. James, Ms. Susan Murphy (NAACP), Mrs. Rosalee Hennigan (President), Mrs. Iola Beverly; (back row) Mrs. Margaret Valentine (Vice President), Mrs. Clara McCrea (Financial Secretary), Mrs. Mary Jones, Mrs. Aletha Nettles (Business Manager), and Mrs. Lillian Martin (Recording Secretary).

During Women's History Month there is no shortage of women to highlight whose contributions have brought positive change to the nation and the world. Often neglected are women whose tireless activism within their local communities are overlooked in history books. Their contributions, however, are no less valuable.

This is the case for the Rosebud Charity Club of Baltimore, Maryland, a group of Black women who gave back to their community through charitable deeds to make life better for those in need. They can best be described as what historian Rhonda Y. Williams calls "community mothers" those who "implemented programs to address people's everyday needs."[131]

Their initial charitable efforts began with organizing Christmas basket and gift deliveries to health facilities such as the Henryton State Hospital, which housed African Americans suffering from tuberculous and moderate mental illness. The club also provided food, clothing, religious and educational instruction, in addition to other necessities such as funds for an amputee who was able to receive a transtibial prosthesis. The Rosebuds, as they were popularly known, were well regarded throughout the city, and state of Maryland. Their charitable efforts extended to the nation's capital and Virginia; and reached as far as Mississippi, Louisiana, and Indiana.

On November 7, 1948, Mrs. Victoria Sully organized a group of women comprised of family friends Mrs. Rosie Watts and Mrs. Sarah Frances Lewis; her sisters Mrs. Althea Nettles, Mrs. Rosalee Hennigan, Mrs. Mary Jones, and their mother Mrs. Mary Frances Thompson Gray to form The Rosebud Social and Savings Club. This meeting took place at 2227 North Howard Street in east Baltimore. The Gray women, as they were known in their former rural community of King George County, Virginia, migrated to the city in the early 1940s. They were members of a prominent family in King George County; the family patriarch Mr. George Allen Gray was the wealthiest African American landowner in the county. They were pillars in

the Good Hope Baptist Church, the first African American church in the
county, and they were known for their generosity. "We were better off than
most of the Blacks and whites," said Rosebud Mrs. Frances Gray James.
"Papa and Mama never turned anyone away."

Following the migration from a farm community in which the needs
of their neighbors were only apparent when they received a knock at the
front door, to the close living quarters of a 1940s segregated Baltimore, the
Rosebuds decided to change the direction and name of the organization to
the Rosebud Charity Club. Their primary goal was to help needy families
and participate more fully in the struggle for civil rights.

The Rosebuds were avid readers of the *Afro American Newspaper*
which "crusaded for racial equality and economic advancement for Black
Americans" since its establishment by John Henry Murphy, Sr. in 1892.
They became actively involved with the local chapter of the National
Association for the Advancement of Colored People (NAACP), which by
1946 was one of the largest branches (now the organization's headquarters)
in the country and known for its female leadership. Lillian Carroll Jackson
served as president of the chapter from 1935 to 1970. Jackson's empowering
image and influence proved instrumental in the Rosebuds' decision to
become NAACP lifetime members.

The Black church played a fundamental role in the Rosebuds' civic
engagement. To increase their outreach, the Rosebud women collaborated
with their home church, Unity Baptist Church. It was one of dozens of
Black churches in Baltimore at the time, which built upon a long and rich
history of Black social activism in the city. By the mid-nineteenth century,
Baltimore possessed "the largest denominational variety of African American
churches in the country," from Sharp Street Memorial United Methodist
Church founded in 1787 to Bethel AME incorporated in 1811 to the
Oblate Sisters of Providence — an order of Black Nuns founded in 1829

in Fells Point, an area of the city where Frederick Douglass made his daring escape a decade later.

Black churches in Baltimore continued as a hub for civil rights activism during the twentieth century with women at the helm. Two young sisters, Juanita and Virginia Jackson, for example, organized a city-wide Young Peoples forum at Sharp Street in the 1930s to challenge discrimination in housing and employment—advocacy that continued throughout the post-World War II era.

The Rosebuds reflected the long tradition of charitable organizations that provided relief to many throughout the Charm City.

The Rosebuds also participated in voter registration drives, which were instrumental in two historic elections when Verda Freeman Welcome became the first Black woman elected to the Maryland House of Delegates, and in 1962 when she was elected to the Maryland Senate to become America's first Black female state Senator. By this time, segregation had begun to lose its grip on the city. Baltimore was also undergoing drastic changes. One, whole neighborhoods were forced to relocate because of the city's urban renewal agenda and two because of white flight.

The Rosebuds relocated to west Baltimore during this period and continued their charitable activities as members of Wayland Baptist Church. Following the deaths of Mmes. Gray, Watson, Sully, and Lewis, the Rosebud Charity Club became a family organization comprised of seven sisters and one niece. Additional members included Mrs. Margaret Valentine, Mrs. Iola Beverly, Mrs. Lillian Martin, and Mrs. Clara McCrea.

The Rosebuds did not miss a beat. These eight women continued their charity work in Baltimore, raising money for various social and political causes with their biannual dinner sales, cross-country eight day scenic and historic tours, baby contest, and church events. Always looking for an opportunity to educate the community about Black History, the Rosebuds invited Frank Wills, the Black security guard who discovered the Watergate break-in, to speak during a Sunday evening program at their church in 1974. Before that event, which drew hundreds of local residents, few knew that a Black man was a Watergate hero. By the end of the decade, their steadfast devotion to community service had been honored with an NAACP Lifetime Membership Award presented by Ms. Susan Murphy of the famous Murphy family of Baltimore.

The Rosebuds continued their charitable work until 2000. As of this writing, my grandmother Mrs. James (98) is the last surviving member of the Rosebuds. While their charitable work is finished, the legacy of the Rosebud Charity Club continues in the numerous organizations in Baltimore, which are working tirelessly to bring about positive change in the community. ▨

40

A PLAN TO TAKE THE GEORGE FLOYD CASE TO THE U.N. HIGHLIGHTS A DECADES-OLD TENSION BETWEEN CIVIL RIGHTS AND HUMAN RIGHTS

TIME MAGAZINE, JUNE 10, 2020

As people across the globe take to the streets to demand justice in the wake of George Floyd's killing, the case against the four now-former Minneapolis police officers involved in his death has already begun: Derek Chauvin, the white officer who pressed his knee to Floyd's neck for nearly nine minutes, has been charged with second-degree murder, and the three other officers present with aiding and abetting. But lawyers representing the Floyd family, S. Lee Merritt and Benjamin Crump, are not looking only to the U.S. criminal-justice system. They have announced that they also plan to take the matter to the United Nations Human Rights Council.

Merritt and Crump also represent the families of two other African Americans who deaths have shocked the public in recent weeks—Breonna Taylor and Ahmaud Arbery — and have in the past worked on other high-profile homicide cases involving police brutality, such as Eric Garner and Michael Brown. And this isn't the first time their clients have gone to the U.N.: in 2014, Michael Brown's parents gave heart-wrenching testimony before the United Nations Committee Against Torture, in Geneva. That same year, the office of the Commissioner on Human Rights announced that the Garner and Brown cases "have added to our existing concerns over the longstanding prevalence of racial discrimination faced by African-Americans, particularly in relation to access to justice and discriminatory police practices."[132]

BC BEN CRUMP
TRIAL LAWYER FOR JUSTICE

Attorney Ben Crump and Family of George Floyd Appeal to UN to Intervene in Floyd Case, Make Recommendations for Systemic Police Reform

Nationally renowned civil rights attorney Ben Crump, the legal team, and the family of George Floyd has submitted an Urgent Appeal to the United Nations to intervene in the case of Floyd's death, encourage the U.S. government to press Federal criminal charges against the involved officers, and make recommendations for systemic police reform in the United States. The requested reforms include deescalating techniques, independent prosecutions and autopsies for every extrajudicial police killing in an effort to stop further human rights abuses including torture and extrajudicial killings of African Americans to protect their inherent and fundamental human right to life.

Attorney Crump issued the following statement about the request:

"The United States of America has a long pattern and practice of depriving Black citizens of the fundamental human right to life. I have sought the protection of the Federal government on innumerable cases involving the torture and extrajudicial killing of Black men and women by police including Martin Lee Anderson in Florida, Michael Brown in Missouri, Breonna Taylor in Kentucky, and George Floyd in Minnesota. The United States government has consistently failed to hold police accountable and did not bring Federal criminal charges even in cases with irrefutable video evidence. When a group of people of any nation have been systemically deprived of their universal human right to life by its government for decades, it must appeal to the international community for its support and to the United Nations for its intervention. We echo the words of Emperor Haile Selassie I in his 1963 speech to the United Nations in which he pledged to continue to fight for equality and justice, "until the philosophy which holds one race superior and another inferior is finally and permanently discredited and abandoned...until the colour of a man's skin is of no more significance than the color of his eye."

International legal strategists and advocates Jotaka Eaddy and Jasmine Rand further stated: "The United States of America's systemic failure to appropriately address police violence has weaponized racism against African Americans, abridging their human rights. The comments made by President Trump on June 1, 2020, wherein he highlighted protecting citizens' right to bear arms above African Americans' right to life, heightens the urgency of the appeal to the United Nations, as we believe his comments will incite vigilante behavior and violence against African Americans, leading to more violations of their fundamental human rights.

As Merritt and Crump approach the U.N., the involvement of the international community draws attention to a tension that has existed for more than half a century within the movement for African American rights. For much of the history of the Black Freedom Struggle in the United States, civic leaders and politicians used the term *civil rights* to characterize the objective of the movement to gain equal rights in this country; the period to which the current moment has been compared is known as the civil rights movement. But not everyone at that time thought that civil rights were the goal.

Malcolm X — who abandoned the philosophy of Black Nationalism in favor of the more inclusive Internationalism, a philosophy that aimed to encourage allyship with oppressed people globally — admonished Black Americans in the mid-1960s to abandon the domestic agenda for *civil rights* in favor of an international agenda for *human rights*. In fact, this effort has been called the "unfinished work of Malcolm X," which came to a tragic halt when he was assassinated on Feb. 21, 1965. The problem with civil rights, Malcolm argued, was that such a framing defined the matter as a domestic issue, focused on guaranteeing African Americans equal access to the rights of U.S. citizens. In his view, that limited the potential of the movement and left Black people at the mercy of a government that had ignored its pleas for equality since the post-Civil War era.[133]

Malcolm X was no stranger to police brutality. In *Malcolm X: A Life of Reinvention*, Manning Marable recalls a notorious incident involving Los Angeles police and the Nation of Islam (NOI) in 1962, which reads like a story ripped from today's headlines. On April 27, 1962, while members of the Nation were delivering clothes from the dry cleaner to their mosque, two white police officers who were on a stake-out approached the men, believing the clothes were stolen. The details are murky on what followed. After some pushing and shoving and a call for back up, which bought at least 70 additional officers to the scene, the mosque was raided. What is clear is that 15 minutes later when the dust was settled, "seven Muslims were shot," Marable explains. They included Ronald Stokes, a Korean War vet who was fatally shot from behind while trying to surrender. Less than a month later, Malcolm X delivered a blistering speech against L.A. city officials for their willingness to tolerate police brutality.

By 1964, Malcolm X had split with his spiritual mentor Elijah Muhammad and NOI to launch what he called the Organization of Afro-American Unity, with a rallying cry for Black people to set their differences aside for the common goal of Black Liberation. In his classic speech "The Ballot or the Bullet" — delivered twice, on April 3 and 12, 1964, less than a year before he was assassinated at the Audubon Ballroom in Harlem — he channeled the sentiments of Revolutionary War patriot and slave owner Patrick Henry who in 1775, ironically, cried, "give me liberty or give me death." Malcolm echoed these sentiments nearly 200 years later when he stated in the second iteration of the speech, "It's the ballot or the bullet. It's liberty or it's death. It's freedom for everybody or freedom for nobody."

At the conclusion of this speech, Malcolm admonished Black Americans to approach their freedom struggle from an international viewpoint, which would reframe the struggle as one not for civil rights but human rights, for which they would be entitled to seek the aid of the international community. "When you expand the civil-rights struggle to the level of human rights," he stated on April 3, "you can then take the case of the black man in this country before the nations in the U.N." He also explained how he saw the difference between civil rights and human rights:

> You can take Uncle Sam before a world court. But the only level you can do it on is the level of human rights. Civil rights keeps you under his restrictions, under his jurisdiction. Civil rights keeps you in his pocket. Civil rights means you're asking Uncle Sam to treat you right. Human rights are something you were born with. Human rights are

your God-given rights. Human rights are the rights that are recognized by all nations of this earth. And any time anyone violates your human rights, you can take them to the world court.

His focus on human rights, however, didn't mean he had given up on the possibility of winning civil equality within the United States. In fact, Malcolm believed that, while revolutions have historically been bloody, the U. S. was uniquely positioned for a revolution devoid of bloodshed, "[Today]," he stated, "this country can become involved in a revolution that won't take bloodshed. All she's got to do is give the black man in this country everything that's due him, everything."[134]

Malcolm X, whose political philosophy of freedom was underscored by the mantra "by any means necessary," called for a revolution that would overthrow the system of white supremacy rather than integrate Blacks into it. Even so, like Martin Luther King Jr., Malcolm believed that such a revolution could be achieved through nonviolent means. While he believed Black people had a right to defend themselves if attacked, he counseled white America to listen to King rather than face the alternative.

Just the month before this speech, Malcolm X and Dr. Martin Luther King Jr. had met for the first and only time. The two men were on Capitol Hill to attend a Senate hearing on school segregation and employment discrimination. Malcolm, who had attempted on several occasions to reach out to King and had conversed extensively with King's wife Coretta, approached the Southern minister with his hand outstretched. While cameras flashed as the two men greeted each other, Malcolm expressed his desire to be more involved with King's movement. "I am throwing myself into the heart of the civil rights struggle," he told King. He clarified his intent further in his speech the following month: "We have injected ourselves into the civil rights struggle," he stated, "and we intend to expand it from the level of civil rights to the level of human rights."[135]

Today, as Black America is still pressed under the weight of white supremacy and violence, including extrajudicial killings, that struggle continues. With a new generation embracing Malcolm X's idea that human rights is the path to Black liberation, the work of expanding the struggle continues too. ■

CODA

A TALE OF TWO PROTESTS

IN THE MATTER OF BLACK LIVES: WOMANIST PROSE
FEBRUARY 23, 2021

"This is not America," a woman said to a small group, her voice shaking. She was crying, hysterical. "They're shooting at us. They're supposed to shoot BLM, but they're shooting the patriots."

—Andrew McCormick, The Nation

This was the chaotic scene at the U.S. Capitol on January 6, 2021, as pro-Trump supporters violently descended on The People's House in an attempted coup to stop Congress from counting the electoral college votes and officially declaring Joseph R. Biden president-elect of the United States. Images of rioters/insurrectionists breaching police barricades, ascending the steps and scaling the walls of the Capitol, breaking down windows and doors, storming the Capitol rotunda now filled with rioters engaged in hand-to-hand combat with Capitol Police, the take over and vandalism of the House and Senate Chambers, and offices of esteemed lawmakers who were hiding in fear for their lives as violent rhetoric echoed throughout the building, "Hang Mike Pence, hang Nancy Pelosi," were at once stark and surreal. Time seemed to standstill as the peaceful transfer of power, the cornerstone of American Democracy which had gone uninterrupted since

1804, was now under assault instigated by the President of the United States, Donald Trump.

Weeks prior to the deadly assault. which resulted in the deaths of six people including Brian Sicknick a Capitol police officer who was beaten to death by rioters with a flagpole (the flag was attached to the pole) Trump put out a nationwide call to his supporters to come to the nation's Capital to his "Stop the Steal" Rally based on a multitude of false claims and conspiracy theories that the 2020 presidential election had been stolen from him, claims he began making long before the November election. These unsubstantiated claims stoked the anger of his loyal cult followers which included a majority of rank-and-file white citizens, white nationalists, and neo-Nazi groups, white (and some Black) evangelicals, business owners, law enforcement officials, conservative media outlets, and most Republicans in the House and Senate. In his December 19th Twitter post Trump's call to American "patriots" was unambiguous. "Big protest in D.C. on January 6th. Be there, will be wild!"

During this unbridled assault, a whopping 400,000+ Americans (now 500,000+ as of this writing), disproportionately Black and Brown, had died of complications from the novel COVID19 virus; but the agony of this real-life tragedy was not the issue that kept this president awake at night.

During his stump speech at the rally which preceded the Capitol assault, it was clear that the only thing that mattered to Trump was remaining in the White House by any means necessary. He repeated his false claims of a stolen election and then gave the order to his followers to head to the Capitol.

And after this, we're going to walk down, and I'll be there with you… we're going to walk down to the Capitol, and we're going to cheer on our brave senators and congressmen and women. . . I know that everyone here will soon be marching over to the Capitol building to peacefully and patriotically make your voices heard.

Yet after repeating the laundry list of conspiracy theories about the "stolen election," Trump's tone turned aggressive. Echoing the sentiments of Alabama Republican Mo Brooks who told the crowd, "It's time to start taking names and kicking asses," and Rudy Gulianni's statement, "Let's have trial by combat," Trump admonished the crowd:

> We fight like hell. And if you don't fight like hell, you're not going to have a country anymore. So we're going to walk down Pennsylvania Avenue . . . and we're going to the Capitol, and . . . We're going to try and give them the kind of pride and boldness that they need to take back our country. So let's walk down Pennsylvania Avenue.[136]

But as the throng of rioters headed to the Capitol, Trump and his motorcade drove in the opposite direction to the White House and watched the mayhem on television.

As many Americans watched the terror at the seat of our government unfold, the double standard in policing white bodies and Black bodies was quickly expressed on numerous mainstream and social media outlets. Days prior to the rally, requests for extra security made by D.C. Mayor Muriel Browser to keep the peace at the rally were denied. This, despite explicit plans posted by pro-Trump and alt-conservative social media sites like Parler, which expressed an intent to violently overtake the Capitol and derail the certification process. Is it any wonder that the Capitol was seized with such little effort? Washington's attorney general Karl Racine told CNN:

> There was zero intelligence that the Black Lives Matter protesters were going to "storm the capitol," he remembered, after ticking down the many police forces present in June. Juxtapose that with what we saw today, with hate groups, militia and other groups that have no respect for the rule of law go into the capitol. . . . That dichotomy is shocking.[137]

Former Capitol Police Larry Schaefer, who retired in 2019 after 34 years also expressed shock at the unpreparedness of his former co-workers.

> It's not a spur-of-the-moment demonstration that just popped up. We have a planned, known demonstration that has a propensity for violence in the past and threats to carry weapons — why would you not prepare yourself as we have done in the past?[138]

While some Capitol Police fought to protect the sacred building constructed with the use of slave labor from 1793-1868, others removed barriers and even took selfies with rioters. Even after Metropolitan Police and the National Guard arrived on the scene, rioters moved at a snail's pace to clear the Capitol and defied Mayor Browsers 6 p.m. curfew. Few arrests were made that day as rioters exited the Capitol building without incident.

Yet, this was in stark contrast to the treatment Black Lives Matters protesters received during their 100 days of protest in the aftermath of the police murder of George Floyd. According to *The Guardian*, approximately 1,000 incidences of police brutality were reported during the summer-long BLM protest which covered the period from June through September 2020. Even journalists were subjected to police harassment. According to *The Guardian:*

> Retaliation by police against civilians and the press was widely documented in the first wave of protests, but as the protests have continued, so too has the violence. There has not been a single week without an incidence of police brutality against a civilian or a journalist at a protest in the U.S. since the end of May. Of the instances of police misconduct the data shows:
> - more than 500 instances of police using 'less-lethal' rounds, pepper spray and teargas;
> - 60 incidents of officers using unlawful assembly to arrest protesters;

- 19 incidents of police being permissive to the far right and showing double standards when confronted with white supremacists;
- five attacks on medics;
- and 11 instances of kettling.[139]

For certain, as numerous commentators pointed out, BLM protesters would have never made it past the police barricades. The arrests and fatalities would have been innumerable.

One of the most poignant examples of the police assault on BLM peaceful protesters was demonstrated on June 1, 2020, as Lafayette Square was filled with protesters demanding justice for George Floyd and other victims of police brutality and white vigilantism. The president had just given one of his time-worn law and order speeches demanding that governors use police and the National Guard to take back the streets which had been overtaken by the longest sustained protest in recent history. Then Secretary of Defense Mark Esper concurred stating, "We need to dominate the battlespace." As noted by *NPR*, "The plaza between St. John's Church and Lafayette Park was full of people nonviolently protesting police brutality late Monday afternoon when U.S. Park Police, [the Secret Service], and National Guard troops, with the use of tear gas [and rubber bullets], suddenly started pushing them away for no apparent reason." But the reason soon became apparent. As the smoke from the teargas cleared Trump, along with several of his family members, Attorney General Bill Barr, and the chairman of the Joint Chiefs of Staff Mark Milley (who later apologized for his participation) walked through Lafayette Square to St. John's Episcopal Church—also known as the President's Church (and for its social justice activism)—for a photo-op with the president who stood in front of the edifice and held up the Bible (albeit upside down). "We have the greatest country in the world," he said. "Keep it nice and safe." This callous act drew the ire of many around the country including members and clergy of St. John's Church. Gina Gerbasi, a former minister of St. John's who was helping the protesters, witnessed the entire scene and later lambasted the president on social media stating:

PEOPLE WERE HURT SO THAT [President Trump] COULD HAVE A PHOTO OPPORTUNITY IN FRONT OF THE CHURCH!!! HE WOULD HAVE HAD TO STEP OVER THE MEDICAL SUPPLIES WE LEFT BEHIND BECAUSE WE WERE BEING TEAR GASSED!!!![140]

The next day, in preparation for the Washington, D. C. primary, according to ProPublica:

Law enforcement officers appeared on every corner, heavily armed in fatigues and body armor. Humvees blocked intersections. Buses full of troops deployed into military columns and marshaled in front of the Lincoln Memorial in a raw show of force. Police kettled protesters in alleys. Choppers thudded overhead for days and sank low enough over protesters to generate gale-force winds.[141]

Perhaps the most egregious example of the disparity between policing Black and white bodies occurred on August 25, 2020, when a white cop shot an unarmed Jacob Blake, a Black father of six, in the back seven times leaving him paralyzed from the waist down. Protest ignited all over the country including Kenosha, Wisconsin, Blake's hometown. Two nights later August 27th a white 17-year-old vigilante armed with an AR-15 arrived from Antioch, Illinois to Kenosha driven by his mother to the BLM protest. Rittenhouse fatally shot two men and wounded another. As people were shouting, "Get him, he shot somebody," Rittenhouse walked past police with his rifle slung over his shoulder and his hands in the air. Officers let him go. The following day, he surrendered to police in his hometown of Antioch. Rittenhouse was extradited to Wisconsin and faces multiple charges, including intentional homicide. Yet, Rittenhouse pleaded not guilty by reason of self-defense claiming he was protecting businesses from looters. Conservatives have hailed him as a hero and raised enough money to post his $2 million cash bail. In late September, Rittenhouse's mother Wendy attended a Waukesha County, Wisconsin GOP event and was invited on stage by ultra-conservative commentator Michelle Malkin. Malkin praised mother and son for their bravery. Wendy received a standing ovation. The officer who shot Blake was not charged.[142]

Indeed, the double standard between the police response to the peaceful BLM protesters, the Rittenhouse murders, and the violent acts of the insurrectionists at the Capitol was shocking but nonetheless unsurprising.

And this leads us back to Donald Trump. Trump's election to the U.S. presidency was the consequence of years of racial fearmongering. Unfortunately, too many whites, especially the overwhelming number of white women who voted for Trump in 2016 and 2020 have fulfilled the prophetic words of Belle Kearney who stated during a National American Woman Suffrage Association meeting in 1903, "The enfranchisement of women would insure immediate and durable white supremacy honestly attained. . . the enfranchisement of women would settle the race question in politics." Indeed as New York Congresswoman Alexandria Ocasio Cortiz stated in a 2019 Twitter post regarding Trump:

He can stay, he can go. He can be impeached or voted out in 2020. But removing Trump will not remove the infrastructure of an entire party that embraced him; the dark money that funded him; the online radicalization that drummed his army; nor the racism he amplified+reanimated.[143]

While I wholeheartedly agree with Congresswoman Cortiz the truth is, the Republican Party is not solely responsible for Trump's rise and the damage he has done to this country. Americans want their politics to be both serious and entertaining. It is the latter that helped catapult Trump, a reality TV star, to the highest office of government. Indeed, many liberals and progressives prayed for Trump to run for president because "it would be so much fun!" During the 2015-2016 primary season, they could not get enough of the vile soul that is Donald John Trump—watching every cable news show, reading every article and blog about him—then tweeting and posting about every foul move he made and word he said, LMAO—ad nausea. Their contribution to cable news ratings made them accomplices to Trump's rise.

It was so funny then; but when he clinched the Republican nomination and the potential of a Trump presidency seemed more a reality than a show, the laughter came to a screeching halt. On November 11, 2015, Larry Wilmore of The Nightly Show declared, "This isn't funny anymore." Anymore?!!! Trump was never funny. He was always dangerous. This is the same guy who published four op-eds calling for five innocent teens infamously known as the Central Park Five, to receive the death penalty for the 1989 beating rape of a white woman. And lest we forget, Trump pushed the Birther conspiracy theory which claimed Barack Obama was not born in the U.S. falsely claiming America's first Black president was illegitimate; and it was certainly clear the day he announced his candidacy as Trump's white nationalist/birtherism politics was on full display:

> The U.S. has become a dumping ground for everybody else's problems. When Mexico sends its people, they're not sending their best. They're not sending you. They're not sending you. They're sending people that have lots of problems, and they're bringing those problems with us. They're bringing drugs. They're bringing crime. They're rapists. And some, I assume, are good people. But I speak to border guards and they tell us what we're getting. And it only makes common sense. It only makes common sense. They're sending us not the right people. It's coming from more than Mexico. It's coming from all over South and Latin America, and it's coming probably— probably— from the Middle East. But we don't know. Because we

have no protection and we have no competence, we don't know what's happening. And it's got to stop and it's got to stop fast.[144]

Cable news and social media ate it up. Trump's daily racist, sexist, xenophobic rantings, and ignorant rhetoric provided enough fodder for the 24-hour news cycle and then some. By the time the laughing gas wore off, Trump was at the gate of the White House. Hence, while many grieved his triumph few dealt with their own personal guilt for enabling hate. This is what happens when bigotry passes for cheap laughs and is not immediately put in check. Now the laughter had turned into fear as tangible as a hurricane. As the saying goes, "Be careful what you pray for!" Yet, the obsession with Trump continued. Many who claimed to hate him could not stop watching, tweeting, and posting about him—still; that they find the 1000th malfeasance more shocking than the first is, in a word, pathetic.

Yes, Trump is out of the White House, we have a Black female Vice President, Kamala Harris, and the nauseous rollercoaster ride that is American politics continues.

Today marks the one-year anniversary of the murder of 25-year-old Ahmaud Arbrey who was shot to death when he was attacked by two white men who claimed they were making a citizen's arrest while a third man videotaped the incident. Arbrey's crime was jogging while Black. Now the defense lawyers for the perpetrators have asked a judge to restrict the use of the word "victim" during the trial (which has been delayed due to the pandemic) because the use of the term would imply the guilt of the defendants. "If granted," Slate.com contends, " the motion would reinforce one of the most treacherous effects of the nation's proliferating 'stand your ground' laws: the retroactive role reversal of victim and perpetrator."[145]

I want to believe with all of my heart that in this era of racial reckoning, the court will see through this farce and deny the motion. But THIS IS AMERICA, and I ain't holding my breath! ▪

#AllBlackLivesMatter

POSTSCRIPT: On April 20, 2021, former Minnesota police officer Derek Chauvin was found guilty of second degree-manslaughter, second-degree murder, and third-degree murder for the death of George Floyd who died on May 25, 2020, when Chauvin pressed his knee into Floyd's neck for 9:27 seconds. As of this writing, the sentencing phase of the trial is not yet underway.

ENDNOTES

1   Arica L. Coleman, *That the Blood Stay Pure: African Americans, Native Americans and the Predicament of Race and Identity in Virginia* (Bloomington: Indiana University Press, 2013).

2   For more on the 1994 Crime Bill and its impact on Black communities see Michelle Alexander, *The New Jim Crow: Mass Incarceration in the Age of Color Blindness* (New York: New Press, 2012); Nathan J. Robinson, *Superpredator: Bill Clinton's Use and Abuse of Black America* (W. Somerville, Massachusetts: Current Affairs Press, 2016). For the politics of welfare reform see Sanford F. Schram, et.al., *Race and the Politics of Welfare Reform* (Ann Arbor: University of Michigan Press, 2003).

3   For more on the 2008 Presidential Primary see Beverly Guy-Sheftall and Johnnetta Betsch Cole, eds., *Who Should Be First? Feminists Speak Out on the 2008 Presidential Campaign* (New York: SUNY Press, 2010); Christopher Beam, et al., The Hillary DeathWatch," *Slate*, March 27, 2008, https://slate.com/news-and-politics/2008/03/gauging-the-odds-that-hillary-clinton-will-win-the-nomination.html.

4   Peter Wallenstein, "AfAm 2—finishing up," Email, May 4, 2020; Kareem Abdul-Jabbar, "Don't Understand The Protest: What You Are Seeing Is People Pushed To The Edge," *Los Angeles Times*, May 30, 2020, https://www.latimes.com/opinion/story/2020-05-30/dont-understand-the-protests-what-youre-seeing-is-people-pushed-to-the-edge

5   Ibid. By invoking the metaphor of the burning house Kareem echoed the sentiments of Dr. Martin Luther King Jr as recalled by actor-activist Harry Belafonte during a conversation with King not long before his assassination. "I remember the last time we were together, at my home, shortly before he was murdered," Belafonte stated. "He seemed quite agitated and preoccupied, and I asked him what the problem was. 'I've come upon something that disturbs me deeply,' he said. 'We have fought hard and long for integration, as I believe we should have, and I know that we will win. But I've come to believe we're integrating into a burning house.'" See "Harry Belafonta Reflects On Working Towards Peace," The Markkula Center for Applied Ethics, Santa Clara University, https://www.scu.edu/mcae/architects-of-peace/Belafonte/essay.html.

6 Alice Walker, *In Search of Our Mothers' Gardens: Womanist Prose* (New York: Open Road Media, 2011).

7 Layli Maparyan, *The Womanist Reader* (New York: Routledge, 2006) Kindle Edition. The book was published under the name Layli Phillips. She has since married and now uses her married name.

8 Ibid; AnaLouise Keating, *Transformation Now!: Towards a Post-Oppositional Politics of Change* (Champaign: University of Illinois Press, 2012), Kindle Edition; Lata Mani, *Interleaves: Ruminations on Illness and Spiritual Life* (New Delhi: Yoda Press, 2011), 74.

9 Randy Turner, "Transcript Provided for Clinton Indiana Victory Speech," *The Turner Report (blog)*, May 8, 2008, https://rturner229.blogspot.com/2008/05/transcript-provided-for-clinton-indiana.html.

10 Nico Pitney, "Dianne Feinstein to Clinton: Show Me Your Plan," *The Huffington Post*, May 15, 2008, https://www.huffpost.com/entry/diane-feinstein-to-clinto_n_100658; Michael Barnicle, "Race is All The Clintons Have Left," *Huffington Post*, May 7, 2008, https://www.huffpost.com/entry/race-is-all-the-clintons_b_100660.

11 Steven Kornacki, "Clinton, Obama In An Epic Dual," NBC News (Online), July 29, 2019, https://www.nbcnews.com/politics/elections/2008-clinton-obama-epic-duel-n1029626; Toni Morrison's statement that Clinton was "the first Black President" has been woefully misinterpreted. For her own words see Toni Morrison, "Comment," *The New Yorker*, October 5, 1998, https://www.newyorker.com/magazine/1998/10/05/comment-6543. Earl Ofari Hutchinson, *The Assassination of the Black Male Image* (New York: Simon and Schuster, 1997).

12 Christopher Beam, "The Hillary Deathwatch," *Slate*, May 8, 2008, http://www.slate.com/articles/news_and_politics/deathwatch/2008/05/the_hillary_deathwatch_12.html#7s8d6f87; M. S. Bellows, Jr., "Clinton Camp Stoops to Language Games and Overt Racial Strategizing," *Huffington Post*, May 15, 2008, https://www.huffpost.com/entry/post-indiana-clinton-camp_b_100708 . Clinton lost the support of many of her surrogates due to her reply that she was staying in the race because "Bobby Kennedy was assassinated in June;" see Arica L. Coleman, "Hillary: Stop Asking Bernie to Suspend His Campaign!," *LA Progressive*, June 5, 2016, https://www.laprogressive.com/bernie-can-still-win/.

13 Kathy Kiely and Jill Lawrence, "Close Up: Hillary Clinton," *USA TODAY*, May 2008, https://usatoday30.usatoday.com/news/politics/election2008/2008-05-07-clintoninterview_N.htm.

14 Alice Walker, "Lest We Forget: An Open Letter to My Sisters Who Are Brave," in Guy Sheftall and Cole, *Who Should Be First*, Kindle Edition.

15 Fernando Suarez, "Union Boss Says Clinton Has Testicular Fortitude," *CBS News*, April 30, 2008, https://www.cbsnews.com/news/union-boss-says-clinton-has-testicular-fortitude/.

16 Catherine Price, "Hillary's 'Testicular Fortitude'," Salon. com, May 2, 2008, https://www.cbsnews.com/news/ union-boss-says-clinton-has-testicular-fortitude/.

17 Eleanor Clift, "Obama Needs A Knock Out Punch Against Clinton, " *Newsweek.com*, May 1, 2008, https://www.newsweek.com/ clift-obama-needs-knockout-punch-against-clinton-89807.

18 For more on the invention of the Caucasian race see Nell Painter, *The History of White People* (New York: W. W. Norton, and Company, 2010), chapter 6. Kindle Edition.

19 Daniel Geary, "The Moynihan Report: An Annotated Edition: A Historian Unpacks 'The Negro Family: The Case for National Action' On Its 50th Anniversary," The Atlantic, September 14, 2015, https://www.theatlantic.com/ politics/archive/2015/09/the-moynihan-report-an-annotated-edition/404632/. Moynihan's report was used to justify the overrepresentation of Black men conscripted for the Vietnam War.

20 Maureen Dowd, "Mincing Up Michelle," New York Times, June 11, 2008, https://www.nytimes.com/2008/06/11/opinion/11dowd.html; Leonce Gaiter, "Michelle Obama Is Ungrateful? For What?," *Huffington Post*, August 8, 2008, https://www.huffpost.com/entry/michelle-is-ungrateful-fo_b_114774.

21 Pam Spaulding, "Obama Daughters Labelled 'Nappy Headed Hos,' In 'Art' Exhibit," *Shadow Proof*, June 13, 2008, https://shadowproof.com/2008/06/13/ obama-daughters-labeled-nappy-headed-hos-in-art-exhibit/; Barbara Christian quoted in Patricia Hill Collins, *Black Feminist Thought: Knowledge, Consciousness, and the Politics of Empowerment* (New York: Routledge, 1990), 68.

22 Gloria Steinem, "Women Are Never Front-Runners," *New York Times*, January 8, 2008, https://www.nytimes.com/2008/01/08/opinion/08steinem.html; Vanessa Tyson, "Response to Steinem," *Huffington Post*, January 14, 2008, https://www.huffpost.com/entry/response-to-steinem_b_81464.

23 Adele Logan Alexander, "She's No Lady, She's a Nigger: Abuses, Stereotypes and Realities from the Middle Passage to Capitol (and Anita) Hill," *Race, Gender, and Power in America: The Legacy of the Hill – Thomas Hearings*, Anita Faye Hill and Emma Coleman Jordan, eds. (New York: Oxford University Press, 1995).

24 Anne Goodwyn Jones, "Belles and Ladies," *Encyclopedia of Southern Culture*, Charles Reagan Wilson and William Ferris, eds. (Chapel Hill: University of North Carolina Press, 1989), 1528; W. J. Cash, *The Mind of the South*, (New York: Vintage Books, 1941), 84. Cash's "proto-Dorian pride" is reference to the racial bond forged by white men regardless of class.

25 Jones, "Belles and Ladies," 1529; for more on the writings of Drew, Harper and Fitzhugh see Kent Anderson Leslie, "A Myth of the Southern Lady: Antebellum Proslavery Rhetoric and the Proper Place of Woman," *Southern Women*, Caroline Matheny Dillman, ed. (New York: Hemisphere Publishing Corporation, 1988), 19-33.

26 Gerda Lerner, *The Majority Finds Its Place: Placing Women in History* (New York: Oxford University Press, 1975), 26.

27 Barbara Welter, "Cult of True Womanhood, 1820-1860," *American Quarterly* Vol 19, No 2 Part 1 (Summer 1966), 152.

28 Lerner, *The Majority Finds Its Place*, 26.

29 Quoted in Paula Giddings, *When and Where I Enter: The Impact of Black Women on Race and Sex in America* (New York: William Morrow & Co, 1984), 48.

30 Ibid., 48-49.

31 Evelyn Higginbotham, "African American Women's History and the Metalanguage of Race," Signs, Vol. 17, no. 2 (Winter 1992), 262.

32 "The Negro Problem: How It Appeals to a Negro Southern Woman," *The Independent*, Volume 54, Issue, 2, 1902, 2222.

33 Alexander, "She's No Lady."

34 Trudier Harris, *From Mammies to Militants: Black Domestics in Black American Literature*, (Philadelphia: Temple University Press,1982), 4.

35 Ed Kilgore, "Michelle Obama: Iron Woman," *The New Republic*, June 30, 2008, https://www.cbsnews.com/news/michelle-obama-iron-woman/.

36 Josephine Harvey, "Fox News Host Lauds Michelle Obama's DNC Speech: 'Sliced and Diced Trump," *Huffington Post*, August 18, 2020, https://www.huffpost.com/entry/fox-news-panel-michelle-obama-dnc_n_5f3b5f24c5b61100c3aba3f1.

37 Barack Obama, "Statement of Senator Barack Obama Hurricane Relief Efforts," September 6, 2005, http://obamaspeeches.com/029-Statement-on-Hurricane-Katrina-Relief-Efforts-Obama-Speech.htm.

38 Obama rightfully labeled Kanye West "A jackass" after his infamous Taylor Swift moment at the 2009 Video Music Awards.

39 The meeting between Obama, Gates, and Crowley was infamously dubbed "The Beer Summit."

40 Adele Logan Alexander, *Homelands and Waterways: The American Journey of the Bond Family, 1846-1926* (New York: *Pantheon Books*, 1999); also see *Princess of the Hither Isles: A Black Suffragist's Story From the Jim Crow South* (New Haven: Conn., Yale University Press, 2019).

41 Jamil Smith, "Melissa Harris Perry's Email to Her #Nerdland Staff," *Medium*, February 26, 2016, https://medium.com/@JamilSmith/melissa-harris-perry-s-email-to-her-nerdland-staff-11292bdc27cb.

42 Ibid.

43 Tonya Pinkins, "Full Statement On Her Departure from CSC's *Mother Courage*," *Playbill*, September 6, 2016, https://www.playbill.com/article/exclusive-tonya-pinkins-issues-unedited-full-statement-detailing-abrupt-departure-from-cscs-mother-courage-com-377196.

44 Martin Luther King Jr., "The Other America," (speech, Grosse Point High School, March 14, 1968), https://www.gphistorical.org/mlk/mlkspeech/.

45 "Prizefighting: With Mouth and Magic," *Time Magazine*, March 6, 1964, http://content.time.*com*/time/subscriber/article/0,33009,938476-3,00.html.

46 Alexandra Sims, "Muhammad Ali: Why Did the Boxing Champ Change His Name From Cassius Clay," *The Independent*, June 4, 2016, https://www.independent.co.uk/news/people/muhammad ali-death-cassius-clay-why-did-he-change-his-name-nation-islam-a7065256.html.

47 Taylor Lewis, "Kirk Franklin Apologizes to Gay Community For 'Homophobia' in Black Church," *The Grio*, November 12, 2015, https://thegrio.com/2015/11/12/kirk-franklin-apology-homophobia-black-church-gay-community/.

48 Michael Barbaro, "Hillary Clinton and Donald Trump Are Winning Votes, But Not Hearts," *The New York Times*, March 15, 2016, https://www.nytimes.com/2016/03/16/us/politics/hillary-clinton-donald-trump.html? r=0&register=facebook.

49 Eddie Glaude, "My Democratic Problem With Voting For Hillary Clinton," *Time Magazine*, July 12, 2016, https://time.com/4402823/glaude-hillary-clinton/.

50 W. E. B Du Bois, "I Won't Vote," *The Nation*, October 20, 1956, https://www.thenation.com/article/archive/i-wont-vote/.

51 David Levering Lewis, *W. E. B. Du Bois: A Biography 1868 – 1963* (New York: Henry Holt and Company, 2009); W. E. B. Du Bois, "Another Open Letter to Woodrow Wilson," *Teaching American History*, September 1913, https://teachingamericanhistory.org/library/document/another-open-letter-to-woodrow-wilson/.

52 Du Bois, "I Won't Vote."

53 Rachel L. Swans, "Georgetown University Plan Steps To Atone For Slave Past," *New York Times,* September 1, 2016, https://www.nytimes.com/2016/09/02/us/slaves-georgetown-university.html? r=0.

54 Jaeah Lee, "Uncovering the Painful Truth About Racism On Campus," *Mother Jones*, November 20, 2015, https://www.motherjones.com/politics/2015/11/racism-campus-protests-mizzou-yale-craig-wilder/.

55 M4BL, "Invest – Divest." *Vision for Black Lives: Policy Demands for Black Power, Freedom, and Justice*, 2016, https://m4bl.org/policy-platforms/invest-divest/.

56 Alan Dershowitz, "Black Lives Matter Must Rescind Anti-Israel Declaration," *The Boston Globe*, August 12, 2016, https://www.bostonglobe.com/opinion/columns/2016/08/12/black-lives-matter-must-rescind-anti-israel-declaration/EHDYV3gNLwrTTwfp0JA8QN/story.html; Rabbi Dan Dorsch, "As a Rabbi, I Can't Support Black Lives Matter When They Call to Boycott 'Apartheid' Israel," *Haaretz*, July, 8, 2016, https://www.haaretz.com/opinion/.premium-i-can-t-support-black-lives-matter-when-they-back-bds-1.5421652.

57 Lily Rothman, "Read TIME's Report on the Crown Heights Riots of 1991," *Time Magazine*, August 19, 2015, https://time.com/3989495/crown-heights-riots-time-magazine-history/.

58 Ben Sales, "Black Lives Matter Platform Author Defends Israel 'Genocide' Claim," *The Times of Israel*, August 10, 2016, https://www.timesofisrael.com/black-lives-matter-platform-author-defends-israel-genocide-claim/; Michael Schuerman, "King's New York Connection: MLK Jr.'s Friendship with Stanley Levison," *WNYC News*, January 17, 2011, https://www.wnyc.org/story/108985-martin-luther-kings-hidden-friend-and-advisor/.

59 Gene Roberts, "S.N.C.C. Charges Israel Atrocities," *New York Times*, August 15, 1967, https://timesmachine.nytimes.com/timesmachine/1967/08/15/issue.html.

60 Wilson Dizard, "Hundreds of Jews March For 'Black Lives Matter' In New York," *Mondoweiss*, August 12, 2016, https://mondoweiss.net/2016/08/hundreds-lives-matter/#sthash.OgTLFbtF.dpuf.

61 The poem which later became the lyrics to the U. S. National Anthem was written by slave owner and pro-slavery advocate Francis Scott Key who came from a prominent slave owning family in Maryland. See Christopher Wilson, "Where's the Debate on Francis Scott Key's Slave-Holding Legacy," *Smithsonian Magazine*, July 1, 2016, https://www.smithsonianmag.com/smithsonian-institution/wheres-debate-francis-scott-keys-slave-holding-legacy-180959550/.

62 Jamie Stiehm, "The Star-Spangled Banner's Racist Lyrics Reflect It's Slave Owner Author, Francis Scott Key," *The Undefeated*, September 6, 2018, https://theundefeated.com/features/the-star-spangled-banners-racist-lyrics-reflect-its-slaveowner-author-francis-scott-key/.

63 Josh Peter, "Descendent Of National Anthem Songwriter Rips Colin Kaepernick, *USA Today*, September 14, 2016, https://www.usatoday.com/story/sports/nfl/49ers/2016/09/14/colin-kaepernick-national-anthem-star-spangled-banner/90374620/.

64 Julian Bond and Sondra Kathryn Wilson, *Lift Every Voice and Sing: A Celebration of the Negro National Anthem;100 Years, 100 Voices* (New York: Random House, 2001; see also Imani Perry, *May We Forever Stand: A History of the Black National Anthem* (Chapel Hill: University of North Carolina Chapel Hill, 2018).

65 "Poetic License Raises A Star-Spangled Debate," *NPR All Things Considered*, July 3, 2009, https://www.npr.org/2009/07/03/106257394/poetic-license-raises-a-star-spangled-debate.

66 Marian Wright Edelman, "Black History, American History," *Huffington Post*, March 5, 2009, https://www.huffpost.com/entry/black-history-american-hi_b_163049.

67 Daniel White and Sarah Begley, "Everything We Know About the Charlotte Police Shooting," *Time Magazine*, September 16, 2016. https://time.com/4502543/charlotte-police-shooting-keith-lamont-scott/; Eugene Robinson, "In America, Gun Rights Are For Whites Only," *Washington Post*, September 22, 2016, https://www.washingtonpost.com/opinions/in-america-gun_rights-are-for-whites-only/2016/09/22/3990d370-80f2-11e6-8327-f141a7beb626_story.html?tid=ss_fb&utm_term=.e6e125255cd3; Erica Evans, "Does The 2nd Amendment Apply to African Americans," Los Angeles *Times*, July, 8, 2016, https://www.latimes.com/nation/la-na-second-amendment-20160707-snap-story.html.

68 Carl T. Bogus, "The Hidden History of the Second Amendment," *U.C. Davis Law Review*, Volume 31, Winter 1998 No. 2, https://docs.rwu.edu/cgi/viewcontent.cgi?article=1316&context=law_fac_fs.

69 Gerald Horne, "Historian: You Can't Disconnect History of the 2nd Amendment from the History of White Supremacy" *Democracy Now*, July 12, 2016, https://www.democracynow.org/2016/7/12/historian_you_cant_disconnect_history_of.

70 Arica L Coleman, "When The NRA Supported Gun Control," *Time Magazine*, July 29, 2016, https://time.com/4431356/nra-gun-control-history/.

71 Zach Stafford, "America's New TV Violence: Videos of Black Men Dying On Loop," *The Guardian*, May 11, 2016, https://www.theguardian.com/commentisfree/2015/may/11/when-we-watch-videos-of-black-men-dying-on-loop-it-harms-us; Amel Ahmed, "Ferguson Fallout: Black Americans Grapple With Victim Blaming," *Al Jazeera*, August 21, 2014, http://america.aljazeera.com/articles/2014/8/20/ferguson-and-victimblaminganationalpastime.html; Carlos Maza, "How News Networks Criminalize Black Victims of Police Violence," *Media Matters*, July 7, 2016, https://www.mediamatters.org/cbs/how-news-networks-criminalize-black-victims-police-violence.

72 "Best Practices For Journalists Reporting On Police Killing Of Black and Brown People," *Race Forward*, July 8, 2016, https://www.raceforward.org/press/releases/best-practices-journalists-reporting-police-killings-black-and-brown-people; Chauncey DeVega, "The Hard Truth About Terence Crutcher and Tulsa: What Kind Of White Person Do You Want To Be?," *Salon*, September 21, 2016, https://www.salon.com/2016/09/21/the-hard-truth-about-terence-crutcher-and-tulsa-what-kind-of-white-person-do-you-want-to-be/.

73   James Allen and John Littlefield, "Without Sanctuary: Photographs and Postcards of Lynching in America," https://withoutsanctuary.org/.

74   Equal Justice Initiative, *Lynching in America: Confronting the Legacy of Racial Terror,* https://eji.org/reports/lynching-in-america/; Campbell Robertson, "History of Lynchings in the South Documents Nearly 4,000 Names," *New York Times,* February 10, 2015, https://www.nytimes.com/2015/02/10/us/history-of-lynchings-in-the-south-documents-nearly 4000-names.html.

75   Frederick Douglass, "Why Is The Negro Lynched?" (Bridgewater, Conn., John Whitby and Sons, Limited, 1895), https://archive.org/details/whyisnegrolynche00doug.

76   LZ Granderson, "The Political Michael Jordan," *ESPN Magazine,* August 13, 2012, https://www.espn.com/nba/story/_/id/8264956/michael-jordan-obama-fundraiser-22-years-harvey-gantt.

77   "Nate Scott, "Kareem Abdul-Jabbar rips Michael Jordan For Choosing 'Commerce Over Conscience'," *USA Today,* November 4, 2015, https://ftw.usatoday.com/2015/11/kareem-abdul-jabbar-rips-michael-jordan-for-choosing-commerce-over-conscience.

78   Mahita Gajanan, "Michael Jordan Speaks Out on Police Shootings: 'I Can No Longer Stay Silent'," *Time Magazine,* July 25, 2016.

79   Sam Roberts, "Gwen Ifill, Political Reporter and Co-Anchor of 'PBS NewsHour,' Dies at 61," *The New York Times,* November 14, 2016, https://www.nytimes.com/2016/11/14/business/media/gwen-ifill-dies.html.

80   Ibid.; Alana Horowitz Satlin, "Watch Gwen Ifill Call Out Fellow Journalists For Not Standing Up To Racism," November 15, 2016, https://www.huffpost.com/entry/gwen-ifill-racism-don-imus_n_582aea71e4b0c4b63b0e5c7f; Ifill was personally insulted by the late Don Imus when he quipped in 1993 that the *New York Times* had let "the cleaning lady cover the White House."

81   Julia Zorthian, "This Is How February Became Black History Month," *Time Magazine,* January 29, 2016, https://time.com/4197928/history-black-history-month/.

82   Kevin Liptak, "Obama on Dallas: 'Vicious, calculated, despicable attack on law enforcement'," *CNN,* July 8, 2016, https://www.cnn.com/2016/07/08/politics/obama-dallas-police-shootings/; "Attorney General Loretta Lynch Statement On Dallas Shooting," *The United States Department of Justice,* July 8, 2016, https://www.justice.gov/opa/speech/attorney-general-loretta-e-lynch-delivers-statement-dallas-shooting.

83   Jason Howerton, "Exclusive; New Details Emerge As Parents of Dallas Cop Killer Micah Johnson Break Silence," *The Blaze,* July 11, 2016, https://www.theblaze.com/news/2016/07/11/exclusive-parents-of-dallas-cop-killer-micah-johnson-speak-out-for-first-time-since-attack.

84   Miles Moffeit, "Dallas Shooter Called Mentally Unstable Back In 2011 In Mesquite Police Report," *Dallas Morning News, July 29, 2016,* https://www.

dallasnews.com/news/2016/07/29/dallas-shooter-called-mentally-unstable-back-in-2011-in-mesquite-police-report/.

85　Brendan McGarry, "Dallas Police Shooter Was Army Reserve Vet Who Served In Afghanistan," *The Military Times*, July 8, 2016, https://www.military.com/daily-news/2016/07/08/dallas-police-shooter-identified-as-former-us-soldier-reports.html.

86　Robert Jablon, "Mom: Gunman Would 'Pretty Much Lose It,' On Police Shootings," *Associated Press*, July 22, 2016, https://apnews.com/article/b114be7 05b344656a05458c8eb84a961; Gavin Long, "Convos With Cosmos," *Twitter*, July 17, 2016, https://twitter.com/convoswithcosmo.

87　Monica T. Williams, "The Link Between Racism and PTSD," *Psychology Today*, September 6, 2015, https://www.psychologytoday.com/us/blog/culturally-speaking/201509/the-link-between-racism-and-ptsd.

88　"Note: The Root Of The Negro Problem," *Time Magazine*, May 17, 1963, http://content.time.com/time/subscriber/article/0,33009,830326-1,00.html; Tony Morrison, "JAMES BALDWIN : HIS VOICE REMEMBERED; Life in His Language," *New York Times*, December 20, 1987, https://archive.nytimes.com/www.nytimes.com/books/98/03/29/specials/baldwin-morrison.html.

89　"James Baldwin Speech," *C-Span*, January 15, 1979, https://archive.nytimes.com/www.nytimes.com/books/98/03/29/specials/baldwin-morrison.html; James Baldwin Documentary: The Price of the Ticket, Excerpt, Youtube, April 28, 2015, https://www.youtube.com/wtch?v=OCUlE5ldPvM.

90　Martin Luther King Jr., "Beyond Vietnam—A Time to Break Silence" (speech, Riverside Church, April 4, 1967), *American Rhetoric Online Speech Bank*, https://www.americanrhetoric.com/speeches/mlkatimetobreaksilence.htm.

91　King was the lone Black and only southern member of the CALCAV. According to Hanh in his book *Vietnam: A Proposal* (see footnote 36) "The word 'Thich' has been widely but erroneously interpreted as meaning 'Venerable' or 'Reverend.' Its actual purpose is to replace, for the monks and nuns of Vietnamese Buddhism, the family names to which they were born . . . and represents the family name of the Lord Buddha, Sakya (in Vietnamese, Thich-Ca; abbreviation, Thich), of whose spiritual 'family' they have become a part. The appropriate title in Vietnamese, which is the equivalent of 'Venerable' or 'Reverend,' is Dai Due."

92　Thich Nhat Hanh, "In Search Of The Enemy Of Man (addressed to (the Rev.) Martin Luther King," *African American Involvement In The Vietnam War: Letters, June 1, 1965*, http://www.aavw.org/special_features/letters_thich_abstract02.html; E. B. Cowell, *Jakata Or Stories Of The Buddha's Former Births, New Edition (New Delhi, India:* Motilal Banarsidass, 2014).

93　Hanh Letter to King.

94　King, "Beyond Vietnam."

95   Thich Nhat Hanh, "Our Green Garden," *Viet Nam Poems* (Santa Barbara, CAL: Unicorn Press, 1972).

96   Robert D. Bullard, et al., *Toxic Waste and Race at Twenty: 1987 – 2007 (United Church of Christ Justice and Witness Ministries, March 2007)* https://www.nrdc.org/sites/default/files/toxic-wastes-and-race-at-twenty-1987-2007.pdf; for a recent study on environmental racism in Dallas, Texas see Darryl Fears, "Shingle Mountain: How A Pile of Toxic Pollution Was Dumped in a Community of Color," *Washington Post, November 16, 2020,* https://www.washingtonpost.com/climate-environment/2020/11/16/environmental-racism-dallas-shingle-mountain.

97   Cord Jefferson, "The Racism Beat: What It's Like to Write About Hate Over, and Over, and Over," *Matter,* June 9, 2014, https://medium.com/matter/the-racism-beat-6ff47f76cbb6.

98   Charlie Rose Show interview with Bryant Gumbel, PBS, August 6, 2015, https://www.youtube.com/watch?v=w6QbOgOPRbQ; Bryant Gumbel, "Commentary: Black Tax," *Real Sports with Bryant Gumbel,* June 23, 2020, https://www.youtube.com/watch?v=VvKPBJVAPWE.

99   Jane Elliott, "Being Black," *YouTube,* January 2, 2016, https://www.youtube.com/watch?v=VvKPBJVAPWE.

100 Angel Kyodo Williams, *Twitter,* November 14, 2016, https://twitter.com/ZenChangeAngel/status/798152703809617920.

101 "Confederate States of America Treaty With the Cherokee," *Boston Athenaeum Digital Collection,* October 7, 1861, https://cdm.bostonathenaeum.org/digital/collection/p16057coll14/id/90842/.

102 "Cherokee Emancipation Proclamation," *Black Past,* February 18, 1863, https://www.blackpast.org/african-american-history/cherokee-emancipation-proclamation-1863/.

103 Kat Chow, "Judge Rules That Cherokee Freedmen Have Right To Tribal Citizenship," *NPR,* August 31, 2017, https://www.npr.org/sections/thetwo-way/2017/08/31/547705829/judge-rules-that-cherokee-freedmen-have-right-to-tribal-citizenship.

104 Marianne Williamson, "Our Deepest Fear," *A Return To Love: Reflections On The Principles In A Course In Miracles* (New York: Harper Collins, 1992), 190-191.

105 Abigail Abrams, "President Trump Once Again Says There Were 'Bad Dudes on the Other Side' in Charlottesville," *Time Magazine,* September 14, 2017, https://time.com/4942797/donald-trump-tim-scott-both-sides-charlottesville-antifa/.

106 Emma Bowman and Ian Stewart, "The Women Behind The 'Alt-Right'," *NPR*, August 20, 2017, https://www.npr.org/2017/08/20/544134546/the-women-behind-the-alt-right; Flavia Dzodan, "The New Alt-Feminism, When White Supremacy Met Women's Empowerment," *Medium.com*, January 6, 2017, https://medium.com/this-political-woman/the-new-alt-feminism-when-white-supremacy-met-womens-empowerment-b978b088db33.

107 Toni Morrison, "What The Black Woman Thinks About Women's Lib," *New York Times*, August 22, 1971, https://www.nytimes.com/1971/08/22/archives/what-the-black-woman-thinks-about-womens-lib-the-black-woman-and.html?mcubz=0;

108 Salamishah Tillet, "'Black Panther': Why Not Queen Shuri?" (Guest Column), *Hollywood Reporter*, February 16, 2018, https://www.hollywoodreporter.com/heat-vision/black-panther-why-not-queen-shuri-guest-column-1086012?utm_source=twitter&utm_source=t.co&utm_medium=referral.

109 Sylvia Serbin, *The Women Soldiers of Dahomey*, UNESDOC Digital Library, 2014, https://unesdoc.unesco.org/ark:/48223/pf0000230934.

110 Nathan Connolly, " How 'Black Panther' Taps Into 500 Years of History," *Hollywood Reporter*, February 16, 2018, https://www.hollywoodreporter.com/heat-vision/black-panther-taps-500-years-history-1085334.

111 Jewel Allison, "Bill Cosby sexually assaulted me. I didn't tell because I didn't want to let black America down," *Washington Post*, March 26, 2015, https://www.washingtonpost.com/posteverything/wp/2015/03/06/bill-cosby-sexually-assaulted-me-i-didnt-tell-because-i-didnt-want-to-let-black-america-down/.

112 Bill Cosby, "Pound Cake Speech Excerpt," YouTube, May 9, 2009, https://www.youtube.com/watch?v=_Gh3_e3mDQ8.

113 Sarah Begley, "Watch Poet Nikki Giovanni Rip Bill Cosby to Shreds in 2007 Speech," *Time Magazine*, November 21, 2014, https://time.com/3599976/nikki-giovanni-bill-cosby/.

114 Robert Joiner, "Cosby Throws Stones From Glass Castles," *St. Louis Dispatch*, June 18, 2005, https://journalstar.com/lifestyles/cosby-throws-stones-from-glass-castle/article_d45684af-3693-589d-95b5-b5c99b5aeb85.html.

115 Reid Nakamura, "Watch the Hannibal Buress Stand-Up Act That Helped Trigger Bill Cosby's Downfall (Video)," *The Wrap, April 26, 2018,* https://www.thewrap.com/watch-hannibal-buress-stand-act-helped-trigger-bill-cosbys-downfall-video/.

116 Eduardo C. Robreno, *Andrea Constand v. William H. Cosby Jr. Decision*, July 6, 2015, https://www.paed.uscourts.gov/documents/opinions/15d0578p.pdf.

117 "Bushman Shares A Cage With Bronx Park Apes," *New York Times*, September 9, 1906, https://humanzoos.org/wp-content/uploads/sites/18/2018/01/bushmannyt091106.pdf; Pamela Newkirk, "When the Bronx Zoo Exhibited A Man In An Iron Cage," *CNN*, June 3, 2015, https://www.cnn.com/2015/06/03/opinions/newkirk-bronx-zoo-man-cage/index.html.

118 Beyoncé Knowles, "Beyoncé in Her Own Words: Her Life, Her Body, Her Heritage," *Vogue Magazine*, August 6, 2018, https://www.vogue.com/article/beyonce-september-issue-2018.

119 Brenda E. Stevenson, "What's Love Got To Do With It: Concubinage, and Enslaved Women and Girls in the Antebellum South," *Journal of African American History*, Volume 98, No. 1, Winter 2013, 99-125.

120 Thomas A. Foster, "The Sexual Abuse of Black Men Under American Slavery," *Journal of the History of Sexuality*, Volume 20, No, 3, September 2011, 445-464.

121 Martin Luther King Jr., "Palm Sunday Sermon on Mohandas K. Gandhi," Delivered at Dexter Avenue Baptist Church, March 22, 1959, https://kinginstitute.stanford.edu/king-papers/documents/palm-sunday-sermon-mohandas-k-gandhi-delivered-dexter-avenue-baptist-church.

122 Martin Luther King Jr. "My Trip to the Land of Gandhi," *Ebony Magazine*, July 1959, https://kinginstitute.stanford.edu/king-papers/documents/my-trip-land-gandhi.

123 B. R. Ambedkar, *The Annihilation of Caste: The Annotated Critical Edition, S. Anand and Arundhati Roy, eds. (New York: Verso, 2014);* Ambedkar is known as the Father of India's Constitution, which he helped drafted but later denounced.

124 Sander Vanocur Interview with Martin Luther King Jr, *NBC News*, May 8, 1967, https://www.youtube.com/watch?v=2xsbt3a7K-8.

125 "US, Israel Pull Out of Racism Conference," *ABC News*, January 6, 2006, https://abcnews.go.com/International/story?id=80564&page=1; Errin Harris, "King's Widow Reflects On Husband's Legacy," *NBC News.com*, 2005, http://www.nbcnews.com/id/6830276/ns/us_news-life/t/kings-widow-reflects-husbands-legacy/#.X44_g9BKiM8.

126 "Cherokee Nation Responds To Release of Senator Warren's DNA Test," *Twitter*, October 15, 2018, https://twitter.com/CherokeeNation/status/1051965527214776321.

127 Francis Galton, "Eugenics: Its Definition, Scope, and Aims Paper," School of Economics London University, May 16, 1904, http://galton.org/essays/1900-1911/galton-1904-am-journ-soc-eugenics-scope-aims.htm.

128 American Anthropological Association, "Statement On Race," May 17, 1998, https://www.americananthro.org/ConnectWithAAA/Content.aspx?ItemNumber=2583.

129 Amy Harmon, "Why White Supremacists Are Chugging Milk (and Why Geneticists Are Alarmed)" *New York Times*, October 17, 2018, https://www. nytimes.com/2018/10/17/us/white-supremacists-science-dna.html.

130 Dana Owens, "Veteran Congressman Still Pushing for Reparations in a Divided America," *NBC News, February 20, 2017,* https://www.nbcnews.com/news/ nbcblk/rep-john-conyers-still-pushing-reparations-divided-america-n723151; see also Ashley D. Farmer, "The Black Woman Who Launched The Modern Fight For Reparations," *Washington Post,* June 24, 2019, https://www. washingtonpost.com/outlook/2019/06/24/black-woman-who-launched-modern-fight-reparations/.

131 Rhonda Y. Williams, "'We're tired of being treated like dogs': Poor Women and Power Politics in Black Baltimore," *The Black Scholar,* Volume 31, Issue 3-4, 31-41.

132 Family of Michael Brown, et al., "Written Statement on the Police Shooting of Michael Brown and Ensuing Police Violence Against Protesters in Ferguson, Missouri," *53rd Session of the United Nations Committee Against Torture,* November 3-28, 2014, http://i2.cdn.turner.com/cnn/2014/images/11/11/ fergusonreport.pdf; "Legitimate concerns" over outcome of Michael Brown and Eric Garner cases – UN rights experts," United Nations Human Rights Office of the High Commissioner, December 5, 2014, https://www.ohchr.org/EN/ NewsEvents/Pages/DisplayNews.aspx?NewsID=15384&LangID=E.

133 Krissah Thompson, "The Unfinished Work of Malcolm X" *Washington Post,* February 15, 2019, https://www.washingtonpost.com/lifestyle/ style/fifty-years-after-his-death-malcolm-x-speaks-to-the-current-moment/2015/02/19/4dba5ca4-091e-4303-b3ee-6a655c583655_story.html.

134 Malcolm X, "The Ballot Or The Bullet," Cleveland , Ohio; April 3, 1964, http://www.edchange.org/multicultural//speeches/malcolm_x_ballot.html; King Solomon Baptist Church, Detroit, Michigan, April 12, 1965, https:// americanradioworks.publicradio.org/features/blackspeech/mx.html.

135 Ibid.

136 C-SPAN, "Rally on Electoral College Certification," Washington, D.C., January 6, 2021, https://www.c-span.org/video/?507744-1/ rally-electoral-college-vote-certification.

137 Quoted in Logan Jaffe, et al., "Insurrection: Capitol Rioters Planned for Weeks in Plain Sight. The Police Weren't Ready," *ProPublica,* January 7, 2021, https://www.propublica.org/article/ capitol-rioters-planned-for-weeks-in-plain-sight-the-police-werent-ready.

138 Ibid

139 Tobi Thomas, et al., "Nearly 1,000 Instances of Police Brutality recorded in US Anti-racism Protest," *The Guardia*n, October 29, 2020, https://www.propublica.org/article/ capitol-rioters-planned-for-weeks-in-plain-sight-the-police-werent-ready.

140 Tom Gjelten, "Peaceful Protesters Tear-Gassed To Clear Way For Trump Church Photo-Op," *NPR*, June 1, 2020, https://www.npr.org/2020/06/01/867532070/trumps-unannounced-church-visit-angers-church-officials; Helene Cooper, "Milley Apologizes for Role in Trump Photo Op:'I Should Not Have Been There'," *New York Times*, June 11, 2020, https://www.nytimes.com/2020/06/11/us/politics/trump-milley-military-protests-lafayette-square.html.

141 Logan Jaffe, "Insurrection."

142 Stephen Groves and Scott Bauer, "17-Year-Old Arrested After 2 Killed During Unrest in Kenosha," *U.S. News & World Report*, August 27, 2020, https://www.usnews.com/news/us/articles/2020-08-26/kenosha-police-3-shot-2-fatally-during-wisconsin-protests; Matthew Impelli, "Kyle Rittenhouse's Mother Receives Standing Ovation at Wisconsin GOP Event," *Newsweek*, September 29, 2020, https://www.newsweek.com/kyle-rittenhouses-mother-receives-standing-ovation-wisconsin-gop-event-1534364.

143 Belle Kearney, "The South and Woman Suffrage," *Woman's Journal*, April 4, 1903; Alexandria Ocasio Cortiz, *Twitter*, March 29, 2019, https://twitter.com/aoc/status/1109877625265229824?lang=en.

144 Jelani Cobbs, "The Central Park Five, The Criminal Justice System, and Donald Trump," *The New Yorker*, April 19, 2019, https://www.newyorker.com/news/daily-comment/the-central-park-five-criminal-justice-and-donald-trump; Andrew Serwer, "Birtherism Of A Nation," The Atlantic, May 13, 2020, https://www.theatlantic.com/ideas/archive/2020/05/birtherism-and-trump/610978/; "Here's Donald Trump's Presidential Announcement Speech," *Time Magazine*, June 16, 2015, https://time.com/3923128/donald-trump-announcement-speech/.

145 Caroline E. Light and Janae E. Thomas, "Ahmaud Arbery's Killers Want to Ban the Word Victim at Their Trial," *Slate.com*, February 22, 2021, https://slate.com/news-and-politics/2021/02/ahmaud-arbery-jury-mcmichael-trial-georgia.html

SELECTED BIBLIOGRAPHY

Alexander, Adele Logan. *Homelands and Waterways: The American Journey of the Bond Family, 1846 – 1926.* New York: Vintage, 2007.

Allen, James. *Without Sanctuary: Lynching Photography in America.* Santa Fe: Twin Palms Publishers, 2000.

Anderson, Carol. *White Rage: The Unspoken Truth of Our Racial Divide.* New York: Bloomsbury, 2017.

Arajuo, Ana Lucia. *Reparations for Slavery and the Slave Trade: A Transnational and Comparative History.* New York: Bloomsbury Publishing, 2017.

Asim, Jabari, *We Can't Breathe: On Black Lives, White Lies, and the Art of Survival.* New York: Picador, 2018.

Baldwin, James, and Toni Morrison. *Baldwin Collected Essays.* New York: Library of America, 1998.

Bay, Mia. *The White Image in the Black Mind: African American Ideas About White People, 1830-1925.* New York: Oxford University Press, 2000.

Bell, Derrick. *Faces at the Bottom of the Well: The Permanence of Racism.* New York: Basic Books, 2018.

Berry, Mary Frances. *My Face Is Black Is True: Callie House and the Struggle for Ex-Slave Reparations.* New York: Vintage Books, 2009.

Blee, Kathleen M. *Women of the Klan: Racism and Gender in the 1920s.* Berkeley: University of California Press, 1992.

Bond, Julian, and Sondra Kathryn Wilson. *Lift Every Voice and Sing: A Celebration of the Negro National Anthem;100 Years, 100 Voices.* New York: Random House, 2001.

Coleman, Monica A. ed. *Ain't I A Womanist Too: Third Wave Womanist Religious Thought.* Minneapolis, MN: Fortress Press, 2013.

Collins, Patricia Hill. *Black Feminist Thought: Knowledge, Consciousness, and the Politics of Empowerment.* New York: Routledge Classic, 2009.

Darity, William A. and A. Kirsten Mullen. *From Here to Equality: Reparations for Black Americans in the Twenty-First Century*. Chapel Hill: University of North Carolina Press, 2020.

Desai, Ashwin and Goolem Vahed. *The South African Gandhi: Stretcher-Bearer of Empire*. CA: Stanford University Press, 2016.

Douglas, Kelly Brown. *Stand Your Ground: Black Bodies, and the Justice of God*. New York: Orbis Books, 2015.
	Sexuality and the Black Church: A Womanist Perspective. New York: Orbis Books, 2018.

Du Bois, W. E. B. *The Philadelphia Negro: A Social Study*. Philadelphia: University of Pennsylvania Press, 2010.
	The Souls of Black Folk. New York: G & D Media. Original Edition, 2019.

Feldman, Keith P. *A Shadow Over Palestine: The Imperial Life of Race in America*. Minneapolis: University of Minnesota Press, 2015.

Floyd-Thomas, Stacey M. *Deeper Shades of Purple: Womanism in Religion and Society*. New York: New York University Press, 2006.

Forbes, Jack D. *Africans and Native Americans: The Language of Race and the Evolution of Red-Black Peoples*. Champaign: University of Illinois Press, 1993.
	Columbus and Other Cannibals: The Wetiko Disease of Exploitation, Imperialism, and Terrorism. New York: Seven Stories Press. Revised Edition, 2011.

Foster, Thomas A. *Rethinking Rufus: Sexual Violations of Enslaved Men*. Athens: University of Georgia Press, 2019.

Fredrickson, George. *The Black Image in the White Mind: The Debate on Afro-American Character and Destiny, 1817-1914*. 2nd Edition. Ann Arbor: ACLS Humanities E-Book, 2008.

Giddings, Paula J. *When and Where I Enter: The Impact of Black Women on Race and Sex In America*. New York: W. Morrow, 1984.

Gordon-Reed, Annette. *The Hemingses of Monticello: An American Family*. New York: W. W. Norton, 2008.

Greenburg, Cheryl Lynne. *Troubling the Water: Black – Jewish Relations in the American Century*. New Jersey: Princeton University Press, 2010.

Guy-Sheftall, Beverly and Johnetta B. Cole. eds. *Who Should Be First?: Feminists Speak Out On The 2008 Primary Campaign*. New York: SUNY Press, 2010.

Hanh, Thich Nhat. *Vietnam: Lotus in a Sea Of Fire—A Buddhist Proposal For Peace*. New York: Hill & Wang, 1967.

Harris, Trudier. *From Mammies to Militants: Domestics in Black American Literature*. Philadelphia: Temple University Press, 1982.

Ifill, Gwen. *The Breakthrough: Politics and Race in the Age of Obama*. New York: Anchor, 2009.

Joseph, Peniel E. *Waiting Til the Midnight Hour: A Narrative History of Black Power in America*. New York: Henry Holt and Co. 2007.

King, Martin Luther, Jr. *The Autobiography of Martin Luther King Jr*. Clayborne Carson, ed. New York: Grand Central Publishing, 2001.

Lipsitz, George. *The Possessive Investment in Whiteness: How White People Profit from Identity Politics*. Philadelphia: Temple University Press. 20th Anniversary Edition, 2018.

Marable, Manning, Malcolm X: A Life of Reinvention. New York: Penguin Books, 2011.

McKittick, Katherine. Demonic Grounds: Black Women and the Cartographies of Struggle. Minneapolis: University of Minnesota Press, 2006.

Mitchell, Korithia. *Living with Lynching: African American Lynching Plays, Performance, and Citizenship, 1890-1930*. Champaign: University of Illinois Press, 2012.

Miles, Tiya. *The House on Diamond Hill: A Cherokee Plantation Story*. Chapel Hill: University of North Carolina Press, 2010.
The Ties That Bind: The Story of An Afro–Cherokee Family in Slavery and in Freedom. Berkeley: University of California Press, 2015.

Moore, Leonard M. *Black Rage in New Orleans: Police Brutality and African American Activism from World War II to Hurricane Katrina*. Baton Rouge: LSU Press, 2010.

Morton, Patricia: *Disfigured Images: The Historical Assault Against Afro-American Women*. Westport. Conn.: Praeger Publishers, 1991.

Newkirk, Pamela. *The Astonishing Life of Ota Benga*. New York: Harpers Collins Publisher, 2015.

Obama, Barack. *Dreams from My Father: A Story of Race and Inheritance*. New York: Random House, 2005.

Obama, Michelle. *Becoming*. New York: Crown, 2018.

Philips, Layli. *The Womanist Reader*. New York: Routledge, 2006.

Ransby, Barbara. *Making All Black Lives Matter: Reimagining Freedom in the 21st Century*. Berkeley: University of California Press, 2018.

Roberts, Dorothy. *Fatal Invention: How Science, Politics, and Big Business Re-Create Race in the 21st Century*. New York: The New Press, 2011.

Rothman, Joshua D. *Notorious in The Neighborhood: Sex and Families Across the Color Line, 1787 - 1861*. Chapel Hill: University of North Carolina, 2003.

Shabazz, Rashad. Spatializing Blackness: Architectures of Confinement and Black Masculinity in Chicago. Champaign: University of Illinois Press, 2015.

Tallbear, Kim. Native American DNA: Tribal Belonging and the False Promise of Genetic Science. Minneapolis: University of Minnesota Press, 2013.

Taylor, Dorceta E. Toxic Communities: Environmental Racism, Industrial Politics, and Residential Mobility. New York: NYU Press, 2014.

Van Sertima, Ivan. Black Women in Antiquity. New York: Transaction Publishers, 1995.

Wells-Barnett, Ida B. The Red Record Tabulated Statistics and Alleged Causes of Lynching in America. CreateSpace Independent Publishing Platform, 2015.

Wilder, Craig Steven. Ebony and Ivy: Race, Slavery, and the Troubled History of America's Universities. London, England: Bloomsbury Publishing, 2014.

Wilkins, Robert Leon. Long Road to Hard Truth: The 100 Year Mission to Create the National Museum of African American History and Culture. Ashland, Ohio: Proud Legacy Publishing, 2016.

Zimring, Carl A. Clean and White: A History of Environmental Racism in the United States. New York: NYU Press, 2016.

CONTRIBUTORS

 **ARICA L. COLEMAN** is an independent historian and political commentator of race and ethnicity in the United States and founder of SistahGurl Books. She has lent her expertise to a broad range of academic and popular venues which include *Time Magazine*, the *Washington Post*, *Cheddar TV*, and *NPR*. She is the author of the award-winning book *That the Blood Stay Pure: African Americans, Native Americans, and the Predicament of Race and Identity in Virginia.*

 **MARITA GOLDEN** is a bestselling author, speaker, and workshop presenter. The author of over a dozen works of fiction and nonfiction, Golden's works are favorites with book clubs, used in college courses from literature to sociology around the country, and are recognized as having added depth and complexity to the canon of contemporary African American writing.

**STEPHANIE VANCE PATIENCE** (*Stefani Vance*) is a highly gifted and talented self-taught artist and graphic designer. She was raised in suburban Philadelphia in a home filled with art and music which nurtured her creative curiosity. Further exposure to the art world via her parents' community art gallery deepened her love for art and she became an avid reader of the art profession and studied the works of nationally acclaimed artists to perfect her own technique. In addition to graphic design, Vance has lent her expertise in corporate America as an art director in both national and international venues, creating designs in more then a dozen industries, including book covers and interior design.